LINK AND COMMUNIQUÉ

A personal psychic experience

LINK AND COMMUNIQUÉ

A personal psychic experience

by

J. E. BEST

DR. JOHN. BEST,
"WHITE GABLES"
WELLINGFORD RD,
SOUTH STOKE,
READING,
BERKS. RG8 OHY.

Regency Press (London & New York) Ltd.
125 High Holborn, London WC1V 6QA

ISBN 0 7212 0827 4

Printed and bound in Great Britain by
Buckland Press Ltd., Dover, Kent.

CONTENTS

APPENDIX

FOREWORD

By Frank T. Farmer, OBE, PhD, F. Inst P, FIEE, Emeritus
Professor of Medical Physics, University of Newcastle upon
Tyne and formerly Head of Regional Department of Medical
Physics, Newcastle General Hospital.

The issue of this book is *survival*. The subject is of growing interest, yet one which has attracted much controversy. The concept of life after death contrasts with the view which has tended to dominate in the last century, that human life is – bleakly – an emergence from nothingness which after a brief span returns to that same nothingness. Between the two bounds of birth and death there is the experience we call life; outside is only darkness.

This view is not, by its nature, susceptible to proof. Those who hold it are prepared often enough to accept they may be wrong. But there is a strong feeling that it is massively supported by the knowledge we have today in science.

The author of this book is a scientist. He and I were research students together at Cambridge working on different aspects of a geophysical field, and from our many discussions, often running late into the night, I came to know his mind well. He was deeply interested not only in our field of study but also in searching questions at the heart of physics. When on leaving the University he entered industry and I the medical field, we continued our close touch and his enquiring and analytical mind naturally found wide scope for further thought. John Best has written as he has because he became certain that life holds in itself the evidence by which the question of survival can be decided – and answered positively.

If he is right, the picture of the world *in toto* must be different from commonly held views. With the almost incredible developments in science this century, the basic knowledge to support his conclusions is *already there*, he argues; and it leads straight to a more complete picture. The present book is increasingly taken up with this picture of a wider world. In his own experience the start lay in recognizing that the human mind possesses an inbuilt capacity to grasp something at least of this greater reality.

Thus with certain initial events which unexpectedly and tragically broke in on his life, Dr. Best came to realize that communication across the barrier between our present life and that other kind of life outside the bounds of birth and death was personally an achievable thing. Until this point he had felt that survival still remained an open question. Just how events changed his mind is something he describes in the early sections of his book.

However, the main force of his narrative lies not in the personal experience,

7

interesting though that is, but rather in the question what, if communication across such a barrier is a fact, can it reveal about the nature of life beyond and its relationship to this one.

Enquiry of this kind in the past seems never to have got very far. Two reasons may be given: firstly the belief that science has virtually shut the door against it, and secondly those engaging in it have not been equipped with the concepts necessary to do justice to the task.

Dr. Best, because of his knowledge of modern physics, saw that the popularly conceived 'obstacle' from science should not be taken seriously, but even more importantly still he was able to turn to far-reaching advantage the circumstances he encountered in the wake of tragic accident.

It is often said that truth is stranger than fiction. In his explorations he met with things each outstanding and unparalleled to a point which strained belief. As a result of his studies, however, he found that these things possessed common rational explanation along lines now made available to us through the advances in physics of the last fifty years.

In outcome, his message is clear. In man's continuing quest for knowledge and understanding the journey of the human spirit beyond this present world is a subject now accessible to the processes of human intellect and study. But Dr. Best's writing is not simply an intellectual exercise. The story is also a very human one by virtue of the aspirations which, undefeated, carried it forward.

Dr. Best's book brings, in an entirely modern way, the comfort which has always and invariably been sought by the human spirit. The world is now open to a more complete and rational understanding; and it is not a bleak world.

INTRODUCTION

The special events of this account forced themselves upon me from the entirely unexpected. They are far from the domain of organized, calculated happenings which personifies our age. One could say that the computer is now our emblem. By what other means could man have gone to the Moon, landed on it, and safely voyaged back to Earth? That was a triumph epitomizing our time. My upbringing was of this climate: a climate in which the regularities of the world are clearly recognized and widely made to serve our purpose. If perhaps thirty years ago it had been predicted how I should embark on an account like the present, I must simply have been unbelieving. My world was particularly of a kind where the radically unexpected did not happen.

That at least pictures the practical turn of my mind then: the way I ordinarily took things and looked on them. In armchair mood I should have thought this too closed a view properly to match the real world. From the science which had formed my mind I knew the way major advances had shaped science in its progress: it paid tribute to the worth of unanticipated things. The need to be open-minded seemed imperative. Many scientists and non-scientists, I was aware, saw the world as at last all coded up: leaving no room for a basically new vista. That possibility is weighed in Appendix I; but I felt instinctively it was a view time would prove mistaken. What was farthest from my mind was that anything I might experience could influence the subject.

Yet events happened that way.

As the title of this book is intended to convey, my account of them is of direct meeting face to face with the psychical world. In earlier days I had become lightly acquainted with studies of psychical phenomena. I did not know what such studies truly implied; nor did I think the facts of psychical mediumship necessarily demonstrated human survival of death. These things impinge upon a great paradox. If human beings fail to survive the ending of this life, then life may hold the greatest paradox of all. The success of life lies with development. That is something very real. The truth of non-survival would it seems imprint contradiction deeply upon human nature. If there is a general lesson from science it is that the clarity of truth is not muddied ultimately by contradiction. Once again the subject was something on which I never anticipated any experience of mine to throw light.

In that I was proved wrong – and as by chance. My fiancée, Marjorie, and I found ourselves mutually participating in phenomena which, as we studied them, appeared altogether beyond the limits of physical explanation. On those grounds we inclined to think of the phenomena as psychical (meaning by that phenomena essentially different from happenings of a purely physical order). They were

9

highly personal to us, and became a part of our life. In one of their facets they opened up for us a new if rudimentary communication link. They were not interrupted by Marjorie's sudden death in 1971 – though we had never looked on them in that form of context. It was then I knew human personality survives death – on a level of personal knowledge, rather as one knows for example that one loves and is loved. In addition, very differently, but once more unlooked-for, psychical research crossed my path three years later. The two separate threads converged significantly; and I came into closer touch with Marjorie. In October 1975, I met with her very definite wish that I should write this book.

She particularly wanted me to relate her experiences since her death. My account though – as I learned better her idea – must be more than that. It was important to include my approach: how the truth of what had happened became clear, as it did, to me. There was more still: it should give an intelligible picture of her present wider view of life – which she, with her scientific mind, had come to see made sense along lines that modern science has established this last half century.

The things I had been learning were deeply interesting and absorbing. I found myself fascinated. But this new step was disconcerting. It certainly meant making public what was private. And on the scientific point I had no notion of Marjorie's meaning. Marjorie, on the other hand, was positive and confident. The months and years as they went by showed her justified.

Setting out the facts here as I have, I have regarded it important to give an indication of the extent to which my mind was prepared for the experiences I shall be describing.

What I also wish to say in advance and want to stress is that, rather than forming an avenue of expression just for interpretation of my own, the events of the book carry an inbuilt element of interpretation. They carry, as part of an intention which dominated and directed them, a communication about the phenomena with which they are concerned. This communication leads to the intelligible and wider picture of life which Marjorie held in mind. For this reason the pattern of events has naturally divided the narrative into Parts I and II. The first describes how I was increasingly introduced to main features of unaccustomed terrain – this with growing if not deep understanding. The second shows the way that understanding was progressively and markedly strengthened: to the point that the unaccustomed became a fresh, important, and rational aspect of a more extensive world.

For some readers the Appendix will be an integral part of the book – it aims to look much more fully into questions that come to the fore at various junctures. This introduction has already provided an illustration in point; and there are many other instances throughout Parts I and II. But as the reader comes across any such reference there is no necessity to interrupt the flow by turning to the Appendix.

PART I

Chapter One

TRAGEDY AND DISCOVERY

Marjorie died on the morning of 3rd August, 1971. It was late in the morning, and in hospital after a motor accident. She had been driving from her flat in Reading to her work at the Government Establishment at Aldermaston. I was also driving to work at the time. I had to travel from my home in South London to Hayes in Middlesex.

As I was passing through Twickenham – and I remember the occasion in sharp clarity, even to the exact location – my body suddenly went chill. An hour later, now in my office, but still feeling that cold grip, the telephone rang. The call was from the Aldermaston Establishment. Marjorie was injured in a car crash, how seriously it was not known. She would be taken to Battle Hospital in Reading.

With this terribly disturbing news the sense of bodily cold left me as suddenly as it had come – to be replaced by the foreboding that Marjorie would not recover. One thought was overmastering: I must hasten to Reading. On my way I prayed – as human beings invariably do – but it was not with words, only with the intensity of my feeling. My foreboding did not lift; and I thought how bright the day before had seemed when the letter came saying that the mortgage arrangements on our house were settled.

I arrived at the hospital before the ambulance. The waiting was not long; though the minutes scarcely moved. Then the ambulance drove in . . . and still there was the limitlessness of waiting. What I had yet to wait was half an hour.

The news brought me what I knew already I did not know how to face. One of the doctors who had tried to save Marjorie's life walked slowly to me: Marjorie was dead. My world froze.

Perforce there were pressing matters. Marjorie's brother who had shared the waiting, shared these also. Looking back I so greatly appreciated his unspoken support. With immediate things done, I returned home and to telephone my office. I spoke to my boss. I told him the reason for my absence all day; and – as a good friend – I told him of my devastation. I made some other calls.

The events of the night were of a most far-reaching and exceptional kind; but to see them in proper perspective I must first set down rather more about Marjorie and myself.

To say that we were close, very close, is most certainly true; and undoubtedly most important. Yet in realizing what occurred during the night I need to say that closeness in the sense of customary standards by no means conveys the full truth. There was more to it; and to explain just how is a necessity. I start though with facts by no means encroaching upon the unusual.

Marjorie lost her father when she was still very young. Eventually it was decided that she should be brought up by her paternal grandmother. This was in a large house in Datchet. The arrangement gave her the opportunity of a wide education. She enjoyed it; and it brought out her natural potentialities. She found she had an instinct for the scientific way of thinking. That was something – becoming incisively evident later on – of great relevance for this book. And meeting with Marjorie it was personally one of the many things that aided the bond between us.

Recognizing this fact – and with it the natural activity of enquiry common to our mental make-ups – Marjorie had called my attention to it more than once. Almost in the earliest days I have reason to quote her on this. I remember exactly the way she first put it. "With us," she exclaimed, "Greek had met Greek." It was an expression of her delight and typical of her vivid way with words. It spoke a wealth on the cast of her mind; yet very specially I quote her because her words verbatim are of distinct importance in the context of certain occasions I shall come to.

The Greek love of enquiry apart, Marjorie's interests and experience of the world extended much beyond the academic. She had met with the problems and traumas of life head on. They had stressed her taut; but as people saw her, particularly with her bright speech and outgiving personality, it was difficult to detect how much she had needed to battle and contend. Here was another entrée of the spirit – another part of an important access – *via* which the stream of understanding flowed emotively between us. I knew in practical terms how such stresses could strain soul and body. In this dimension, like with science and in other avenues, empathy ran deeply in support of mutual feeling.

I can add some detail, some light and shade, to these bare outlines. Marjorie's mind was penetrating, and rapid. She was quick to see the true essence of a situation. Because it came so unequivocally and readily to her it was hard for her to realize how others could draw the wrong conclusion . . . worse that some – for extraneous reasons – could pretend the wrong conclusion was the truth. Set against her very frank way and against her wide generosity and warmheartedness, it was a frame of mind which caused her inevitably to divide her acquaintances most markedly into two camps – in which those who were her friends were greatly her friends. While however she was instinctively critical of what she saw as false or hypocritical, and was open about it, she rarely if ever failed to perceive and give a just weight to the good elements in an opposing point of view. It would be true that on this account she was a bad advocate in her own defence; and that, with this kind of sympathy, any personal quarrel tended to dissipate itself quickly. Her friends noted all these traits of her character and esteemed her for them. I recognized with my own pleasure her great qualities of spirit. Again, our natural attraction was supported by interflow at the level of the spirit.

The unity which grew in such an atmosphere was nevertheless a unison of distinctly differing personalities. The difference is perhaps most simply told in the fact that Marjorie normally found the greater interest in people whereas I found it in ideas.

But I state that – and it is what I was initially asserting – the factor of the spirit on the pattern I have been trying to sketch, while most important, is not the ultimate basis of the special experiences I shall be describing. The real basis lies beyond the background thus far. It is of the spirit certainly; but of a mould which is less easy to grasp. I will turn to it now.

On reflection it was present I think right from the start. We tended to talk when on our own together as if we had always very closely known each other. This stood out in our first long conversation. We both remarked on it afterwards, and more than once. There seemed to be some direct mutual recognition, and access which overrode the use of words and normal modes of communication. It developed more and more; and in a parallel progression it became part of our lives. I could influence Marjorie's thoughts and she mine even when separated and by whatever the distance. At one time, some hundreds of miles between us, I was certain I had received instructions from her to carry out a particular wish she had. Looking at it logically, and in the light of the facts as I believed them to be, it made no sense to me – I thought I should be on a pointless errand. Marjorie was most disappointed I had not done as she wanted: I *had* received the message; and, concerning what I *thought* were the facts, with more care I could have got them right. I cannot say that personally I had known anything akin to this deeper interrelation – not at least in this acute degree in which a transferred thought was not to be brushed aside on account of a believed conflict with fact. Marjorie on the other hand had met with something partly like it. When her father had died he was in hospital and she naturally at home; but despite the separation – and she was positive on the point – she had become aware at a certain time, ordinary communication apart, that he was no longer alive. They did not tell her of his death until two days after she had gained this direct and accurate knowledge.

Such direct access to knowledge may be called intuition. It tends today not to be taken with any great seriousness – beyond doubt because it does not fit in well with popular ideas of the nature of our world. Deeply entrenched, there are signs of the tendency weakening. Marjorie and I for ourselves integrated this direct access increasingly into our mutual existence – precisely as we would any other natural activity.

Our direct influencing of each other, we discovered before long, was not confined just to our thoughts. We found we could affect each other in a bodily way. It was a thing totally new to us, which we subjected to many tests; both when we were together in the same room and when we were separated even up to a thousand miles apart. We checked it when one of us was screened from the other by metal screening or by intervening high ground. The screening made no difference at all; and in the circumstances we came to the opinion that the effects had no conceivable explanation in terms of the science we knew. It strengthened our growing view that in ourselves we were dealing with something of the spirit: in which the material world was not playing a fundamental part.

When we first noticed the effects we were in fact not in each other's company. We were pursuing our ordinary respective tasks; but, as we established later, we were each at the time thinking of the other. The effects had arisen spontaneously. Neither had intended them – for as I have indicated we then did not know that such effects could exist. However we discovered that they could be induced at will; and it was this that easily allowed of our scientific testing. With more experience we found we could operate a variety of rather different forms. We could induce a flow of pleasing warmth; or a muscular tensing like the pressure of a handclasp; or even the movement of a limb.

State of mind it appeared was always present in the situation. When operating the effects, we each were well aware of the other's mood. Once when for two days we had fallen out it was impossible to achieve anything at all. I tried many times. Each time I was faced with a state of deadness – I made great efforts to achieve contact but it was, I felt, just like working into sponge. Marjorie tried similarly with like result. Strikingly as she expressed it to me "it was like working into sponge" – words I had never used as I told her of my own difficulties. Fortunately the grounds of our defeat on this occasion never arose again, and our 'messages' as we called them became very much part and parcel of our way of life.

To go more into the nature of our messages, what would normally happen was that one party might decide to induce one of the variety of particular effects in the other. It would usually get through in the first instance to a weak extent. If weak, this was because the other party was preoccupied at the time. The sender would be fully aware of the poor degree of reception. However, as soon as the receiving party could give attention, the transmitted effect would increase strongly – and again the sender would be well aware of the receiving situation. When the receiving party could no longer give attention, and so might be said to have 'gone off the air', the sending party sensed at once that the received effect had resultingly dropped in intensity. We called the weak state of transmission – when the receiving party could not give true attention – 'single mode'. When the receiving party could be attentive, and the effects were correspondingly strong, we called the state 'double mode'.

We wondered often if such messages might be operated by other people sensitive to each other in the selfsame way that we were. We speculated it was unlikely to be common; or we should have heard of it. We considered it impossible that we should be unique. Not long after Marjorie's death it was fascinating to be told by a scientific colleague that he and his wife possessed similar abilities – which they frequently utilized. I knew exactly what he meant when he said – and without any prompting – that "one can always tell if the other party has switched off". Like ourselves they had conjectured whether other people could operate this kind of link; but, as he remarked, it is not a topic that is easily raised. I have however met with another instance of the same ability.

Our own special link lies at the heart of the events of the night; though there is still more to be said. There were the events leading up to those of the night. Inevitably there was my own inner state of being.

Grief from its nature is resistant to *a priori* analysis. Just as trying to describe colour fails with the colour-blind, so the human mind fails to know just what grief is like until its actual impact. Here, and despite the difficulties and my own inclinations, are things I cannot leave out. They stand in context to the events which shortly were to surprise me. Fortunately, I need go little further than to convey a core of facts centring around my most inward feelings.

The experience of grief – with its intrinsic privacy – is immensely isolating. Then, stunning the mind, there is little ability to recover and find a way to cope with the disaster. But – set against these difficulties – other people just by their presence, and more than they may realize, are able to help with the vital problem of rallying and coming to some terms with what has happened.

16

One of the calls I made by telephone on my arrival home late in the afternoon was to a friend, Jim, with whom both Marjorie and I had shared motoring interests. Marjorie held a natural feeling for things mechanical; and for the handling of a motor car – and what contributed to a motor vehicle of competition kind. Jim had competed in car rallies with success and was the director of a motor business. Our common interest was enthusiastic; and it had built up with Jim into a real friendship. So I naturally telephoned him. It was the briefest of calls; but he left work immediately to drive over to me.

My mind when he came was still paralyzed beyond feeling. I was in a state of icy detachment. I told him the facts of the accident – slightly as I knew them – but I was little more than speaking words. I know, however, I was greatly appreciative that Jim had come. In my continuing detachment we discussed the subject of death. Exactly what we said I cannot recall. I remember I was aware that my mind was holding itself aloof. Possibly that reminded me of the dispassion of Socrates as death was closing on him – when he indicated to his gathered friends his personal expectation of escaping extinction. I mentioned the kind of reasons in support and present to his mind. The thoughts were coming into my consciousness and I was expressing them; but I confess in my own crisis and crucial test all such arguments, telling certainly, offered me no great certainty of the survival of the human consciousness. It was then that my sister, Grace, arrived.

Jim left us together; and I found it hard telling Grace even the small information there was. Grace herself was shocked and deeply saddened – she had found in Marjorie a great friend. My detachment began to falter; and then ceased altogether. That beyond doubt was just a *good*. Grace stayed with me till two in the morning. At that time she suggested I went to bed; even then she sat with me.

It was about four o'clock that my feelings had subsided sufficiently for me to recognize certain facts: that on several occasions during the evening, and in the morning hours also, I had experienced particular sensations in my body – sensations which in the ordinary course of events I would have perceived at once and identified as 'messages'. I recalled too that they had seemed to carry a burden of pain. Then I remembered how my left leg had moved many times as though someone had been tugging at it to attract my attention. I had been aware of these things; but in the flood of my emotion they had been swamped out. My mind did not fasten on to them. Now that I was calmer I was beginning to attach meaning to them. Moreover I was experiencing them again. Neither Marjorie nor I had spoken to anyone else of our special mutual sensitivity. We both thought we should not be believed; therefore we might as well save ourselves the trouble. But I started to tell Grace. She listened with an intent interest; and when I went on to my experiences of the moment she exclaimed: "It *must* be Marjorie!"

My mind regained its full grasp. I saw that Marjorie had been making sustained – and strenuous – efforts to get in touch with me and all the time my reaction had been nil.

I sent at once a reply message such we would use normally. As I sent it I knew that Marjorie was receiving me. Immediately the laboured efforts to rouse my attention, and so fraught with pain, ceased. I was aware of a great sigh – and then of Marjorie's voice in forthright exclamation: "The big nit's got the message at last!" Next I was sensing directly Marjorie's further surge of relief. An immense heave swept up through my body. After a brief pause, we settled to more normal exchanges, but conveying our emotion. I felt at peace; and, concerning Marjorie, I knew not merely that she existed as herself – an issue which was no longer an issue – but very importantly *she also* felt at peace. Grace saw the change and left the room. Whereas there had been no trace of sleep in me, all was different. Shortly I dropped off, and slept two hours.

The total experience lay close to a kind of experience that since has been given close attention – mostly over the past decade and primarily by medicals and psychologists. With the technical abilities of modern hospitals to resuscitate patients who otherwise almost certainly would have died there has come to the fore personal accounts by such patients of a highly characteristic type: of vivid encounters for instance with deceased near relatives, the encounters ending with injunctions from those relatives to return to life. The essentially characteristic facts have proved inconsistent with conjectures that the experiences are simply hallucinations – or induced by medication or by a lack of oxygen in the medical circumstances. Such experiences have invariably had a profound effect upon those experiencing them.

My experience had its profound effect upon me. Yet it contrasts somewhat. While *near-death*, the death was not my own; and, while the studied experiences have been described as prior to the deathpoint, my experience must be seen as post death-point. In its special way, although highly personal to me, it was not solely personal to me: it was a shared experience – it was acutely bi-personal. Moreover the orientation was reversed – Marjorie came to me. But these contrasts only widen the range of the near-death experience.

Most importantly from the time of my own encounter Marjorie and I were able to call one another over our link, and achieve emotional contact: speaking for myself a contact of inestimable value – and especially in the earlier months. We looked more to the emotive transfer of 'messages' than to thought transfer. I know, and knew then, that Marjorie equally wanted and set store by these occasions when we could be present each to the other. I recall how, often when through work or otherwise I was preoccupied, and so could not establish our fully-working link, I sensed directly her wish and intense longing that we should commence our accustomed exchanges. Necessary preoccupation was a state with which we had always been forced to contend. We could recognize it at once, often sensing something of its nature.

For the record to be exact, I must include one or two early occasions, very shortly after Marjorie's death, when for periods of hours I was not able to make, or sense any contact with her whatever. It was not that I felt she was preoccupied; and it was not like anything I had met before. It was as though she had ceased to exist. I have, as I will show, since come to some understanding of these blank periods. They were the result of deep recuperative sleep.

One such period was during the morning of the second day after Marjorie's death. I had to look up her bank manager, and this compelled a journey to the Aldermaston area. In the morning, on my waking, we had been in enlivening touch. Settled down to the drive, I thought it would be good to call Marjorie again, and I did so in our usual manner or rather I tried to, only to realize immediately that I was failing. I seemed altogether cut off from her. This remained so for the whole of the rest of the journey.

18

Later in the day we regained contact in a way that was dramatic. Phyllis was a close friend of Marjorie, and she was employed in the same Government Establishment. I knew her well, and she had suggested that it might help me if, after completing my morning's business, I collected her midday at Aldermaston when she could give me a quick lunch. The lunch was almost devoid of conversation. Our common unhappiness was inhibiting – yet I wanted Phyllis to know what I now knew. The lunch almost over, I told her in a very few words. She listened, saying nothing, and then I had scarcely finished when Marjorie released in me the strongest discharge of emotional energy I had ever experienced. It carried immense joy with it as it surged in me. To my astonishment Phyllis looked strangely at me, gasped, and flushed red. I knew I had not betrayed in physical expression my reception of the message. What flashed in my mind, as I saw her staring at me, was that she had receieved the message also. "What was that!" she exclaimed, trying to maintain her poise; but clearly disturbed, perplexed, and embarrassed. "It was Marjorie," I said, "– you too picked up the message."

Phyllis told me months afterwards that she had been greatly puzzled by all I had said, and by what she had sensed. She was inclined to think there must be some psychological basis to account for it. Could people really be alive after they were dead?

Phyllis's psychological reflections form an issue of some consequence; and I turn to it. It concerns possibilities I had inevitably felt a duty to consider with care – despite my clear consciousness of a real relation with Marjorie since her death. Over our link I experienced just that positive relationship one feels when talking over the telephone with someone one knows. What sort of weight could be placed upon a psychological explanation as an alternative view of my experiences?

Certainly such an explanation has been argued and the force of it – if it were valid – would be this: that what at first sight *seems to be the truth* (that Marjorie in some way continues a conscious existence after her death) is really a false interpretation – because what in fact has happened is radically different.

Instances in which this form of argument operates to useful effect abound in medical practice; and the argued form of psychological explanation of 'survival' experience, such as that with which we are here concerned, is drawn from these instances.

In the medical field a patient may say to his doctor that he is troubled by certain physical symptoms. The doctor, we will suppose, begins by treating him for these symptoms at their face value. But then the treatment fails. When other attempts – within the field of practical medicine – also fail, the doctor may form the opinion that the symptoms are not really symptoms of a physical origin. If so, he may refer the patient to a psychiatrist. Suppose that he does, and that the patient goes to the psychiatrist. The psychiatrist will endeavour to discover those facts which mentally could have induced the condition. In this way, and with the patient's intelligent co-operation, he may succeed in a cure. If he succeeds, it becomes abundantly clear that the explanation of the illness, although the illness seemed at first sight to be physical, was not physical at all but mental.

From such cases there emerges a principle: that the human mind can act unsuspectedly in certain happenings that are observed in the clinical field. The psychological argument concerning survival looks to this principle.

To see just how, one must go further. In the first place, thinking of the clinical field and given the principle, it is not unreasonable to contemplate the possibility of the presence of an element of purpose – acting in some degree and in some special way to mitigate or compensate for a troubling contingency. The assumption is often found to be supported. Characteristically the patient is not naturally aware of any such purpose. On this account the mental factor present is thought of as an activity of *unconscious mind*. A kind of illness is thus recognized in which the patient has deliberately, although unconsciously, brought into being a *compensation mechanism*. He has himself been the unconscious source of events to meet with his particular difficulty. This assessment of the situation is well supported by the overall facts in any such case.

The essence of an argument now becomes evident how invoking no more than psychological ideas it might be possible to explain the special events I experienced with and ever since Marjorie's death: I was generating them – not knowing that I was – to compensate for what I had lost.

Looking back in the light of extensive experience it is far easier to estimate the strength of such an argument than it was at the time. What I saw then was that the compulsion forcing the argument lay with the impossibility – such as that might be – of conceiving the reality of personal survival. That impossibility was really a matter of opinion; and opinion only must be a weak substitute for the clinical logic of practical psychology. There, it was very much fact which compelled the validity of the psychological interpretation: the patient did not respond to practical medicine whereas he was cured entirely apart from it. Substituting opinion for factual logic must greatly detract from the argument – measured against my actual experience I did not see that these psychological ideas were to be taken seriously.

In retrospect, and in overall survey, it is clear that the argument faces immense difficulty in a less personal logic. The difficulty arises through the form of development of the special events. This is discussed in Chapter 14; and the point is made that in such development the basic character of the psychological theory – in which I am the essential and sole source of happenings – becomes a matter of severe embarrassment: events are encountered which do not fit in well with so restricted a form of explanation. Their understanding seems to require some altogether broader basis than just my psychology.

Round about the beginning of the present century – and particularly for those attaching much significance to science – there might have seemed some point in seeking yet to find this broader basis and still to find it, if possible, in strictly non-survival terms. Established science held no easy accord with the likelihood of survival (Appendix IV). At the time however it was becoming apparent that this science was, quite separately from any matter of psychical events, in increasing conflict with the facts even of the physical world (Appendix IV). On this account existing science was replaced by a radically new science of far wider horizons. This new science has a formal structure clearly capable of accommodating the conception of survival (Appendix I). If ever there seemed a real compulsion in favour, for example, of a purely psychological interpretation of survival events, that moment has long passed.

The psychological compensation theory is typical of a very wide desire in popular thought this century – one in fact far from successfully borne out – to perceive every aspect of human activity falling solely within the laws of physics (Appendix IV). The special experiences of Marjorie and myself prior to her death, we had agreed, do not conform with such conceptions. It seemed to be eminently likely that human nature rests not only in the physical world but also in something rather differing – a factor we felt could be termed psychical.

Because of radical difference from matter there was no reason why this factor should not survive the terminal failure of the body. That was of course following logic used in traditional philosophy. We could not see however that *consciousness* must by this argument also survive death, of necessity. Consciousness, in logical possibility, might be a purely interactive effect between the brain and the psychical factor – that was something we did not see how to rule out; and it was not on the face of it consistent with the continuity of consciousness. Consciousness might happen to rest solely with the psychical factor. If it did, that would ensure continuity; but we did not *know* how it rested. On the Sunday before Marjorie's death, and as we were driving down the motorway from a weekend visit to my sister at her cottage in Leicestershire, Marjorie broke a long silence. She said: "You know, I think we do consciously survive death." That may well have been her intuition. I was left still wondering. Within seventy-two hours she was to prove her point completely to me: not in any remotest way either of us would have wanted.

But it was the route I entered upon discovery which previously I had felt was *ultra vires:* the question of survival, I was inclined to hold, was one undecidable by the human mind. That must be true of some methods of approach; on the contrary I now knew it was not undecidable in the logic of personal experience.

From that initial logic I went on eventually to perceive how the fact of survival is part of a more extended rational view. In the meantime many questions were calling to be raised and answered. In what way did Marjorie continue her consciousness? What was the nature of her present world? I doubted if my own sensitivities were up to the task. It might be said that this was the time to turn to the mediumship of recognized mediums. Yet I knew so little of this subject I held back. I considered that in my ignorance it could provide me with inaccurate, perhaps greatly inaccurate, information. I wanted to avoid this possibility. Thus far, I knew that the little I had learned and discovered was firm ground – that was how I wanted matters to stay. The problem in the end was solved quite unexpectedly. This led to a powerful stream of information.

Without the role of such a stream – a flux of elucidation which can be thought of as a communiqué – there would have been no writing of this book. But there happened in the meantime – and about fifteen months after Marjorie's death – two experiences, each impressive. I was at loss to understand them. Understanding eventually came. One of them was instrumental to the new viewpoint on the world which is an important part of this book. I give both, but with little comment now.

The first took the form of a greatly dramatic dream. Its content strongly and personally concerned me. At the start of the dream I was in a theatre, empty of audience as far as I was aware, and seated immediately in front of the stage. Marjorie was on the stage wearing a long blue gown and standing in the brilliance of a spotlight. Between the stage and myself was a black pit which could have been of infinite depth; and at the back of the stage simply a wall of darkness. We reached out towards one another over the blackness of the pit. Though she did not appear to speak, the words "I *am* with you" impinged upon my consciousness; but then she moved away and towards the back of the stage, and disappeared into its nothingness. As she did this my mind entertained the fear that something might take her from me. Nevertheless with the day and waking, our normal interchanges which had never been interrupted hitherto continued in the mutually supportive way they always had. Moreover, later events showed that this dream was not a communication in the sense that Marjorie *intended* me to dream it. It represented my sensitivity to her thought – when she was reflective and pondering what was to be the course of the future.

The second experience was not a dream; and I then did not appreciate its true nature; but I can certainly describe it as a vision. It occurred some days after the first. I had turned in for the night, and switching off the bedside lamp the room was left dark. I was half sitting up in bed thinking back over the day. Thinking like this for a few minutes in the darkness and – with my eyes wide open – I was distracted by seeing near my right shoulder there in front of me what looked like the folds of a black velvet cloth undulating slightly, almost rippling, and faintly illuminated. It was glinting. The next moment there was no cloth, but Marjorie's face scarcely more than nine inches from mine – and looking totally real. It poised motionless, and serenely smiling. Her eyes strangely were closed; yet I was conscious that she was looking directly at me. Her skin was perfect and brightly illuminated. In my mind I heard her voice say quite clearly: "All is well, darling." Then the bright form disintegrated in many slightly glowing fragments, and was gone. From the depths of my being I yearned for it to return. For a few seconds only it was there once more. Quickly it broke up again and vanished; but I was left with a pre-eminent happiness.

I shall be able to explain subsequently that the sense of assurance which I experienced *was intended*. I shall also go on to the way the vision was accomplished. That will not be my own theorizing; rather, what Marjorie herself had to say on the subject.

Chapter Two

SEQUEL TO A HOLIDAY

In the summer of 1974 – about eighteen months after my vision of Marjorie – I spent a short holiday with a friend of mine, and his wife, down in Devon. Bob and I had long shared professional interests. As an outcome of mutual enthusiasm for motor sport, and as relaxation, we had constructed more than one streamlined vehicle – in which concern about weight owed more to aircraft design than that of motor cars. We also found no small pleasure in the piloting of these very quick vehicles.

Two years earlier Bob had remarried and retired early with Doreen to a large and old house in Torquay. Once settled in, they wanted me to visit them and make a holiday of the visit; but this did not work out until the summer I have mentioned. By then unfortunately Doreen had become ill. I knew that she had recently developed thyroid trouble. It was only with my arrival that I gathered the problem was serious. I shall omit the details of her hypothyroidism other than to say that the doctors in charge took an extremely grave view. Doreen, trained as a nurse, may have realized the true character of her illness. During my visit, Jack – a friend of theirs and a professor of medicine – also came to stay; and I was present when he talked over the matter with Bob. What he impressed upon Bob was that he must expect the illness to prove fatal. Bob told me afterwards that three doctors at the Torbay Hospital had already given their opinion, and they saw the illness as terminal. Doreen, they considered, had just nine more months to live. This view was to be confirmed by Hammersmith Hospital – the hospital at which Doreen had gained her medical training.

Depressing as the situation might have looked and for no reason that I could have advanced – rather as if happier events were casting their shadows before – I did not feel the outlook so sombre. Without being uncaring, those are the facts; and I remember I was able greatly to enjoy some private flying with Jack. He was an enthusiast with light aircraft; and he was keen for me to have a first practical lesson in aerial navigation. My experiences with him in the air gave me the most profound respect for the pioneer flyers who found their way over great distances just by compass – and with none of the radio aids with which our Cessna was equipped. When contending with the misty moors of Cornwall and Devon, almost devoid of feature, it seemed we needed all the means we had. Jack certainly was not content with my dead reckoning. During a long leg between airfields which we had picked as markers, he insisted on a fix by radio beacons, even if this confirmation was only rough.

That holiday I met also Roger, another friend of Bob and Doreen, who after graduating at Exeter had in his lively way built up an antiques business. The meeting with Roger prompted Bob to tell me an extraordinary story about Roger's father.

He had, Bob said, suffered an abdominal illness. He had also received surgical treatment for it; but the operation had left him with a permanently irritable bowel. About this the doctors were unable to do very much. One day he entered into an eventful conversation. As it started it was just a polite formal exchange. His wife was affected by an incurable blindness. At her wish he took her as appointments fell due to a 'healer' practising at Bath. The day was that of one such visit. Guiding his wife into the healer's consulting room, the healer greeted him with: "Hello, Mr. Chubb! – and how are you today?" Mr. Chubb was in fact feeling the worse for his chronic condition; and his response conceded his poor tone.

"Oh," said the healer, "let's have you on the couch." Next, Mr. Chubb was listening to the facts concerning his operation; and then, with the diagnosis of his trouble, he heard also the confident assurance: "But I can put that right for you." For a short time the healer's hands appeared to be at work. From then on Mr. Chubb ceased to be haunted by his distressing condition.

While Bob was telling this, I was recalling a story I had encountered about William James, eminent psychologist and leader of early work in philosophy on pragmatism. He like Mr. Chubb had been beyond medical skill to cure. More seriously ill by far than Mr. Chubb, the visits of a healer – if the story was right – put him securely on the road to health. I felt there could be something to such stories. "Why," I said to Bob, "don't you take Doreen to this man at Bath?" Bob replied that he had already contemplated it but the healer – George Chapman – had a long waiting list: too long Bob believed for an appointment to be of help to Doreen. I urged him, nevertheless, to make all effort.

The sequel was more than interesting – and it worked a great change in Doreen. By a special arrangement an appointment was made: Doreen would attend at Bath in early September. I remember learning of this on my return from a caravanning holiday in Suffolk. By then Bob had discovered rather more concerning George Chapman's practice. I am not sure that Bob believed what he told me. Knowing Bob, I should have been surprised had he said that he did. He was simply reporting information given to him and this was that George Chapman did not *consciously* perform healing at all. He was only the trance vehicle used by a totally different personality Dr. William Lang, a noted physician who had died in 1937. When I learned of this, Doreen was to go for her appointment in a few days time. I said how keenly I looked forward to hearing of the outcome.

The hours of George Chapman's practice were rather limited: from 12 noon to 2 p.m. or thereabouts. This was because (so I gathered) his trance activity placed on him a considerable strain. Doreen's appointment was at twelve o'clock; and Bob brought her in by car in good time – in fact before George Chapman himself arrived.

Waiting in the reception room with Doreen, Bob said he saw an MGB sports car drive up. It was about five to twelve, and a man of middle years got out and walked though the reception room with a brisk step. Giving them a breezy "Hullo!" as he went by he entered the consulting room. At twelve o'clock Doreen was asked by the receptionist to go through for her appointment.

Her feelings were mixed. From what she had heard it seemed that the interview must surely be 'spooky' – but she knew she was desperately ill; and if her anticipation was frightening, as she confessed that it was, nevertheless she was spurred on.

The curtains of the consulting room were drawn, so that the light in the room was subdued; also the man sitting before her appeared both different in feature from and older than the George Chapman who had quickly steppped through the reception room. Much as she wanted healing, an underlying scepticisim compelled restraint. She heard a voice not sounding to her like George Chapman's enquiring: "What can I do for you, young lady?" Her response was a less-than-helpful "The doctors can do nothing for me."

From this point I shall continue the account, in recognition at least of the semblance of change in voice and personality, as though Doreen was not in fact now speaking with Mr. Chapman, rather (and to be seen more clearly in due course) with Dr. Lang – who asked her to be seated as he rose and walked slowly towards her. She observed that his eyes – remarkably – were closed. Indeed, as she noted, she never once saw him open them. As he approached her he said: "You are suffering from a lack of thyroxine." Then, as he ran his fingers down her side and his hands continued – so it looked to her – in general appraisal of her condition, he informed her of several other disorders. They were resultant, he explained, upon her thyroid underfunction – but he promised to correct them. First though he must, he stated, restore the functioning of her thyroid gland.

Telling her to lie on the couch, he was active for a period of about twenty minutes. He did not actually touch her. At the same time his hands were near different sites in turn. Most strikingly, he appeared to be in conversation with an entire medical team. Amongst names she could not remember, she heard those of *Basil*, *Susan* and *Lawson*. Basil, she later ascertained, was Lang's son – a brilliant surgeon who died early in life from pneumonia. Susan was Lang's first wife; and Lawson a hospital colleague of his. In due course Dr. Lang turned to Doreen again. "You have a bad headache," he commented. She admitted it was true: of late its hold on her had been constant. To Doreen's great relief he freed her of it. "You need energy," he continued; and, with his promise to remedy this deficiency, she felt warm sensations running up through her. "Now do not exert yourself too much to begin with," he advised her. "Rest in the afternoons – and come to see me in a month's time." Doreen got off the couch. Not only was her headache gone, but she seemed much better in herself. As she expressed her thanks and walked out she was experiencing admiration for an order of medical skill which – while it baffled her – she felt was masterly.

Bob held her hand as they drove home and, so he informed me, whereas it had been icy cold now it was warm. In a couple of days she was working all day in the house, and helping Bob with certain problems of packing – practical domestic problems arising because on the advice of the doctors they had sold their house and made plans to live in a much warmer climate.

Doreen had told Dr. Lang as she left of an outstanding appointment to attend at Hammersmith Hospital. "Go along," he said, "go along." At the hospital the advice was that she now showed a more balanced endocrine state; and that a steady deterioration in her white-cell count had been arrested.

Bob and Doreen held to their decision to go to the West Indies; but, before leaving, Doreen paid a further visit to Dr. Lang as he had instructed – this time at Aylesbury, where George Chapman for a long time had been running a separate and main practice. The treatment then dealt solely with a muscular condition of her arm. There was no need, Dr. Lang said, for any further visits. She told him that they were following plans to go to Trinidad made before ever the appointment at Bath was fixed. "That is excellent," said Dr. Lang, "– the climate can only do you good."

There is little more to say concerning Doreen. The terminal outcome of her illness – predicted, one has to assume, in all correctness by the doctors – was averted; and she returned to a physical well-being that enable them both to enjoy fully their new surroundings.

But questions will be teeming. On hard fact, and for one thing, who exactly was Dr. Lang when he was alive? If it was this Dr. Lang who cured Doreen, how actually was he able to return and treat her? And if he did treat her, what were his methods? Might not any idea of a return, however, be unrealistic? Was it not much more likely that the 'Dr. Lang' who diagnosed Doreen's illness and restored her health was simply a 'personality role' of George Chapman which comes to the fore in his healing sessions? What, and again for hard fact, is there to be said about George Chapman?

The developments of this book throw light in greater or lesser degree on all these questions. Some – principally those of hard fact – I can briefly touch on now.

Taking firstly George Chapman, he was a commando in the Royal Air Force during the Second World War – just after which he became a member of the Fire Brigade at Aylesbury. It was there he developed mediumistic abilities (Chapter 18) that, before long, were to be devoted to healing in the way I have been describing.

Dr. Lang early in his medical career practised as eye surgeon at the Middlesex Hospital. Later, from 1884, he was at the Central London Opthalmic Hospital – now the Moorfields Eye Hospital. Amongst his various activities he pioneered new surgical methods; and he was instrumental in founding the Opthalmic Society. He became a leading authority on diseases of the eye; and when he died in 1937, it was at the age of eighty-four, after enjoying a long retirement.

As to his return – in view of my experiences with Marjorie's death – I saw no *basic* difficulty myself in accepting the present participation of Dr. Lang. And, if it was fundamentally feasible for Dr. Lang to act through George Chapman as a channel, then it was only a matter of adequate testimony, to establish the fact. It was on record, as I discovered, that people who knew him well in his lifetime recognized him speaking through George Chapman: to discern clearly their former medical colleague, or their doctor who had attended them. His granddaughter talking with him was in no doubt he was her grandfather.

On the notion of a personality role of George Chapman, this is one of those ideas comfortable to live with so long as one does not have to meet with actual experience. It fits in well with a wide spread of thinking that looks to the science of the very early part of the century. It is the kind of idea which seems to be demanded by this thinking. The much more developed and competent science of today does not make the demand (see in particular Appendices I, IV and VI).

With the evidence I could bring together at the time, it appeared to be the truth – astonishing as the statement may sound in isolation – that Doreen had in her visit to Bath encountered the eminent eye surgeon William Lang thirty-seven years after his death. Certainly I took this as a provisional conclusion. My own acquaintance in due course with Dr. Lang placed it beyond doubt. (This raises a point of style – as a surgeon Lang in his lifetime was known as Mr. Lang, not Dr. Lang. In his practice through Chapman he has preferred the less remote form *Dr. Lang*.)

Bob, for all his natural scepticism, arrived at a conclusion like my own. This he told me before he and Doreen left for Trinidad. It is of interest that taking Doreen to her appointment at Aylesbury he himself met with and talked to Dr. Lang. He especially wished to thank him for his remarkable treatment of Doreen. It is also of interest that Bob regarded our common conclusion a proper ground for further enquiry.

Would it be possible, he wondered, to ask Dr. Lang some questions. The same thought had been formulating itself in my own mind. But then of course what would be the most instructive questions to ask. There was the very natural question of the nature of the existence now normal to Dr. Lang. It could presumably take a very different form from the one to which we are accustomed. If we asked the question, would we necessarily be able to understand the answer we might get? But it would be most interesting to know whether there was any counterpart to the physical body of this present existence. Then again and amongst fundamental topics, Bob had always inclined to doubt the existence of God: could Dr. Lang, he wanted to know, throw any light – as he might now be able with his extended knowledge – upon this subject. Considerations like these held their intellectual attraction. Beyond all such general enquiry I had particular and personal motivation: concerning Marjorie and her new life. The thought flickered in my mind that through Dr. Lang I might extend my contact with her. Was I hoping for too much? I was not even sure that Mr. Chapman – by all accounts dedicated to medical treatment – would be ready, in the interests of these non-medical matters, to make time available out of the all too little he was able to give.

Chapter Three

FIRST VISITS TO AYLESBURY

Marjorie, identifying with a classic pattern, had had a real fear I would not get along well with her mother, Hilda. This fear had some practical force since we felt that Hilda, with her advancing age, ought to come and live with us after we had settled down; perhaps quite soon. I could not have resisted such a plan even if I wanted – Marjorie had been so good and helpful when my own mother's health was finally failing. From my point of view I saw no actual difficulty. Her mother and I – so it seemed to me – had a true regard and liking for one another; but it was hard to persuade Marjorie she had no cause for doubt. As it all turned out, and with the tragedy of which neither of us dreamed, my standpoint seemed to be confirmed.

One might say that, with Marjorie's death, the loss which her mother and I shared could have brought the two of us more closely together: in fact I am sure that it did. Equally I am sure of origins in the mutual friendliness which earlier had sprung up spontaneously. It naturally happened that on Marjorie's death I formed the habit of visiting her mother frequently: we would chat and the time would slip by rapidly.

Coming to know her better, I felt I might be able to put to her the special experiences which I have related in Chapter 1. I did not think that she really believed me. I know now that she did not – her kindness restrained her incredulity. She had been brought up with traditional Christian instruction; but her mind ran to the practical. As is often true of people cast in her mould she found it difficult to be assured – in all honesty – that traditional Christian teachings, apart from those of purely moral aspect, could or must command the assent given so freely in the past. Therefore she had no convictions on a continuation of life beyond death. From a knowledge of psychology, she was aware of argument (on lines set down in Chapter 1 – but which we never entered upon in depth) that led her to put a weight upon what I had told her which I myself could not regard as realistic. The truth was – in terms she has since expressed it – that the knowledge which I had was hardly knowledge for her: at best and with all further reflection it was only half persuasive.

This half state was apparent when in the October of 1974, some few months after my stay in Torquay, she became ill. A month before she had been to Yugoslavia on a pleasurable holiday visit. On her return she seemed remarkably fit and well; so her illness was quite unexpected. The initial trouble, on the diagnosis of a Harley Street specialist, derived from damage to the base of the

28

spine. When shortly she became worse, tests at the West Middlesex Hospital showed she was suffering also from an inoperable stomach ulcer. Pain was continual, often great. Besides this and her seriously affected mobility, her nervous system was clearly reacting badly. Assailed in these various ways, the outlook did not betide well.

I had been keeping in good touch with Bob. At this point he wrote concerning Hilda with some advice – about which I was at first uncertain: but his own conviction that it was valid stood out clearly in his characteristically brief sentences. I decided to follow his suggestion.

What he advocated was no more than that I should write to George Chapman, and tell him the situation. No travelling on Hilda's part was entailed – something which strongly commended itself. The difficulties of a visit to Aylesbury were great – even supposing in the first place I had succeeded in putting over the idea. If I wrote to George Chapman, Bob insisted, I could count upon help somehow being given. It was termed 'distant healing' – a form of treatment not always so effective as when going to see Dr. Lang like Doreen, but well worth while to ask for. It seemed unbelievable – but I recalled what I had already encountered. I wrote stating the details; and soon I received a short reply. Treatment, George Chapman said, had already commenced. He would like a report in a month's time.

When I looked in a day or so later, to see how Hilda was, I perceived immediately from her voice and appearance that she was distinctly better. She was still far from well – that was clear. But there was this marked improvement. I said nothing about my writing to George Chapman; yet with travelling difficulties plainly eased, I felt I ought to tell her about Doreen's remarkable appointment at Bath. I went into it fully, and explained George Chapman's participation and Dr. Lang's. Not expecting too much, I was surprised but delighted to hear Hilda say: "I wish he could heal me." I asked her if she *really* meant what she had just said. She assured me she was in earnest – and if I would obtain an appointment, and take her by car, she was she told me prepared to make the effort of a visit to George Chapman's clinic at Aylesbury.

I wrote to George Chapman again. He proposed a date in January, and added that the distant healing would continue meanwhile. When the time arrived, I took Hilda to my home in Oxfordshire. This was two days before the appointment – so as to break the travelling into two parts and, before setting out on the second shorter journey, to give her time to recover from the first.

The appointment was in the afternoon; and during the morning she told me she was feeling tense, apprehensive, and frightened. I reminded her that Doreen's reaction had been exactly the same – and, after all, if the appointment was what I felt sure it would be then it must be a strange very extraordinary occasion. We talked, and the conversation wandered. It was clear Hilda did not fear any physical harm to herself. She seemed quite certain of that. While she was not sure she would actually benefit, she had a clear expectation that she would – it was definitely her motivation in making the great effort now. On this vital issue of benefit, she had some particular questions: would it depend on her at all? – would it depend upon her deeper beliefs? If the latter, it was really a lost cause: faith of that kind with her was meagre. I said that, the way I understood it, Dr. Lang's achievements depended upon the operations he performed and not upon the convictions of his patients – adding (on evidence *via* Bob) that I was quoting Dr. Lang himself on the subject.

This carried us back to her state of apprehension. Intellectually she questioned whether the matter was one in which Dr. Lang could *possibly* be involved – and yet she suspected that he might. In that case it would not be just George Chapman she would be meeting: it was this that troubled her – this radical element of the unexperienced. Beyond going over the good that had ensued to Doreen, and the elation of spirit her experience had brought her, there was not a lot I could say at the time.

It is unfortunately a fact that a multitude of apprehensions centre upon the question of death. Even in the abstract, it is not a subject that anyone usually cares to discuss or contemplate – it is natural to shy away from it. When it affects one personally it tends deeply to depress.

In all this, lack of knowledge is a potent factor. It gives freedom to those inmost mistrusts. Quite objectively, death at large is a dread subject. And the question of the impact of the dead carries all the same undertones and colouration. Mental vacuum, reinforced in vicious circle by taboo of silence, tends to tie the human mind to this state.

In the event, it was remarkably natural. When Hilda was called to the consulting room, I heard Dr. Lang's cultured, authoritative, nevertheless kindly voice greeting her: "Hello, Mrs. White." She told me the story ten minutes later – as soon as we were back in the car. First he had invited her to be seated. Then he asked her to tell him which was the worst of all her various troubles. It was her back, she answered – and her left leg. He came over to her, and felt carefully down her spine, remarking that she had an arthritic condition. "I will give you an injection for that," he told her; and she heard him speak to certain persons that like the injection were not visible. Next he wanted her to lie on the couch – indeed he helped her on to it. "Close your eyes and relax," he said. "You have a constriction," he continued, "which is preventing the proper flow of your gastric juices. I must do an operation to relax it." She was not aware of anything happening – she simply continued to recline on the couch. Then he said to her: "Now what do you drink?" She informed him that occasionally she liked a sherry; but she did not drink much. "Oh, a sherry will be all right," he told her. Then she remarked that sometimes she liked a glass of Advocaat before going to bed. "That's good," he exclaimed: "that's very good. You must have that – it will do you good." He assisted her down from the couch and as he said goodbye to her he added: "Come and see me again in two months time."

Hilda's spirits were excellent on the journey back. She felt able to make the drive directly to London, and I noticed a tinge of colour had replaced her previous pallor. I was not sure whether this might mark only the excitement of the occasion, or whether it went further. Perhaps it was in part a nervous reaction; but from then on some natural colour became the norm with her, rather than the exception. Gradually too, as the weeks passed, she appeared more nourished – and she was able to go for short walks. Her friends remarked that she was looking better. Certainly she was greatly improved – but there were troubles that remained: mostly it was that she still had some stomach pain – and a long standing catarrhal condition was still trying her. When I wrote to George Chapman, I mentioned these things. He arranged a second appointment in March.

Taking her once more to Aylesbury I was keen to gather her further account. As last time, I had heard Dr. Lang's raised but friendly tones: "Come in Mrs. White, come in. How are you now?" She told him she still had pain in her back, and in her leg; and then, although her stomach trouble was less, it still worried her – and her catarrh was a sore trial. She remarked with a tinge of humour in her voice that it was a rather long list. "Sit down on the stool," he said, "and I will examine your back." He felt carefully down her spine. "I will give you another injection, and in a few days you should feel very much better." Then he wanted her to recline on the couch again. "You have a stomach ulcer," he remarked, " – but I will repair that. Then I will increase your blood flow." A little later he told her: "I have also operated at the back of your nose, for your catarrh." Relating these facts to me, Hilda said she could not omit the kindliness of his manner. This had greatly impressed her.

What were the results of this second visit? Principally I heard much less, or little at all, about the more serious troubles – though her ills were not all removed. Her catarrh at times practically disappeared; and at others it was still apparent. On the whole she steadily improved, and became able to get out and about, and to enjoy life very much, though not entirely, as she had before. Casting my mind back to her previous serious decline, her pain-racked condition and general collapse, the reversal of trend – just as with Doreen and following immediately upon this kind of treatment – was something which challenged normal understanding. I felt myself wanting, even more, to talk with Dr. Lang.

In May 1975, two months after Hilda's second appointment, I was at length able to meet him at Aylesbury. But there is a background of anterior events in which I was personally concerned that trace through to this meeting.

I go right back to my student days when I was researching and when I went down with a long illness.

It was before the arrival of antibiotics. Their availability, it was the medical opinion, would have saved much later trouble. A major difficulty I encountered after my protracted illness was a general lowering of my powers to resist infection.

It had all started with an attack of infective hepatitis; but there were complications difficult then to treat. They led to my ensuing various susceptibilities to infection. Over the years these susceptibilities had slowly diminished, but not disappeared. Catching a cold, for instance, usually led to bronchitis – or tracheitis. I had pneumonia several times.

Even with the help of modern antibiotics, secondary infections of this kind can be very depleting. At the time of the developments of this chapter I had for some years been finding it more difficult to cope; and the latter part of November in 1974 I was facing the respiratory trouble to which I was liable. Although antibiotics quickly enabled me to take on my usual tasks, I felt far from well. The rest from a week's holiday at Christmas seemed to put me right. With the usual pressures of work again, the improvement was short lived. I had seen at first hand with Hilda the change that distant healing – which I took to be some form of attendance by Dr. Lang – could bring about; and, knowing this, it was I thought foolish not to write to George Chapman and ask for such treatment for myself. On the first weekend of the New Year I sent off a letter explaining the medical details – in fact I remember posting it on the Sunday afternoon.

Next day and after work I went to fulfil an invitation to dinner with some friends in London. The drive home to Oxfordshire inevitably took over an hour, and I was late to bed. Feeling very tired, I immediately fell asleep; but about four o'clock in the morning I was awakened. At the same moment I felt so overpoweringly the urge to breathe deeply that I was forced into this breathing. If I tried to stop, it seemed as though, I would suffocate; so I had to continue. The state lasted for perhaps, twenty minutes. Finally I had the sensation of a stab in my abdomen. After that I fell asleep, to be called back to consciousness by the insistence of the alarm clock. With my waking thoughts I recollected the happenings of two hours earlier. I could not escape one particular mental comment: Dr. Lang appeared not to lose much time in getting round to his patients!

Then I asked myself if I detected any difference in my physical condition. Quickly I realized that I did. My nasal passages had become free, and the tightness and pain at the top of my bronchials were markedly less. My skin felt dry and warm instead of cold and clammy.

When I went out to the car to drive to work, I felt so much better in myself I put on a light mackintosh rather than the heavier and warmer one I had previously been wearing. The next night I experienced none of the heavy sweating that, since the Christmas holiday, had returned – and in a few days my bronchial passages had healed.

Quite dramatically the improvement in my condition was subjected to severe test. Just after Hilda's first visit to Aylesbury, and when driving her back to London in the late afternoon, the windscreen of the car crazed – as toughened glass windscreens can do at moments of great inconvenience or hazard. Fortunately we were able to complete the journey despite the crazing. In the evening, when I came to make my journey back to Oxfordshire, the weather had turned to rain; and – so fate had it – getting into the car the windscreen fell in. I remember vividly the rain stinging my eyes as I drove, making them smart, so that it was difficult to keep them open. I finished the journey very cold and wet. Next morning it was frosty; and there was the long run in to work. During lunchtime I took the car to my friend Jim, for him to organize a new windscreen. He loaned me a substitute car, and I was able to complete the day with protection from the elements – to which, since the previous evening, I knew I had been exposed to a degree that on my past form was sure to bring on bronchitis. The day after, making my run home in the evening, and having a meal, I noticed the symptoms of the start of a cold. I feared not merely a severe cold but an incapacitating bout of bronchial trouble.

I am *not* a person of great faith, and I was worried: particularly since I had at work arranged a group of meetings I certainly did not want to see abandoned. I went to bed early, and turned to the possibility of informing Dr. Lang by thought transference.

I focused my thoughts on him, calling him several times by name in my mind, then telling him briefly my experience and worries. The words "It will be all right" seemed to fall into my mind immediately – and, remarkably, to underline the message they flashed momentarily before my vision in luminous letters. Soon I fell asleep. I woke up about three hours later. I thought of the cold symptoms, but they had gone. I sent a quick message of thanks to Dr. Lang; and dropped off

32

again into sleep. When I got up in the morning I felt below par; but of the otherwise certain cold there was no sign; and in a few hours I was my usual self. Since that time I have gone down to cold and influenza infections; but they have not been the problem they used to be. With my ordinary care, they have not normally brought on the handicapping complications which in the past were so difficult to avoid.

For the record I note some interesting circumstances about a month later when entirely unrequested Dr. Lang paid me a further visit in the night. Instinctively I knew Dr. Lang was present. The sequence of events was different – though the time was again about four o'clock. I was awakened to hear clicking sounds in the room. They seemed in some way familiar; but I could not place them, and I dozed off, only to be reawakened by them again and yet again – all within a space perhaps of ten minutes. When dressing later I recalled the clicking sounds; and I knew what they were. I had heard exactly these sounds sitting in the waiting room at Aylesbury, when Dr. Lang was treating his patients.

All this time my mind hopefully was reflecting upon what questions I could usefully put to Dr. Lang – supposing a talk to be arranged. If the meeting led nowhere in regard to Marjorie – as it might – I wanted, nevertheless, to ensure the utmost use of the all-too-brief opportunity to gain knowledge.

There would be no special value in asking Dr. Lang how he achieved the remarkable results that he did. Any reply to that question must rest surely on issues of a more fundamental nature. Without some understanding of these, the answer could convey but little. Questions, therefore, had to be directed to more elementary matters.

Here, developments all along had favoured a dualistic – perhaps pluralistic – outlook on reality. Certainly – and at least – I felt they strongly inclined to a dualism of mind and matter – each possessed of a standing independently of the other. It was on these broad lines it seemed that I had to view the psychical and physical aspects of a person. My thoughts naturally included the long-standing problem in philosophy as to how such differing realities can interact – as clearly they must do.

The ideas with this problem that, in the first place, one must think of are simple – even if the question they raise is not. I move my pen over the paper now – a physical activity – because my thoughts and will are formulating in a particular way – a mental activity. The mental activity is causing the physical. Again, as I physically scan a sentence I have written, mental activity according to the meaning of the sentence occurs in my mind. Mind acts on matter, and matter acts on mind – but how?

Perhaps Dr. Lang could throw some light on this difficult question. So I noted the relation of consciousness to the physical world as a possible starting point – and added many subsidiary questions that sheltered, so to speak, under this broad umbrella. Then I remembered Bob's fundamental question: what could Dr. Lang, with all that he now knew, say about the existence and nature of God? These questions, I thought, must more than occupy any interview I was likely to be granted.

Having reached this point, I wrote asking Mr. Chapman for a meeting with Dr. Lang. I said that what I was looking to now was not medical treatment, rather it was knowledge; and I suggested that, if my request could be granted, then perhaps I could see Dr. Lang after he had attended to his normal patient list – because discussions have a tendency to overrun allotted times.

George Chapman gave me a very early date, but sent me only an ordinary patient appointment card – with a time on it that could hardly have represented the end of the patient list. As it was, the date did not fit in with my commitments; so I asked for another date – and again requested an end-of-the list timing. In this last respect I was still not successful; but I was given the interview date in May 1975 that I have spoken of.

The day came; and I entered Dr. Lang's consulting room. The light in the room was low, with the curtains drawn; and I saw a man seated on a chair by the window in a reclining posture that was relaxed. His features were round, and his eyes closed. He looked an old man, but not markedly so.

He rose to greet me, and asked me to sit down. I said, as he also sat down, that I believed he knew I wanted the interview in order to ask him some questions: questions of interest for science and philosophy, also for religion. He told me he was aware of this; and I added that perhaps before starting on these subjects I could enquire if he remembered Dr. Milne, who before he had become our family doctor had held the position of Senior Consultant at the Moorfields Eye Hospital where he (Dr. Lang) had earlier pioneered in eye surgery. "Yes," he said, "I knew George Milne. Lawson was also a colleague," he added, and he went on to include other names. I continued that Dr. Milne died recently in advanced years; but, as Dr. Lang had no comment, I turned to the main issues.

I made the initial point that he, Dr. Lang, with – as it surely was true – the new advantages he now possessed, and the greater knowledge now at his disposal, might be able to give illuminating answers to difficult questions in the fields I had mentioned.

To lead into my first question, I commented that a human being is distinguished in a fundamental respect from an inanimate object through the possession of consciousness – although in the purely physical respect both human being and inanimate object must fall in the same class. "What," I enquired, "can you say, Dr. Lang, on the relation of consciousness to the physical world?"

Dr. Lang drew himself up from his chair, and looking down at me, said quite firmly, even crisply: "I'm afraid I cannot answer that question." This response was unsettling; and I thought highly disappointing. There was a moment's silence in which I felt that he sensed my state of mind – for he remarked: "I have a long patient list; and I have to consider the strain on my medium. On this subject you have raised I could talk for hours." It sounded final, but I made another try. I ventured, hopefully, that he might nevertheless be able to answer one or two questions if I put them in a form that could be replied to briefly. For instance, I said, could he state categorically whether consciousness is possible in the absence of a body.

The answer to that question, I felt, must by implication be extremely revealing. Dr. Lang's response was quick: "Yes," he said, "certainly it is possible. *The seat of consciousness is not the body, it is the psyche, the soul, the mind, the spirit, however you like to term it. The body is simply the means by which the person himself is enabled to be aware of his physical surroundings. When I take over the use of George Chapman's body, he relinquishes his use of it; and he ceases to be aware of what goes on in this room. What he loses is his physical awareness – his rapport with his physical surroundings."*

I thanked Dr. Lang, and noted that he had given me more than a purely categorical answer. I went on that I should very much like to ask him a question on the subject of God. I said that I could see certainly two broad approaches to this subject: one intuitional, one purely rational. As to the first, it was unquestionable that very many people have the sense that in a universal, or transcendent, way they are cared for or cared about. This sense is often most acute in crises. Then, purely rationally, the paradox has long been known that an explanation which runs back through a never-ending chain of (otherwise fully satisfying) reasons is not explanation at all. There *has* to be a final reason, or the paradox remains.

Dr. Lang was silent while I was speaking – also when, momentarily, I paused. I said to him: "Dr. Lang, does what I say make sense to you?" He replied at once: "Oh yes, it does – but when you have said that, so much still rests on how you finally conceive of God. Many people entering the next life suffer great disappointment; because the form in which they have conceived God is wrong. *There is no God-figure.* People who think of God as one ordinarily thinks of a person are doomed to disappointment."

Again I thanked Dr. Lang for his answer. He, in a charmingly persuasive way, and walking across to me, asked: "May I be of medical assistance to you?" I said that while it had not been my aim in the appointment, yet if he could benefit me, I would readily accept. "After all," I added with a smile and thinking of his night attendances, "I am already a patient of yours, Dr. Lang!" He also smiled at this; and I commented; "You know, I could not help noticing you when you came to visit me." "I am not at all surprised," he remarked; and he told me: "Your psychical activity is more intense than in most people."

This put me in mind of the ability Marjorie and I possessed to communicate in our distinctively psychical fashion; and I remarked on it. He enquired how old Marjorie was when she died; and he also asked how old I was. He told me that he was about my age when he came to be interested in the next existence. "It is a good age to commence such a research," he said. "I learned much before I died. I suggest that you write to George Chapman, and tell him that I would like him to make time for a further talk – when the patient list is a short one, and when we can have an hour at least. You realize I have to safeguard my medium. I have to monitor him, so that too great stress is not placed upon him – but now . . . if you will lie on the couch."

I did this; and he continued: "I want to give you more energy. I will form a psychic link between the medium and you. Now just relax completely, and close your eyes." Very gently he placed his fingers over my eyes; and whereas up to this point I had been keenly alert, now the acuity of my consciousness seemed to fall away. I heard him talking again; and suddenly I realized he was making a statement of the greatest importance. With an effort I grasped at the *first part* of what he was saying, and in doing so totally missed *the rest*. Somehow, I felt I could not break in on the proceedings and ask him to repeat what he had just said – but I realized I had heard these words: "Dr. Best, you *may be interested to know that your young lady is attending this operation.* She . . . " His hands – without touching me – continued to move over my body slowly; then he went on: "I want to increase your blood flow." I heard him speak to Susan, and Basil, also Lawson.

At that point I experienced some extremely loud clicks, white flashes of light appearing intensely before my vision with each click. "Now breathe deeply – and out," he instructed. "Raise yourself. You can get off the couch"

He was telling me now he must say goodbye. But he had some concluding words: "As a physicist, you will be interested to know that my son Basil wanted to study physics – when though I sent him to Cambridge, I told him it was more important that he should train as a medical." Had his eyes not been closed, I judged from Dr. Lang's voice, that I should have seen a twinkle in them. I shook hands, expressing my thanks, and realizing he held given me a full half hour of his time. "Write out your questions in a list if you like," he said as I left the consulting room.

I drove home. I was feeling fitter in myself; and I was wondering how it was that Marjorie came to be present. At least it was clear that the move I had made – to meet Dr. Lang – held promise. What I did not realize was just how much I had failed to catch concerning Marjorie when I was lying on the couch.

Chapter Four

TALKING WITH DR. LANG

I move on to my first long conversation with Dr. Lang. More correctly, I must say it was his highly informative talk with me. At most I did little more than ask a few questions. Listening to him, he expressed specific ideas often quite new to me. While, broadly, I saw that they confirmed my existing outlook yet in part they took me by surprise.

At the strictly human level, I thought the meeting revealed much of the character of Dr. Lang, and of what impelled him. It was evident in some news of Marjorie.

Writing to George Chapman to arrange the further meeting I gave him an outline of the interview I had had with Dr. Lang. I also stated how Dr. Lang wanted him to make available a period of an hour or so for a further conversation and after patients had been dealt with. Mr. Chapman suggested a date in the August of 1975. Generously he asked me to come simply as his guest. The time he set down was ten past two; but, in fact, the treatment of patients continued for a half hour beyond that.

Dr. Lang greeted me cordially; and I began by speaking of the outlook on the world to which I had come. So many of my scientific colleagues were ready to assume that all reality could be broken down and reduced solely to the groundwork of physics – the physical reductionist view. These ideas applied for instance with great illumination and power to the field of chemistry; but I had encountered good reason to regard them as an over-simplification when it came to human personality: what I had in mind to say next was that I hoped very much to learn how one could build on this realization. But Dr. Lang was nodding and smiling; and I saw in his smile a good-natured impatience to start at once on answering my unspoken question – so I relaxed simply to listen.

I was right about his intention. He first made it clear that he wanted to bring to bear – though very differently – much the kind of basic simplicity which appeals in the materialism I had mentioned. He wanted to show me the character of the Universe almost in a word. The operative word was 'drive': the most important aspect of the Universe is its *driving force*. In asserting this, he stressed that he was speaking of force at the psychical level: the level of mind or psyche. But he was not above using an old-fashioned term: he would, for the moment at least, speak of this force as spirit. Spirit is the driving force of the Universe. That is what stands first and foremost – and that is what he wanted me to know as the truth central to the Universe. Spirit is a force differing from the blind tendencies which drive things on inevitably in purely physical circumstances: it is conscious, and it has freedom of intention. It is not only, he went on to say, the most important factor in the Universe – *it is the important common element of our two different existences, mine and his.*

These generalities endorsed vividly the picture which already I had felt must be the truth. Then he turned to particular things, and to the individual psyche. It was not a new conception to me, but it was arresting when he stated that "the individual psyche possesses gender". It is masculine or feminine, he said, just as human beings as we know them here are male or female. It was even more striking when he continued that in the next existence "the male and female psyche can, at will, reproduce the psyche". So new psyches were continually being born – and this in order that they should as opportunity presented participate in life at our physical level. Here, he pointed out, he had taken me to the starting point of the evolution of the individual psyche. This evolution – as he was more than once to reiterate – is a matter of supreme significance in the development of the Universe.

He wanted to elaborate on the subject. It was as though he had sensed the question I was immediately wishing to put: if a newborn psyche is to be understood as relating itself uniquely – and with the opportunity – to an infant body in this existence, then at what point does the association begin? Is it before, at, or after the birth of the child? Dr. Lang asserted that as the norm it commences "when the child first draws breath". Up to the association point, he remarked, the child is only a mechanism – highly complex, but still no more than a piece of biophysical mechanics. The remark caused him to digress. It was for this fact, he said, that he took no very strong view concerning abortion. Prior to the association point there was no fundamental argument against it. It was not murder – in any natural sense of the word. You could not describe the destruction of a machine, however complicated, as the taking of life.

He continued on the subject of the association of the psyche by a statement which came almost as a shock. So he now asserted, the psychical association is not always the association of a newborn psyche: far from it. "Are you saying, Dr. Lang," I broke in, "that the Eastern belief in reincarnation is right?" "Reincarnation," he stated categorically, "is a fact." This was something I had not before seriously entertained; or thought likely. The way on the other hand that Dr. Lang was speaking of it, it appeared but a commonplace – if basic – truth of existence. Its significance must I could see be far-reaching; and many questions were rising in my mind. Is the process inevitable? If it is purely of volition, what aims does an individual have in returning? What lapse of time may there be in the interim? I could not help thinking of Marjorie – I had never (consciously) connected such a possibility with our continuing relationship.

Dr. Lang gave me good answers on all these issues as the conversation worked itself out. For the moment they remained but thoughts hanging in my mind; and Dr. Lang was following up with a most interesting comment. What he was saying exhibited very much his professional interest as a physician. There is usually a strong difference, he stated, between new-psyche children and those of reincarnation. The new-psyche child is much more actively taken up with its surroundings. A reincarnating psyche tends to be more detached. It is often not until the child's brain has developed to the age of five years, that such a psyche begins to take a real interest in life.

I made a note to compare these ideas with the children of families I knew. When I came to this it was clear that the two children of one particular family illustrated Dr. Lang's contrast – and, so it appeared, markedly. The first of the two – without precocious manifestations of genius – had from an early age always seemed remarkably adult in his approach to life. His interest in things was noticeably 'laid-back' and more academic than practical – as if he already possessed an acquaintance of sorts with them. He showed also a generosity above average. These were characteristics hard to miss. With the second child it was scarcely possible to discover traits more different. The child had an avid interest in objects which could only be sated by the dismantling of the objects: by opening them up or dismembering them. Such primitive enquiry was matched by an almost unrelenting and equally primitive acquisitiveness. In one sense or another it was – and it appeared fair to say – a child with all to learn. Given that one of those children was a newcomer to this scene, but the other was not, it could not be difficult to decide which was which. Especially is it so if – and this is at the root of Lang's comparison – the basis of distinction should be taken to lie with the evolutionary matter of learning what life has to teach.

But to go back to my meeting with Dr. Lang, he was wanting to enlarge upon the subject of reincarnation. There are many people walking about today he said, who were here in the time of Queen Elizabeth I – some, he added, even at the time of the apostles. No one returned, however, except of his own choice. It might be for any of various reasons: often it was to make good some deficit of the earlier life; or to offset, perhaps, the effects of regretted actions. Again, it might be purely with the object of new experience or achievement. As I gathered later, the love of adventure influences some – but broadly speaking it was always a question of whether the individual was ready yet to remain in the next existence. Whatever might be the particular reason – and Lang stressed this – the decision to return to this life is always a matter of personal desire.

Accepting his authority in all this, thoughts were beginning to dawn with me in quest of the truth in my own case. As if to answer my silent question he said: "You are very old – you have seen many existences." It was a statement I had not expected. I found it rather halting – my thoughts were slow in reaction. I had been keeping good station with Lang – so I thought – as he had been talking; but this opened up a wide gap. Perhaps I was experiencing unreasoning incredulity. I heard myself exclaiming: "Are you quite certain, Dr. Lang?" "Yes," he affirmed quietly, and definitely, "I am quite certain."

There was a brief pause. Against the broad philosophic background he had laid down initially, I could see the rationale of reincarnation; and that it must bear upon the supreme issue as he held it of the evolution of the psyche. Both this existence and the next, it was appearing, dovetailed in the psychical build-up of the individual. It might be best, I felt, if the question of my own psychical age were left over for the present; and if instead we could consider the more important question for instance of how the transition from the present life to the next is accomplished. This, I reflected, must surely fit in with the broad topic I had raised in my first interview: how does consciousness relate to the world of our experience?

Lang proved ready to talk on these lines. It would be helpful and indeed necessary, he said, to contemplate first the overall nature of the human organism. We in this existence were apt – even at our most realistic – to take too superficial a view. There was indeed the physical body that gives us sense awareness of the physical world in which we live. There was indeed the psyche, the dynamic part of our nature, and the seat of our consciousness But these were not the entire story.

One has to understand, he explained, how in superimposition to our physical body-structure there exist two other body-forms. They are not evident to us *via* our physical senses; but they are present all the same, and they extend right throughout the physical body. One of them extends (usually) somewhat beyond the physical body, though not greatly – about two or three inches. This body is electrical in character; and it stands in what he called an energizing relation to the physical body. It is energy interactive both with the psyche and the physical body in an intermediary activating sense: without such a body and without entering upon details the psyche could not, he said, control – or, reversely, react to – the physical body. Here was a first answer to my question on the relation of consciousness to the physical world. With Lang's approval (there are other designations) I shall call this energizing body-form simply *the electrical body*. The other body-form met my question on the transition from this life to the next.

Lang was content I should call the form the *psychical body*. It is in fact of the nature of a physical body, except that it is not physical in our sense of the term: it is constructed of matter of an order quite different from what we mean when we speak of matter. There is no difficulty in the two kinds of matter interpenetrating – but despite their great disparity and interpenetrability it is not impossible for them to interact. The psychical body is, in many respects, almost an exact replica of the physical body.

Further, the physical and psychical bodies are interconnected. This is by a linkage. Lang did not go into its function – but as an issue of detail I discovered in talks we were subsequently to have that it is to transfer from the physical body energy needed by the psychical body.

The psychical body, so he continued, separates away with the death of the physical body; and the linkage parts. The psyche then substitutes use of the *psychical* body for its previous use of the *physical* body. Memories survive the substitution. In further talks, Lang explained that this was so because – at variance with the common beliefs of neurophysiologists and just as consciousness itself is really a matter of the psyche – the memories of events are not retained in the brain, but in the psyche. To return however to his present explanations, Lang added that with the transition to the next existence the psychical body rapidly gains in strength. It is vitalized by the ambient radiations of the world in which it then finds itself.

You can say, if you like, Dr. Lang remarked, that here and now the next-life body exists in you in a germinal sense. "So St. Paul was right," I observed. "Yes," said Dr. Lang: "St. Paul was quite correct."

My observation was totally a digression, and the conversation was only momentarily diverted by it. But it had struck me forcibly when Lang used Paul's germinal simile to describe entry upon the continuing life. Paul, I had judged, must be using the language of poetry – not of science. On Lang's authority I was

40

wrong: Paul's knowledge was objective. The realization impressed me – hence my remark, almost exclamation. With the opportunity in due course, I looked up what St. Paul actually had to say; and it made remarkably good sense. How did St. Paul know? It was knowledge that had to invoke another dimension, exactly as I was invoking that same dimension in approaching Dr. Lang. Within the natural and normal dimensional limitations of this present existence we do not have such knowledge: the same as within the limitations, in mathematics, of ordinary – non-complex – numbers the truth of propositions of major importance in algebra cannot be decided, though it can if numbers are seen in the light of the added dimension of the complex plane.

It may or may not be evident in just what actual way St. Paul had gained his knowledge. The manner he put it however and the circumstances which took him to this point both bear very much and with illumination upon what Lang was saying. They bring some distinctly basic issues to the fore.

The background is St. Paul's touring of the Roman world and his stay at Corinth, capital of Roman Greece and centre of commercial and intellectual adventure. While at Corinth he was heard with interest and open-minded criticism. It was a visit which lasted for eighteen months, and since it overlapped with the term of office of the proconsul Gallio it must have been about A.D. 51 or 52. The imprint it left on Corinth was the church he founded there. A few years later he wrote two letters to this church – on problems which had arisen since his departure.

One problem was over the Christian teaching of the continuity of personality beyond death. What Paul had said was not criticised in broad terms – but to the Greek mind an important matter of detail was inevitably in dispute. The criticism was not fundamental since Greek thinking much inclined to a continuation of the existence of the self. The difficulty was that it saw this continuity as divested of material trappings. It is in the tradition of this view that we still tend to think of the dead as continuing in the fashion of spirits freed of the body. *Disembodied spirits* – the words highlight this very Greek issue – is a common expression with us. Lang had made it altogether plain that any such view is contrary to fact. In his "First letter to the Corinthians" Paul found it necessary to insist upon the same point.

Paraphrased, the argument he faced goes like this: "If you say that the dead are not just *spirits*, and that they have a *bodily* existence, then how do they come by this body (which you say they have) and what is it like?" In Paul's own words, as translated by James Moffat with his care to approximate the modern equivalent, the points addressed to him were: "How do the dead rise? What kind of body have they . . .?"

Quickly, Paul dismisses any philosophic attractiveness in the pure-spirit theory: that is simply a folly, he exclaims. Perhaps he is overquick in his dismissal – but it is a good exercise to try thinking out in detail what a continued existence would be like if the theory were true. Looked at on these lines I feel some sympathy with Paul's impatience. In our present state of development the loss of a physical type of environment would leave us a content to life that must be abysmally small. What you really need to contemplate, Paul says, is some form of 'physical' continuity. In this lies another major issue. The continuity, he says, is of the kind you have, taking a simple parallel to guide your thoughts, when you sow a seed.

41

Death corresponds to the implanting of the seed in the ground; and there is something in you now which is only waiting for death in order to become your new body from then on. This is what he terms the *spiritual* body; and it is very evident that with his own knowledge of these things he can himself serenely look on death – prime symbol of human frailty – as a wonderful elevation of humanity.

The issues that surface with St. Paul's first letter usefully place Dr. Lang's expositions in perspective. And the practical import of such knowledge, embracing the issue of the outlook on death, is particularly weighty.

It would be expecting too much that Paul should have any grasp of the electrical aspects of the nervous system. So it is not surprising if he is entirely silent on the other body besides the psychical enunciated by Lang: a body having physical nature and also superadded to the ordinary physical body.

It was this body, the electrical body, on which – having listened to all Lang had said – I was wanting to ask an immediate question.

I was curious to know what happened at death with this body. "That," said Lang, "does not survive long: perhaps two hours. It breaks down and is scattered as particles in the atmosphere." So I was to learn, there is no need in the next existence for the electrical type of body. The psyche can use the psychical body directly; whereas it fails in this fashion with the more intractable matter of our world.

Lang had spoken of memory. He took up the subject again to cast light upon the trance relationship sustained between himself and George Chapman. "I have no interest in, or wish to know, the particulars of George Chapman's life, or what he said to his wife at breakfast – nor do I want to be confused by his memories coming into my consciousness. So, when – to give me access to George Chapman's nervous system – we displace his psychical body by about a foot we also inhibit communication with his memory. Poor George then feels, momentarily, that he is being suffocated." It was also a matter of importance that George Chapman should not become perplexed by 'memories' which had no part in his own experiences. Dr. Lang said that one step taken is to interrupt the optical channel at the retinas. I later connected this with an interesting fact I learned, on a subsequent visit, in conversation with George Chapman's son Michael. When his father comes out of the trance state, Michael told me, he cannot see well – a short time, such as five minutes, has to elapse before his optical system settles down and functions normally.

The conversation transferred to the subject of the brain. This was because of a question I had planned to raise. It was this: the brain of man differs particularly from that of other primates by its well developed fore-structure – could this difference constitute the whole basis of the very great powers of reason held by man in comparison with the rest of the members of the animal kingdom? I had been suspecting there might be rather more to it than that; and it seemed important to learn how Lang looked on the question. He answered without hesitation. Man, if he was to become the highly rational being that he is, needed an apparatus which could learn to read. This was provided by the fore-structure of his brain. It was through the power of his psyche however that man achieved his eminence of reason – but he could not do this without a suitable reading mechanism.

With this extra light thrown upon the psyche, I recapitulated the roles of the psyche as I had encountered them with Lang to date. It was the ultimate source of man's reasoning powers, so I had just been told. It was also the origin of his motivations, his creativity, and his volition – additionally too of his awareness. The last prompted me to think of the differing ways the mind knows; and I could not help referring to the psychological studies of Carl Jung (who had then but recently died) in regard to them – and to the categories correspondingly under which he had classified character. We ran over them; and I noticed Lang's pleasure in the subject. When we finished he exclaimed: "How interesting that you should speak of the work of Carl Jung!" And with a beaming smile he told me: "He is a great friend of mine – a very great friend. He was also a patient of mine."

Perhaps Dr. Lang was thinking of the overall impression he wanted me to have as a result of our conversation. Perhaps also he was prompted by our discussion on the variety in human personality. There was, he remarked, the subject of the broad character of the next life – in the sense of how it is lived. This he gave me to understand is various in the extreme: it depends so much on the individual; and the spectrum of human personality is extensive The quality of existence in the next life is in parallel various. So life proceeds, to use Lang's own words, "on a multitude of levels". As by a law of nature people tend to gravitate to their own level: one is own's own arbiter in this sense. Then, just as here, people have homes; and commonly home life is family life too – but families are not necessarily what we on earth mean by families. A human family may re-form in the next life; but it may not. A family can be based simply upon the desire of kindred spirits to be together and, frequently, the bonds that hold families together are very much closer than is experienced here.

It had been of great interest to cover the ground of our conversation; but I had an insistent longing to know more about Marjorie. I felt I had missed out on some major details during my previous visit – and I recalled to Dr. Lang what I remembered him saying as I lay on the couch. Was I correct when I thought I had heard that Marjorie was present at the operation? Yes, I was quite right, he told me. "While you were speaking to me of Marjorie, I sent my wife Susan to find her. When Marjorie arrived, she said she wanted you to think of her each evening at nine o'clock for half an hour. I passed on the message to you." Then, with some asperity, not without its kindliness he ended: "But you didn't do it!"

The afternoon had already brought surprise. This was something far greater. Hearing now what I had missed before, I did not think to explain the way my awareness had faded at the time – I was simply caught in a flood of confusion. I had a main impression of the generosity which had been advanced to me. How extremely good of Lang, and of his wife Susan, to go to the trouble – unasked – to locate Marjorie! How ever must he – and Marjorie – have been rating my total lack of response! Collecting my thoughts, and to be quite sure I had heard correctly, I asked him if he would kindly repeat what he was telling me. He did so very patiently – no doubt because he now realized I had been near to sleep at the crucial time on that first visit. But I was still unsettled; and when he finished I responded: "To think that I would have just been watching the news at nine on B.B.C. 1!"

Then, with my thoughts in better array, I asked him *exactly* what I should do – not stopping to remark on why I had missed his message originally. He stated:

43

"You have some quiet room. Simply retire there, and concentrate your thoughts on Marjorie. That is all you have to do – just think of her."

The session – I sensed – was nearing its close; and there was yet a question I wanted to put – again about Marjorie. It was something which had formed in my mind concerning her when Lang first spoke of reincarnation. If transitions of existence could go both ways – an idea, as I have noted, which I had not seriously regarded before – it did not follow of necessity that, when I died and entered upon the other life, Marjorie would any longer be present in that existence. So far as I could tell, I might remain here for a long time yet – meanwhile Marjorie could have moved to a new field of experience here. It was a possibility that I was unable to rule out; and I expressed it to Lang. He replied with the assurance: "Marjorie will be there – you can take that as certain."

Then he explained that the strain on his medium was becoming too great – he must end the conversation. He wanted to know if I would like a further meeting. I shook him by the hand, and told him that I would.

As I left Aylesbury I felt emotionally and intellectually that events were taking a new and positive turn.

Chapter Five

PSYCHIC IMPRESSIONS AND ADVENTURE

Home again from my talk with Dr. Lang at Aylesbury the nine o'clock periods with Marjorie had to begin at once. I did not know quite what to expect. It could not be a matter of physical messages – if we had done little more we had maintained emotional closeness through them, and everyday since that momentous first night. Now, surely, it was going to be something different.

To help my concentration as nine o'clock approached, I looked at one of the photographs I had of Marjorie.

When the time came I found myself telling Marjorie major personal matters since her death. They were things in which she must be interested; and I felt a full confidence my thought was reaching her. The half hour came to an end like that. It was the same the next day.

On the third evening, I began to talk about her friend Phyllis – with whom I had kept in touch. My mind began to run on to some other matter; but, almost at once, I experienced a mental tug to revert to the subject of Phyllis and to give more news. So I did this; and I then passed on to a different topic – only to be halted again, with the same demand. This time I was aware of actual words: "Go back to Phyllis – tell me more." I returned to Phyllis and followed out the instruction. But then, about to speak of something else, I experienced the identical pattern and demand yet again. Reason argued that I was under test – and, happily, my sensitivity to Marjorie's thought had not become rusty. From the fact moreover that I complied with her demands, she must see that she was accurately influencing my mind.

Almost immediately there was a radical change in events. Random sequences from the Greek alphabet began presenting themselves rapidly to my consciousness – and as they came I was almost saying them out aloud. Was Marjorie I wondered trying out her ability to reach my mind in a more subtle degree. Was she reminding me, by choosing the Greek alphabet, of her early Greek dictum when first we came together? Was *Greek meeting with Greek* here in this new way? I was certain we were extending the communication between us. And I saw that in the Greek approach Marjorie had signed her name. In my emotional reaction I sensed that we were closer to one another than we had ever been – and I expressed this to her.

Our sessions spread as circumstances would allow to other times of the day.

I found next that visual images were coming to me, quite apart from more frequent thought impressions. One evening I felt my mind drawn to Marjorie as I drove home from work, and I experienced her voice, not aloud but the words distinct: "When I was a small girl, I loved my father very much. When I died, he came to meet me." An image formed in my mind. I saw a sunny country setting with a river not far distant. The river was spanned by a bridge. At the same time I knew that it was this setting in which Marjorie found herself in her first conscious moments after her death. I knew also that, as that scene dawned upon her, she experienced the urge to get up and walk towards the bridge. There she became aware of her father coming to her. My impressions did not go further just then; but I believed I was meant to note a basic principle: if someone who has been close to you is already in the further existence, then when you enter it yourself that person may well be waiting to greet you.

Marjorie and my sister had been cordial friends; so it was natural I should give Marjorie news of Grace. When Marjorie was alive, Grace had two dogs, both Jack Russells. They were in fact father and son; and the latter's name was Pickles. Marjorie always had a strong love for animals. The dogs knew she was very fond of them. Unhappily, in the summer of 1973 Pickles was run over and killed. I was telling Marjorie of this, and how upset Grace had been. He was a lovely dog. Suddenly I heard Marjorie's voice announce that she had Pickles with her. I was so astonished at this news that I immediately asked if I had heard her correctly. The response to that question was: "Of course I have Pickles!" – as though I should have known. And it was meant to startle me – to make me think. I had reasoned out that the structure of the total animal organism must be similar to the human; so animal survival was to be anticipated – but in what conditions it was not clear. With these exchanges it seemed Marjorie was asserting something important I ought to have realized by now: that affection has a universal gravitating effect. It was a principle which included Pickles. From a practical standpoint I was confident enough of the present whereabouts of Pickles to pass on the news to Grace without any further check. I had kept Grace in general touch with developments; and against this background she found it reasonable to take the news seriously.

My ability to receive communications from Marjorie increased. We succeeded in accomplishing some degree of conversation, even if rather restricted. The receptive mode was much easier when the subject was a personal one; and I took it that the influence of emotion enhanced the ability to receive. What was characteristic of receiving was that I would suddenly be aware of a whole sentence from Marjorie falling into my consciousness, rather like a pebble into a pool. What I needed to be wary of was the effect of my own reasoning and my imagination. Both could provide 'answers' to a question I might put to Marjorie. Spurious answers like these were normally slowly forming, or they might be coupled with alternatives. Such effects are counterpart to the *noise* of an electronic-type communication channel. The true information, the *signal,* has always to be read or discerned despite the disturbance from an extraneous background. Some radio operators exhibit great skill in picking out signal in the presence of disturbing background. My experience in my reception of communications from Marjorie was that such operators often function with skill much greater than any required of me in distinguishing between 'signal' and 'noise'.

Amidst these things was a development quite beyond the telepathy we were practising. As I have so far described them, my impressions were due for the most part to Marjorie's planning and instigation. My role was primarily passive – setting aside the news I gave her; and, as I looked on the situation Marjorie was in control. In this new development the roles were largely reversed: it was I who took the initiative. What happened was distinctly an adventure. Because of the very strange form which it took, a few explanations are first needed.

My approach to the development lay in my reading. I was, by now, beginning to look into the literature of psychic research. Having made advance such as I have described, this literature was in part assuming significance where before I would not have placed much weight on it. One study to which I was giving attention was a treatise by Dr. R.Crookall, *The Techniques of Astral Projection*, (The Aquarian Press, 1964). It concerned a curious form of extrasensory perception. On reading the book, and reflecting on it in the light of what Dr. Lang had been telling me, I was far from convinced that the author's understanding of the subject was the true one. It called to my mind work that, so I had heard, was being done in the selfsame field at the Standford Research Institute, California. The general nature of this work has now been described by Russell Targ and Keith Harary in their book, *The Mind Race* (New English Library, 1985). As I heard of it, it was of some relation to the American space activities. The highly unusual form of consciousness which some psychically developed persons seem to be able to take on enables them, apart from normal sense, to extend their visual awareness even to vast distances. That is what is entailed. Interplanetary distances are within the ambit, if indeed there are any limits.

Dr. Crookall, so I understood him, was maintaining that this projection of awareness depends upon the individual concerned separating what I have earlier termed the psychical body from his physcial body. Transfer of consciousness from the latter to the former is the key to the situation – if one assumes with Dr. Crookall that the psychical body is now completely free of the physical body and can translate to any location. Distant vision, in this way, then becomes a possibility.

Crookall, I must note, speaks of the *psychical* body as the *astral body:* hence the title of his book. I note, also, that I found Crookall aware of the other superadded body of the human organism which I have referred to as the *electrical body*. Here a term, amongst others, used by Crookall is *electromagnetic body*. With these things, I was broadly on familiar ground. But I was altogether dubious of the unlimited mobility postulated to the psychical body – because of the linkage, as Dr. Lang had said, with the physical body. What I found especially interesting however was the detail Crookall gives on the separation, and return, of the psychical body relative to the physical body.

He describes visual sensations accompanying return. In the return there is, he makes clear, a final impression of fast movement, such as falling – or such as passing rapidly through an avenue of trees. His information was apparently gathered from accounts of practical experience in America and France over the past hundred years – also from reports of mediumistic communications from personalities of allegedly Far Eastern and Egyptian origin.

I put Crookall's ideas to Marjorie. As I saw it, if I could separate my psychical body from my physical, and then transfer my consciousness to my psychical body, I must certainly enter Marjorie's order of existence. The transition might last only for a short time – but it held the possibility of our meeting.

Crookall incidentally but fascinatingly gives his view that some at least of the ancient wisdom was derived in this fashion. He notes – particularly – St. Paul and a statement of his in the "Second letter to the Corinthians" on 'out of the body' experience. Crookall could well be saying something important in these respects even if – on Dr. Lang's authority – he must be in error through overlooking the tethering effect of the linkage.

When I put the idea to Marjorie that we should meet by my contemplated projection, this was greeted by a flat negative. When later I raised it again, the response was: "I think you should consult Dr. Lang first before you try such a thing." Then one evening, still persisting with my idea, the answer was positive: "OK – we'll try."

Crookall had stated that in the condition of sleep the psychical body is partly separated away from the physical body. In such a condition, volition can more easily secure total release. The act of will precedes sleep.

I followed this procedure and in the early hours of the morning I had a thus far unparalleled experience. I was aware that I was in pitch darkness; and I seemed to be tilted backwards at an awkward angle. Next I could sense clearly Marjorie's perfume. A second later I saw her standing in the blackness brightly illuminated – though no source of external light was evident. She was dressed in a long gown of her favourite blue, and she was looking in my direction with arms outstretched. Suddenly, and for a brief instant, she was very close – and then I seemed to pass from reality to a dream state.

I was in a glider flying-in low over tree tops to land in a clearing. I was anxious about my height and avoiding the trees; but there was no landing – I awoke. At first, the dream of the flight over the green tree tops was vivid in my mind – and nothing else; but then, almost with a crash, I remembered the blackness and Marjorie's bright figure standing in it. I felt elated that we must have achieved our aim. The glider dream was plainly part of the return of my psychical body – it fitted in with Crookall's description. Was the experience, though, *all* a dream? I reflected on it; and right or wrong I did not feel that it was. What seemed more important was why the meeting had been so brief.

I got in touch with Marjorie. Clearly she, too, was delighted over our reunion; but equally plainly, there were to be no more attempts – certainly as yet. "You have something to learn," I was told. What exactly this was I could not gather; and it remained a question to raise with Dr. Lang at my next meeting with him.

Shortly – in the October of 1975 – I was talking with Lang at Aylesbury. Keen for his comments on my adventure I asked him firstly whether it might all have been a dream. Lang smiled and shook his head: it was not just a dream. He ought, he said, to warn me – it could have been dangerous. The power of movement I then possessed was in reality very limited. He reminded me of the link – which had been the basis of my doubt with Crookall – between the psychical and the physical bodies. It can be extended, he informed me, to about twelve feet, but not more. Therefore, Marjorie *had* physically to come to me, to what he called the 'dark levels' of the Earth – I could not go to the 'bright levels' of her existence. In the general environment of our meeting there are playboys, as he called them, who are devoid of a serious interest in life. Living, in the positive, trustworthy sense in which we understood it, is contrary to their nature. They could have attacked us both; and Lang added pointedly: "If the link between your psychical and physical bodies had been severed you would have died. Should you want to do this again tell Marjorie to inform me, and I will come with my friends to guard you – or else instruct Marjorie to bring helpers to guard you." I would have liked to ask Lang more questions on the subject; but there were topics he wished particularly to speak about – so for the moment I noted the conclusion which stood out: Crookall's belief in a transfer of consciousness to the psychical body as the means of projecting the consciousness over great distances could not be right. The real basis of any such projection must be different. Leaving my adventure there, I give the rest of our discussion.

Lang wanted me to know he had been in conversation with Marjorie; and that he would especially like to talk of our relationship, which he looked upon as important. He also wanted to talk of male-female relationships in general.

Many such associations, he commented, were ill-founded; and their achievements were negative. The sooner such bonds were broken the better – to avoid the harm they do. Bonds however where there is wide and deep understanding and sympathy, in a mutual sense, are of a great value and enrich life. It is worth every effort to preserve them. He was thinking of unforeseen events. The illness of one of the partners can throw a heavy strain upon the other, calling for large sacrifice. If the bonds are well-founded the strain should be borne, and the sacrifice made – that, at least, is the ideal to strive for; and the effort leads to its own justification.

Short-term views, views which take for instance no account of the actual continuity of existence beyond the present life, can be false because of this disregard. But people who follow the ideal will inevitably find their striving rewards them. This was true to the philosophy of *Karma;* and real love between two people entails the creative sense of duty to the bond that holds them together.

By illness he meant of course to include accident. In our case there had been an accident and, although the accident was fatal, the principle he had been laying down still applied. In the truest sense of the word, he affirmed that we were what he termed soulmates; and there was the inherent duty to preserve the bond. Marjorie for her part was "doing her Karma". Whilst it was to be expected that I would live to a ripe old age – and he smiled as he said this – Marjorie was patiently waiting; and, when it was my turn to enter her world of existence, she would be there for us to take up our life again together.

Lang went on to assert as he had before that the evolution of the psyche is of the essence of living. With certain patterns of living, inferior patterns, the development of the psyche is retarded, or even reversed. To "fail in one's Karma" is to follow an inferior pattern – but, if duties are observed, then the powers and sensitivities of the psyche are inevitably increased.

Marjorie at present, he went on, was working in a hospital. "We have many hospitals," he continued, "for those with medical need when they come into our life on leaving life on earth. Many require special treatment; and there are many traumatic cases arising from accidents – Marjorie is helping with such cases."

He changed the subject entirely with an unsuspected request. It threw me off balance when he explained; all the same finding out what it was I felt pleasure in being asked. He spoke of my writings; then he simply added that Marjorie wished me to publish a book. I divined the task, and its size was obvious. I said that, having my conversations with him in mind, it had seemed to me desirable sometime to produce a publication, perhaps a paper – but he interrupted, smiling and waving his hand: "Not one of your purely academic studies – more the kind of writing anyone might pick up and read; and giving an account of Marjorie's experiences. She wants you to do it." That appeared to be a clinching argument.

Thinking of what I had, as I believed, gathered from Marjorie on her experiences so far – and to start on the work there and then – I told Lang I understood from Marjorie that the person who came to greet her, on her entry into her new existence, was her father. Lang nodded slowly in agreement: "Yes, that is right, the first person to meet her was her father." The confirmation came as distinct encouragement. I asked if Lang would be able to help me with checking on other such points. I was thinking for instance of Grace's dog Pickles; and I explained what had happened to him and what Marjorie had conveyed to me so forcibly. He told me that he did not know about Pickles; but he assured me the story had the ring of truth – and he promised to find out. He promised also he would ascertain other matters which, checking and authenticating what I gathered from Marjorie, would help me with material for the book.

I did not precisely realize how much the book would depend on my sensitivity to Marjorie's thought – and despite remarkable assistance from mediumship such as George Chapman was giving. But I had an impending sense of the fact. It was weighing on me, since I doubted I could measure up to the requirement; and it was almost as to light relief that my mind turned to some questions in philosophy and cosmology I was planning to put. Dr. Lang seemed to know my unvoiced sense of inadequacy for the work Marjorie was asking of me. Before I could start on the first of my questions, he was saying: "Do not be worried about your ability to gain the impressions that Marjorie wishes to give you. You will be able to do this. You have developed psychically since your last visit. I can see it clearly – and your development will continue." Concerning my questions, I felt their answers could guide basic understanding and add to the broad picture of the circumstances in which we as human beings find ourselves. Psychical research is often charged with the triviality of the information which it gathers. My questions were remote from trivial.

The first was one that harked back to my interest (evident in Chapter 3) in the long-debated relation between mind and matter. In the debate and as I said to Lang, there has been the endeavour especially more recently to show that matter is fundamental, and that mind can be explained in terms of it. Conversely, it has been propounded that mind is basic, and that given mind it is then only a question of how matter is to be seen in respect to it. On a third view, the advocates of neither of these theories are right. Matter and mind each rest in their own foundations: it is not true of either that the one depends upon the other for its existence. I said to Lang that it was hardly necessary to consider the first of the three possibilities – but what of the other two? Could matter be understood entirely in terms of mind? His answer was emphatic: it could not. "Matter exists in its own right. God imparts form to matter – but if God should cease to exist, matter would still exist." I note that this statement bears sympathy with the thought of Plato (who incidentally – if only in allegoric form – had almost singularly among Western thinkers shown interest in the principle of reincarnation).

My second question concerned the possibility of the existence of civilizations elsewhere in our own galaxy of stars (the Milky Way), or in other galaxies. I said that, over the last ten to fifteen years, we had come to understand very well the workings of single-cell animals; and that we have seen from laboratory studies how largely the bricks from which, so to speak, they are built could be formed by natural processes. We, furthermore, have gained a good idea of the way that our own planetary system was formed. Wherever, and whenever, the conditions characteristic of our Earth are simulated with some closeness we would expect the formation of primitive life such as I have mentioned – and the possibility of subsequent and similar evolution. Although in any one instance, the probability of suitable conditions arising is very slight yet, taking into account the vast size of the physical Universe (on which immensity of size Dr. Lang, breaking in, himself laid stress), an estimate of the likelihood of life occurring elsewhere in the cosmos could be reached. Making due allowances, the probability of finding *homo sapiens* or his next of kin otherwise than on Earth seemed to amount to certainty. Speaking loosely present day estimates led one to expect the presence, distributed throughout the galaxies, of something like ten thousand, or one hundred thousand, civilizations at least of the level of development we know on Earth.

Lang was signifying his acquiescence as I quoted these figures. "Something like that," he said; and then he added: "You may take it that wherever it is possible for a human being to breathe, there you will find human beings."

I remarked that thought and effort was being given to the possibility of communication with other such civilizations by radio methods. As the distances and thus the transmission delays are inevitably so great however, little more could be done than to indicate the presence of intelligence. Anything resembling a conversation seemed to be out of the question. Was it possible, I suggested, that something could usefully be learned of other inhabited planets by making mental contact with those for instance who in the next existence had previously lived in these places and so knew them?

Dr. Lang was affirmative; and he commented that difference of language would raise no problem. In the next life conversation commonly if not by any means always works by thought transfer – and a thought is the same in any language. The individual who receives it translates it automatically into his own tongue, and hears it in that language. A German who knows no French and a Frenchman who knows no German have no difficulty in talking to one another.

At this point the session came to an abrupt close. Lang was due in the evening, he told me, to perform an operation at a London hospital; and George Chapman must be given the time to travel there.

Leaving the consulting room I spoke to Michael, and I asked him if I might shake hands with his father after he had recovered from his trance condition – I would like particularly to meet him and thank him for the generosity he had shown with these talks. Michael thought it would be possible, stressing there was not much time. But I was glad just to meet George Chapman; and he told me that he had appreciated the outline reports I sent him.

I could not fail to notice that George Chapman's face did not naturally have the same fullness of width which it did when Lang was talking to me; and that he had a good colour – contrasting with the lack I had always observed in my conversations with Lang. His step also was quick, compared with Lang's slow movements. I was reminded of Doreen's account – not only that, I recalled a comment by Lang early in the talks (though I have not to this point specifically quoted it): the *psyche always impresses its own characteristics upon the physical body, and tends to mould it.*

In my session that night with Marjorie, I turned my mind to her meeting with her father. As I did so, I began to sense the flood of her emotions when she hastened to meet him; her joy to see him; the nightmare of her distress at what had happened; his tenderness and understanding; and his taking her to some location – which as I came later on to learn was his domicile.

Just what this place might be I was not however at the moment at all clear. Reasoning was taking over and acting as a hindrance, and a major interference. Must she not have been in need of medical aid? Must that not have been given in a hospital? I went on to put these questions to Marjorie and with a positive feeling they were relevant and appropriate. Yes, oh yes, came back the impression, that was so. Expert aid *was* important. But then, astonishingly, and with a dry humour completely characteristic of Marjorie there streamed in the further impression: if I was going to say – in the notes I was writing down – that she was taken to hospital I would have besides to write that the hospital was a boat!

I did this dutifully, and extremely dubiously: accurately, so it proved.

Chapter Six

KNOWLEDGE – WHY? HOW? WHAT?

It was important to concentrate upon telepathy. In the foregoing chapter I compared it to radio communication. For me the special comparison was with weak-signal reception.

In the receiving of radio waves, signals which are extremely weak can still be detected successfully if the right precautions are taken to control and minimize the inevitable background disturbances. A parallel lies with the surface of water, like that of a river or of a lake. In favourable conditions, when the surface is smooth, the motion of a fish just below the surface can be detected through a small ripple or swirl it causes in the water. With a breeze blowing or with the passage of a power-boat undulations from either may be entirely masking, so that the eye cannot pick out the slight patterns produced by the fish. The perceiving of the slight patterns rests with the conditions. Exactly as with visual perception of this nature, and with the detection of very weak radio signals, the degree of control over what is extraneous is vital to receiving the mental impressions of telepathic communication. *Control* is the operative word. The end of the previous chapter illustrates how easy it is to be off guard against the activities of imagination and reason. They represent well the difficulties to be met with.

Hoping for helpful advice, I had at my last meeting with Lang spoken of the difficulties. His response went little beyond what I knew Marjorie herself had been seeking to impress upon me. He simply said: "Do not be restless. Try to be passive; and let your thoughts dwell upon Marjorie." I could see that the concentration of my mental activity upon Marjorie must tend to exclude, and so control, the thought activity that would confuse me or swamp out what I wanted to receive; but he agreed that my thoughts, for instance – and by no means least – those of work, would be forcing themselves upon my consciousness. All such things had to be *controlled*.

Realizing the difficulties more clearly itself proved helpful; and even if we did not get far at any one time Marjorie and I now forged steadily ahead.

I wanted to discover more about those early moments when Marjorie made her entry into the next world. Concerning her father it was so wonderful, she conveyed to me, to be met by him. It was just what she needed. Everything she had aimed for was in ruins. Who better to turn to, unburdening herself and expressing the havoc to her longings and her feelings. She told me of her distress for me. After some hours, she was more composed. "I knew how terrible you must feel," she said. "My father was marvellously good. When I explained to him about our messages, he encouraged me to get in touch with you. You were totally numbed."

"I tried, and tried – and there was no response." Her father urged her to keep up with her efforts; and medical staff from the hospital at which her father had duties, and where she was later to work, came and built up her energies. The communication she was endeavouring to achieve was distinctly rare. The hospital staff told her they thought she would succeed. She related to me her great sigh of relief when, after an age, she gained a reply. The whole climate of feeling from that moment changed as if by magic. Sleep became possible for her: she needed the deepest and most refreshing sleep. Falling into oblivion, it was greatly vitalizing to her.

Gathering this information, and learning that Marjorie had the benefit of several of these unconscious but revivifying periods, I felt I understood those early patches when, while they lasted, all contact seemed lost. Lang too, when I asked him, placed the cause in Marjorie's sleeping state.

It took her a few days for her state of shock to abate. She became interested in her new surroundings. There were many talks with her father about them; but – inevitably – what had mattered in her previous life dominated her mind.

I asked for some elucidation of the mysterious boat of our recent conversation. "It is where my father lives," I was told, "and he took me there when he met me at the bridge. You could call it a houseboat – but that doesn't give the right idea. It is spacious, and elegant; and it makes a delightfully pleasant home." I was forming an image of a vessel moored to the side of a river, and I described the image. "That is right," came the response. "It *is* moored to the side of a river. My father does a lot of rowing on the river, for relaxation – in a light sculling craft. He enjoys that." Having always understood from Marjorie that her father had loved sport and athletics, I could see that the mystery contained sense.

The times when I received impressions were normally short. After a long day, I needed first to relax. So, at the start of a session, I would pass on some interesting items of news. There was always something to say – and then I would try to free my mind of extraneous thoughts, and assume the receptive role. It would take some little time to write down my impressions, which I invariably passed back for Marjorie's confirmation. With each session, there would be some advance; and gradually a more embracing picture began to build up.

I informed Marjorie of an image in which I could see that the river under the bridge at which she had met her father and the river in which the housevessel was moored were one and the same. Looking from the direction of the bridge, the vessel lay by the right bank. The river, continuing, flowed into an extensive lake; and from the right hand side of the lake there spread back a slowly rising parkland with many large and low buildings. These, I seemed to know, were the hospital at which Marjorie had taken up duties. Beyond the hospital were woodlands.

Marjorie confirmed this description. She liked, she said, to go swimming in the lake – and it was good for some of her patients to take them swimming. The hospital buildings were low since there was no restriction on ground space. The surrounding countryside was beautiful – and it was most enjoyable going for walks with Pickles.

People entering the next existence were in one way and another often in need

54

of expert medical assistance. For that reason, there exist very many hospitals like the one at which Marjorie was giving her help. People who had suffered violent deaths, and had died for example as she had from accident, commonly required special care. They were almost certainly in a low state; and they were usually deeply distressed. With sudden and unexpected separation from those they loved and cared for, that was only natural. Marjorie, because of her own experience, was well able – from the outset – to understand such cases; and her main efforts were with them. Her father's work was not so specialized. He was concerned in general terms with patient needing advice in regard to their new life.

I asked when it was that Marjorie had commenced at the hospital. "Quite early," was the answer. The environs of her new life were delightful and enlivening, and they brought the tone that you find with a good holiday; but then, you didn't want to spend all your time on holiday. Before long the urge had intensified in her to do something of more value. Within three months she was anxious to join her father at the hospital. Started there, she divided her time between attendance on patients and working at studies. Medical work attracted her; and she wished me to think of it as a profession when I came to join her – she was looking on it as a highest form of engineering. But beyond any question, life as she was now realizing it was full of satisfaction. One's brain was clear, and one's body full of life. It was possible to work hard and long and scarcely feel tired. Her leisure she found always enjoyable. The ordinary needs – and Marjorie cited particularly the need to eat – consuming so much time and energy in the old life were non-existent. (It is not true that people never eat. Lang says he often enjoys a bowl of fruit on returning home from surgical work – mainly as a relaxation.)

There was one thing particularly where I looked for more enlightenment: the more exact ideas in Marjorie's mind on my writing of this book. I had more than once put this enquiry to her. Each time I gathered a single basic impression: that, as soon as there seemed the possibility of reliable communication between us, she felt the onus on her to develop the possibility to the point that the book could be written. Now she insisted that when a satisfactory level of communication had been attained then responsibility extended to me also.

It was true that she greatly wanted me to know of her experiences – but the interest and value of such knowledge did not stop there. Ignorance places people at a great disadvantage. On the subject of death, lack of knowledge is the source of much suffering. In a state of not-knowing false notions spring up like weeds. Even though false notions, normally, die hard it was greatly important to state the truth. She did not want to think that, although we had the knowledge, we permitted people to suffer because of our inaction.

If there were people who chose to promulgate views to the contrary of what we had to say – and she anticipated that, human thinking being what it is, there would be no lack of these people – then such people should consider the wide responsibility that in consequence lay with them. On the other hand, and in a rightly critical world, it was little use simply relating the truth – it was necessary to present an account that an unbiased mind would find persuasive and compelling.

Even enlightened quarters, it had to be admitted, can harbour strong taboos. That could not be helped. On the other hand she and I certainly knew what it meant to be sceptical; and we were both well aware of the virtues of scepticism. The sceptical mind is by no means a closed mind; and when it is attracted by adventure what it looks for is a sufficiently secure foothold. Therefore I must write to provide such a foothold; and that she considered was something I would be able to do.

She was not interested to be proved right – simply as such. The incredulous would – eventually and inevitably – come to discover the truth for themselves; but that would accomplish nothing of what she was wanting to achieve. Therefore it was highly important for me to reason out the evidence as fully as I could. An academic treatise would be read and understood by few only. What I must write had to be reasoned and supported; but it must be of general interest.

One thing stood out impressively: Marjorie's objective was that people should *know* – as distinct solely from possessing hopes, or just holding beliefs. Her ideas of *knowing*, I soon learned, embraced also the elucidating influence of modern science.

There were some facts about the next life that she wished to be recognized as basic. These were things which she had had little need to touch on herself since largely I had already been introduced to them by Dr. Lang. They could be collected and summarized in this way:

(i)   life continues for a certainty;
(ii)   it continues in a similar bodily form in a material
         world, and in these respects the broad character of life
         does not change;
(iii)   the matter of the continuing world has rather different
         properties from the matter of our own world – one could
         say it is possessed of a much less tiresome nature;
(iv)   linked with this there is no need of food for the
         maintenance of life;
(v)   the pattern of life is basically home centred, as with
         us;
(vi)   this pattern, also as with us, stretches out in a most wide
         range of activities – mainly in work, relaxation, study,
         art and research;
(vii)   the memories of the previous life tend clearly to be
         retained.

Beyond these elementary facts, Marjorie felt there should be included something on the quality of life. That could most simply be done by explaining two primary principles; laws like laws of nature which, as was clearly evident to her now, could be said at their heart to be universal in the sense they are true both of the life of her present existence and of the life that she had left.

For the moment, and since it bears upon – and leads into – this subject, I will continue with our telepathic transfer and the development of events; concentrating for brevity just on their substance. Firstly, I learned more concerning our own personal relationship.

Thus far since Marjorie's death, there never had elapsed a day in the course of which we were not in touch through our long-established link. It remained a central practical asset. If I still had only the vaguest idea of its operation, that did not matter. How little is known of the working of our ordinary senses. The key thing was that more, much more, than in Marjorie's life here it helped frames of mind and sympathies to be exchanged. People who lose the use of a sense organ tend to gain greater knowledge than normal through their remaining sense abilities. It had been rather like that with us. Our link initially had brought us, for the most part, just physical sensations. With Marjorie's death it acted far more effectively to bring us into contact – so that affection, comfort and strength could flow mutually between us.

It did not therefore at all surprise me that Marjorie should now specifically confirm this vital give-and-take. Speaking for herself, she had been able to detect in it the slow yielding, over the first year, of my insensibility of spirit – to the point that I was becoming more conscious of my being lonely. She wondered whether I might want to fill the gap she had left; and what that might mean. She had wanted – did I not know her clear-thinking mind so well! – to work things out if she could: rather than leave them to drift. She could not at first see exactly what she herself should be doing. That was why with our increased mutual sensitivity I had picked up the uncertainty of her mind, from which I had constructed the vivid theatre dream. Marjorie now positively told me this dream was nothing on which I should have placed much weight. Her real longing was always for our continuing closeness. She came to discern how I felt just the same as she did. That was the solid truth, whatever transitory impression – like my theatre dream of her – she might have gathered from her sensitivity to my thought. When she felt certain on the whole question she made the appearance to me which I have in chapter 1 called a vision. This, she affirmed, was with the precise intention of reassuring me of our future together.

The decision which our minds had made in common at this early stage leads, as Marjorie next conveyed, to one of the two prime and universal principles she wished to come to. Inevitably our decision meant we had to wait for each other; and how long that would be we could not really say. As we saw it the waiting was called for as an act of discipline. We had to forgo the perfectly normal and legitimate opportunity to make good the vacuum created by the accident. It was true we were still able to give much to one another; but the point strongly remained. We both felt the need for sacrifice. Our present discipline was necessary to achieve *the good* of the goal we both looked forward to. We knew this instinctively.

In her world, Marjorie said, things were much more clear – purely in the light of accumulated experience. The bonds of a good relationship constantly developed the psyche. That was partly true in terms of the sacrifices these bonds are always demanding. Our separation was an occasion of this kind of sacrifice. It was a sacrifice to the future, and much worth the making.

The developing of the psyche is development both of its quality and its strength. By strength Marjorie meant something in the broad nature of creative ability and inherent energy. But, enmeshed with development, there was a question of self-interest. Sacrifice and self-interest might seem to be things lying at some variance. It depends rather on circumstance. Self-interest is undoubtedly both natural and reasonable, in principle, as a guideline; but it has its varieties. There are more facile ways of meeting with its calls that do little for the psyche. In fact there are ways that are greatly damaging. Much later, Marjorie told me how next-world hospitals have recently been taking in more and more cases in which the patient is grossly enfeebled by the practises of the permissive society. As Marjorie was now asserting, self-interest is a guiding principle over which one must be wary. It has a wide spectrum of consequences, some good, some bad, some neutral. With the last it is largely a matter of a waste of time. Then, all bad consequences have in the end to be put right. There the waste is even greater. The human mind has its intuition on all these things; and it has long had the intuition that the greatest good (as seen later in the light of experience) is achieved through discipline. This is the intuition of Karma. Karma asserts the principle of duty; and this assertion was the first of her two primary principles. It ties in closely with the purpose of the Universe as Dr. Lang had expressed it to me: the evolution of the psyche.

It was now even more clear what Dr. Lang was saying when he assured me I should find Marjorie waiting for me – because she was "doing her Karma".

Pressing home what she had been putting to me, Marjorie insisted that the understanding which lies central to this principle of Karma is not properly and basically found in terms just of piety, of duty to a belief: it reflects the fabric of the Universe – and it is one of those things that apply like the classically conceived law of nature. It operates functionally and determinately, everywhere and all the time. Lang since has epitomized it as *growing by the wholehearted carrying through of the duties of life.*

Marjorie took up the second of her two principles on the quality of life. She endeavoured to give me clearer ideas on the *circumstances* at large of the next-life – it answered a question I had been asking: what more explicitly had Dr. Lang meant when talking of the individual gravitating to this or that level? I had understood that the individual exercises his choice. Did this relate to the attractiveness – which seemed to be implied – of the level he chose?

Marjorie's first point was that one had to think of the word *gravitation* in its wider meaning – that simply of tending to a particular condition or circumstance: then one could speak correctly of the principle of individual gravitation. Otherwise one could get false ideas. In the common narrow meaning, gravitation implies a force of attraction. The level gravitated to is not *necessarily* what appeals to the individual as attractive. To take a more extreme example, the person whose attitudes are characteristically mean will find himself in circumstances which – despite his naturally taking them up in preference to others – are far from inviting to him: they will reflect so to speak the mean qualities of his nature, and reflecting this character he will not like them. Therefore in the narrow sense of *gravitation* it is to that extent a misnomer to talk of a law of individual gravitation. It gives the right idea, if one likes to put it this way, to say there is a principle of the reflection of an individual in his surroundings – almost as though the individual himself alone fashioned his local world, and by paralleling in it the actual pattern of his own nature. Lang had some rather special corroboration for what Marjorie was here expressing: a mean mind, he said, will *blight its physical environs unconsciously.* This in passing anticipates a strange feature of the next world that I was going to learn more about. The matter of the next world is much more sensitive to the influence of mind than our own here.

Speaking very generally it will be clear, Marjorie said, that the principle of individual gravitation applies widely also in our world: in the sense for instance that birds of a feather flock together. In the next life the mirroring of an individual's inner nature in his surroundings is evident rather in the same way; but in the special circumstances more vividly, even it may be starkly. Hence it is especially true that if the characteristics of a person are poor then his environs will be poor. If his characteristics compare well then his environs will also compare well. This is a principle, once again, like a classical law in science. It is not an edict – it simply happens.

Discussing the principle subsequently with Lang vis-à-vis the element of the individual's free choice, he told me it was always true that a person naturally selects a living situation in which on the whole he is more at ease.

In its operation the principle of gravitation reveals the development of the individual. This operation is in fact continuous. It is not restricted to the transition from this to the next life. By the nature of the law no individual is held to the level of the moment – with development then inevitably the circumstances of his environment change correspondingly.

Both the laws are concerned ultimately with motivation; and as is evident they function together throughout the continuing life history of each individual. The first relates to his inner status – the second to his locale.

The burgeoning of our telepathic activities – from the mere trickle when, in Marjorie's lifetime, we first found it happening to the flood dimensions by comparison of the present – was a most inspiring experience. It seemed to draw back the curtains and reveal the world afresh. At the critical level however, I wanted to move on to verification. With this, having asked for Lang's help, I looked forward to my next meeting with him. Meanwhile I noted that in gathering telepathic information from Marjorie I invariably had the same feeling of validity that was always built into our physical messages. It was similar to the feeling built into ordinary sense perception (regardless of how little or how much understanding one may have – or may think that one has – of the actual mechanism).

In December, 1975, two months after receiving Marjorie's request for this book, I was talking with Lang again at Aylesbury. I plunged straight into the subject of my telepathic impressions: telling him the developing story and starting with Marjorie meeting her father on the bridge. My thoughts concentrating upon the account, as I took it stage by stage, I heard Lang confirming what I said.

But early I digressed with a question. There was one particular matter, I explained, on which I was not clear – there hadn't been the opportunity really to go into it with Marjorie. From the moment, certainly, at which she had died to the time when she found herself near the bridge she was not in a state that we would describe as conscious. I knew this, I stated, because she mentioned she had been "in a dream". "That was so," Lang agreed; and I continued by asking him how it was she came to be by the bridge. I did not think that her father had brought her there. "No," said Lang, "it was not her father. It was staff from the hospital to which her father is attached – where Marjorie herself is now also working."

I described the hospital, and he interrupted me when I outlined the parkland setting and the woodlands I had been able to see lying beyond. Having informed him of that, he remarked, I must be interested – if not perhaps surprised – when he said that the hospital was named *Woodlands*. The various low but extensive buildings of the hospital were called after famous doctors.

The conversation included the matter of the housevessel; and I give what was said virtually in full. I stated first that with her arrival in her new surroundings Marjorie was not, so I understood, taken to hospital – although she was treated by hospital staff. What happened was that her father took her to his home. At this point I exclaimed that I felt diffident about what I was next going to say – yet my impressions were so clear that I must simply put them to him: her father's home was a boat, a ship moored by the side of the river, and not far from the bridge. Was I right about this? "Oh yes," said Lang almost flatly, "that is right."

Not having thus far actually described this boat, except in the briefest way, I correct the lack now. My visual and other impressions from Marjorie, and certain mediumistic conversation I came rather later to have with her, give the idea of a vessel about one hundred and fifty feet long with a transom stern and a beam of just twenty feet – a powered luxury cruiser all in glistening white. It had an upper deck and raking bows. Apart from the well furnished living quarters of the upper deck it was equipped for games and sport: you could play snooker if you wished, or squash racquets. It was taken frequently pleasure cruising on the very large lake.

The time was not sufficient, by any means, to report every impression to Lang; but I was able to cover ten different major issues with each of which I gained clear verification – *except for one*. With this exception I was totally wrong; at the same time Lang's correction of my error opened – most instructively – a window upon his world and particularly upon its scientific and engineering aspects.

It traces back to a mechanical device of which I have not spoken – which however Marjorie told me she possessed or used. She had tried to describe its nature; but despite all her efforts I had remained highly obtuse: in fact so totally undiscerning that I came to believe it could not be a mechanical device after all. It was for reason of this state of muddle that I omitted mentioning the device earlier.

Marjorie, and I think with enthusiasm, had given me the very clear impression: "I can fly." The words formed in my mind in the sense that she had taken up flying – just as we say when a person turns to private aviation. My reaction was of incredulity; though exactly why I can in fact find no good reason. I said in reply, perhaps with a detectable flippancy: "Why, surely not an aeroplane!" "No, not an aeroplane," came the response; and I thought I noticed an atmosphere of disappointment – that I was making so little of so vitally interesting a piece of news. Marjorie did not at that point persist with the subject; though we returned to it on another occasion and quite shortly.

She could "move in a straight line vertically upwards or downwards" was the further information – also she could "hover". Rather dubiously I suggested that she possessed a helicopter. This was met with a negative, as I somehow rather expected.

On a still further occasion I learned: "We have our own specially developed means of high-speed travel" – and the idea of a 'flying saucer' came into my mind. This last idea I just dismissed; and rated it so lightly I did not even record it in my notes.

Marjorie, I assumed in a vague way, must be trying to tell me that she could levitate or somehow project herself. She had certainly informed me that she could "move through the air". Moreover, before ever the subject arose, she had explained she was now possessed of a body so dynamic "you could almost say it was as light as a feather". That, the thought came to me, was an object which might not be so difficult to levitate – or project. On the other hand my suggestion that this was what she was really trying to tell me did not meet with any support.

Taking Dr. Lang over the ground, I found out why. Yes, he remarked, it was possible to project yourself to some other – even far-distant – location.

With such projection, he digressed, but most interestingly, it had to be understood that there can be an important sense in which you nevertheless remained all the time just where you were – unprojected. As he said this, I thought – in yet further digression – of my difficulties with Crookall's view upon projection. Here possibly was some clarification of that particular matter. (Actually the energy considerations as between the psyche and the body's matter are vastly different in the next existence compared with those holding good in this world. It is as a result very easy if one is a next-world person to create another body in another location, to which body one can transfer one's consciousness. The original body may then give the impression of sleeping – but its annihilation at will can recoup to the psyche the energy expended in creating the distant body. So persons of this present existence with strong psychical development can create at will a replica of their psychical body in the presence of a person of the next world: in order to see and talk with that person. This is a situation – one eventually elucidated in mediumistic conversation with Marjorie – which bears very much on the kind of projection contemplated by Crookall. The statements I have made here will be better apparent on reading in particular the passages on physics in Chapter 16; also on referring to Appendix V on the subject of mind and energy. I note that the psyche can be trained to perception of remote events apart from any use of psychical-body abilities. Marjorie has comments on this as reported in Chapter 11.) But Lang was continuing, and to state with some emphasis, that I jumped to an entirely wrong conclusion when I thought Marjorie had been telling me anything about unaided bodily transport – transport of any kind accomplished solely in terms of the self.

"You people here," and he spoke with even greater emphasis, "think we have no mechanical devices. *We have.* Some are very highly developed. We frequently need to travel, and travel great distances. For this travelling we often use flying machines, because of the need to transport also things such as equipment or personal belongings. Marjorie was trying to tell you that she has a flying machine." I remembered how, initially, it had been that precise idea which came over to me. I broke in: "What kind of machine is it?" The answer was of a form I never anticipated. "Well . . . " and he began slowly and with a smile, "you people talk about flying saucers – you know what I mean. *It's a machine like that!*"

There was a moment of acute silence – and all I could do was put the obvious question: "How does it work?" "Oh," said Lang, "it works by jet-thrust: not using petrol of course! – but the principle is jet-thrust." I noticed a flicker of amusement cross his face as he referred to *petrol* – at the same time I was looking back on all Marjorie's efforts, and on her undoubted feeling of disappointment. She had handed me more than clues – she had given me the image of a flying saucer (perhaps even of her own machine). In a fatuously 'wise' reaction, I had made less than nothing of it.

It was a perfect illustration of interference – by prejudice – obliterating the transmission.

Every time, the interview seemed to last scarcely a few minutes. Lang was telling me we must conclude. He summarized the meeting, saying: "You have clearly been receiving psychic impressions from Marjorie." But there was one other thing he wanted to turn to before we said good-bye. It was about my sister's dog called Pickles: "the little dog that had been run over and killed." His description *little dog* struck me as he spoke. I had never told him that Pickles was a small dog. He continued: "I have enquired of Marjorie as I promised. Your impression from Marjorie was quite correct – she does have Pickles."

I wondered if we could fit in one further thing; and I mentioned my cat Chi – who not long after the demise of Pickles had suffered a similar fate. Marjorie, I said, had regarded Chi with much fondness; and it seemed that he had found his way to her. She had told me he enjoyed his excursions in the fields. "I do not know," Lang replied, "but you may be very sure that Marjorie has Chi as well." I apologized for taking time on such a minor matter. Chi I explained had always been a great pal. "Oh," said Lang with a response that appealed to me, "trivialities can be very important."

On the subject of the knowledge Marjorie planned to convey we had made a start. I was at the foot of a stairway.

Chapter Seven

MARJORIE JOINS IN AT AYLESBURY

The meetings with Lang at Aylesbury had been absorbingly interesting. The pity was that they had to be so short, and so infrequent. My mind was full of questions; but there were always things Lang wanted to say; and I had invariably to make a choice of those subjects I felt at that point to be more important to put to him. A queue of topics was always left still to be taken up. With the meeting of Chapter 6 there were remaining over various questions centred closely on Marjorie; and I had asked Lang whether it would be possible for Marjorie to attend at our next meeting – when we could all three of us look at these questions. Lang was entirely enthusiastic; and we had the meeting in March, 1976. Marjorie was not able to use George Chapman as medium; that is to say in the fashion in which Chapman customarily related to Lang in his mediumship. That inability, so I gathered, was due to physiological differences which matter in this mode of mediumship. Lang though often referred to Marjorie and told me what she had to say.

In the run-up to the meeting there were some things of note which in a degree were preparatory to the meeting. They came about with my continuing telepathic communication with Marjorie. For one thing, and my mind disabused of wrong ideas which – by their interference – had made it, as I have noted, difficult earlier for me to gain impressions about Marjorie's flying machine, I went on to learn details of this machine that I found fascinating.

The idea Marjorie now got across to me was of a craft, circular in plan, with a diameter of about fifteen feet. It had a fore-and-aft cabin in which two seats were arranged side by side in front. Further seating was possible behind – and then, of much interest, I could see the vehicle was possessed of a hovercraft form of skirt. The craft did not have any normal landing gear such as a wheeled undercarriage or landing pods, but just this blown skirt. With the skirt the vehicle could equally well be put down on land or water. Marjorie let me see it being set down on water. Because the vehicle was designed for use over very great distances it had highly sophisticated and computerized navigational aids, and was capable of exceptionally fast flying speeds – at which Marjorie only hinted. If she used it for so short a journey as a few hundred miles only, the flying speeds could easily be five thousand miles an hour. With long distances the speed would be *very* much greater. From such high-speed flight, final approach and touch down was assisted by computer control. Marjorie did not try to go into the motor unit (though I know that its operation is based in high-energy physics).

I gained some impressions of terrain seen from the craft in flight – especially some rolling hill country which, I thought, held special attraction for Marjorie. I could see the wooded sides of the hills – it was scenery with which I was in fact going to become much more familiar.

Marjorie told me that the flying machine was constantly used by her in the course of her medical duties. She coupled this with the statement that she was taking medical studies very seriously.

This emphasis on things medical prompted me to interrogate her on her day-by-day work with patients. As her cases were usually of so tragic a kind, didn't she find her task a most wearing one? The answer was that to feel a true sympathy for each patient was altogether important. She was naturally able to give a genuine sympathy – because she had learned at first hand. So her task certainly weighed on her; at the same time, anxiety and feeling did not undermine her energies. This was for the reason she could be entirely sure of a resolution of the patient's problems; and she looked ahead to this – even if it was distant. Like that she possessed a full serenity – and it spread to her patients. As she told me this I thought back to the time when I had seen that look of serenity on her face in my vision of her.

She elaborated on her background of relaxation. It fitted closely with her natural interests in her lifetime here. It included gardening for instance – a great love with her and a long-standing one.

I wondered if Marjorie could expand even more widely on the setting of her present life: what, more explicitly, were the physical characteristics of her world? She had told me they were of a less-tiresome nature than we experience. What was she really saying when she put it like that? The impression entered my mind that it was premature to try to understand such things at this point. But I also learned that a salient aspect of the world I was wanting to know better was a permanence of form, with material things, which is of a special kind unfamiliar to us in our world.

The only other comment to make on events leading up to the meeting is that knowing exactly the various questions I wanted to ask I thought it might save time at the meeting if I informed Marjorie beforehand what they were. Then she could put the points to Dr. Lang prior to the talk. This in fact worked out happily; and at the meeting I often found I was being given answers to questions without my actually expressing them.

In the consulting room again, and after I had shaken hands with Dr. Lang, he announced: "Marjorie is here – she gives you her love." I responded and he turned at once to the subject of the book.

He appeared to know roughly how the draft had been progressing – and he approved particularly of an appendix that would place the scientific issues in perspective. In a book of this kind, which would largely be an effort wasted if it did not deal with problems it might seem to raise, he considered such a step had to be appropriate. He spoke a little on the subject of publishing; and then with a smile he told me that Marjorie had some special news.

Over the past few months she had been building a cottage. Although he did not say so, I shortly discovered it was near the rolling and wooded hills I had seen in the view from the flying machine. He added that she had built it for the two of us to live in when I joined her – although that was still far distant. She had carried through all the furnishing. This was what he described as an old style. She very much hoped I would like both it and the cottage.

The design of the cottage was her own. All this news made a delightful surprise; and I enquired how long it was since Marjorie had commenced on the project. "Oh," said Lang, "it was just about five months". I explained that I asked because I remembered saying to Marjorie one evening, not many months before Christmas, how looking ahead it would be good for us to have a cottage – perhaps like the one we had searched for without success in the year before her death. Recalling this expressed wish I said I could not at the moment remember just when I had put it to her. I discovered on returning home and looking up my notes that the date was the 3rd November: slightly more than five months before this present news.

I asked how Marjorie had contrived so much in so short a time. "She is able," Lang replied, "to cause matter to conform to her concepts."

I would have liked to learn more on this; but to have stayed with the subject would have prejudiced my list of topics. We passed to the subject of Marjorie's accident.

The question of how it happened was one which recently I had been raising with her. The impression I had gained was there were few things she remembered of that time, and nothing of the accident itself. Lang told me that he had gone over the ground with her. From his account I learned corroboratively that she had no recollection of why the accident had happened. She remembered she had been thinking about me; and that there followed what she could only describe as swimmy sensations. The dominating event was that she had awakened to consciousness near the river (as I have described) – *to realize almost at once where she now was.* She wanted me to know it was true when I said that with our reunion she had forthrightly exclaimed: "The big nit's got the message at last!" It was her spontaneous reaction when after her long efforts I had eventually responded. Lang laughed as he repeated her exclamation; and he gave his confirmation of it – he was there at the time.

The talk now became instructive on the vision. I remarked that I knew it had intended meaning. Was it – just possibly – one of those things which happen otherwise unforced, or did it have to be carefully devised? I felt it was devised. "Yes, it was both intended and contrived," Dr. Lang replied. I pressed at once the question: how did Marjorie contrive it? "She used you as a medium," I heard the totally astonishing answer. To adjust to it was difficult. It was hard to think of myself as a medium like that.

Lang continued in explanation. Because of my sympathy with her, he told me, she was able to exercise this power. She had withdrawn matter from my body. This was what I had seen when very briefly I had noticed what had looked like slightly-glinting velvet. With this withdrawn matter she had made, for those few seconds, a model of herself – a model of her head.

At this point I was reflecting on the fact that her eyes had been closed – though as I have said I had the clearest impression she was looking at me directly with her smile. The fact had continued to puzzle me that her eyes were shut; and I asked why they were. The information which I received in reply pointed to an exactitude in the replica that was far beyond superficial. The external form I knew to be precisely like Marjorie – short as was its realization. What Lang now told me made it plain that internal structure (at least in part) was highly complete. There is always, he said, a nervous reaction exerted automatically by the retinas of the eyes back upon the eyelids. This reaction is one which naturally tends to close the eyelids. It has to be overcome by specific effort. That Marjorie's eyelids appeared closed was due simply to the fact she had been unable to accomplish this particular effort simultaneously with the strategic efforts the occasion called for.

Marjorie's ability to control material form once again raised my interest – but again I set it aside and kept to my scheduled topics. I wished for some check upon these detailed impressions of Marjorie's flying machine; and I quoted the diameter of fifteen feet. Lang said that, very closely, the figure was right. He did not appear to refer to Marjorie, and I felt that he was not particularly interested in the technical details; but he confirmed the two seats side by side at the front of the cabin; and he went on to say that Marjorie frequently employed the machine to attend accident cases brought in to hospital on earth. Often she was able to give effective aid – and he stated that with these cases she would pray (by which he meant an activity, as he explained on another occasion, looking to the positive, dynamic and creative power of mind). He paid great tribute to her work. She was now the leader of a medical group. In regard to her attendance upon accident cases on earth, he added with a slight smile and a small wave of the hand: "If the patient dies . . . well, there is always the spare seat in the front of the flying machine!"

He continued that he would like me to pass on some news to Marjorie's mother: Marjorie had met with her brother who had died at a very early age. Her brother had received a good education, and on its completion he had at first entered a hospital concerned with the special medical needs of people starting on the new life; but shortly he left this occupation to train as a surgeon. He was now active in this profession. Lang's next remark was arresting. "People," he said, "have wrong ideas about the bodies of the next-life. They think that the psychical body has no imperfections. It is *not* free from defect – and there is a constant effort being made to improve it. Deficiencies that exist in it at present are often reflected in malignant diseases of the physical body." Marjorie's brother was working in that particular field.

I had a question on my list concerning the great psychical age Dr. Lang had attributed to me on my second meeting with him – the visit of Chapter 4 in August, 1975. I took up the question saying how my intuition or impression was that my psyche had been in existence for about one thousand years. I admitted I felt more accustomed to the idea. Yet was my figure right? He answered that one thousand years was a low figure, but not far from correct; and Marjorie, he said, was of nearly identical age. We had known each other in four out of five previous existences on earth. The countries had been widely different. It was always possible to select the family of one's birth, to ensure a high likelihood of meeting with one another again. We had failed in one instance. On the whole, we had progressed at about the same rate. At one point one of us – he would not say which – had lagged; but that had been made up. He commented that he also knew our psychical parentage.

While listening, I had been writing down some notes; and since Lang had given France, Japan, Egypt and Israel as the countries of our meeting I was noting these countries when I became aware there had occurred – without warning – an entire change of voice. *I was no longer listening to Dr. Lang.* The dialect was Irish and the speech much faster than Lang's. If the circumstances of the switch had been obvious I must have missed them in writing my notes. "Hullo," I had heard the voice begin, "I'm Hughie. We've not met before – but you've heard of me. Shake hands." Looking up I saw he had held out his hand; and I shook it. "Yes," I answered, "Dr. Lang has spoken to me of you. I'm pleased to meet you. You are one of his assistants, aren't you?" "That's right," came a sprightly reply, "and I know Marjorie well."

Observing the facial expression as he was speaking I clearly saw there had been a change of features. The tendency to roundness when Dr. Lang was present was gone. There was a greater width to the lower part of the face, and the lips were quite different – they were much more pronounced. Then also, the posture assumed had that smart erectness of a man trained in physical fitness.

"You'll be interested to know," he went on,"that Marjorie is looking after some young children in her new cottage just at present" – kids, in fact, was the word he used for them. Without stopping he volunteered: "you know, the country in which you and Marjorie failed to meet was India. We have been looking up the records." He reverted to the kids and rattled on about them. It was clear that he felt a warm-hearted care for them – but, impressive and highly interesting as was Hughie's intrusion, there remained in my mind the other points I had listed to put to Lang; and I was keen to come to them before all the time was used up.

Perhaps Marjorie gathered my thoughts, or Dr. Lang. Hughie's voice suddenly stopped – and the features dropped back to those of George Chapman. George Chapman slumped forward deep asleep – in fact I was about to catch him, afraid he would fall from his chair. But Dr. Lang was present again and with a jerk – beaming a smile.

Feeling that my mental reaction towards the end of this quite fascinating episode might have been ungenerous (and could have been obviously so) I asked Dr. Lang if he would thank Hughie for his interlude – which I valued. Lang nodded, plainly pleased by my appreciation. "He's a good fellow, Hughie," he said. "He was blown up in H.M.S. Hood during the last war. You will remember. He was brought up in Liverpool; but his parents were Irish."

Lang did not give me any chance to refer to my list and my next question. Answering the question he simply said: "You wanted to know how it was that you and Marjorie were able to react on one another in your *messages* as, you call them. The interaction is one which operates through the electrical body of which I told you. This body is a special nervous system existing, in a sense, in its own right. It interacts – as you know – with the physical body. Because of the mutual sensitivity between you, you were each able to control this special nervous system of the other and so control each other physically. Marjorie can still use this special nervous system of yours to control your ordinary nervous system and so your muscles. That is how it works." (Lang might have gone on to explain that with Marjorie's death, and in reverse respects, I was able to control her body directly since mind or psyche can influence the psychical form of body without the need of any intermediary. This reverse action will be more clear from passages of Chapter 16 concerned with the principles operating in transfiguration phenomena; and from Appendix III).

I asked Dr. Lang if Marjorie had any difficulty in receiving my thoughts. "She easily receives your thoughts," he answered, "– but you have difficulty in receiving hers, because your mind tends to be preoccupied with so many everyday matters."

Then he diverted to an entirely new subject: "I would like you to get in touch with a young friend of mine. His name is David Young. He lives in Reading. He will be able to give you a new psychic experience of Marjorie." Lang did not say that David Young was a clairvoyant; but I imagined then – and discovered later that this was so. For reasons I have stated, I had been cautious of mediums in general. With Dr. Lang's use of George Chapman as medium the situation seemed different. Speaking in this fashion with Lang, I was talking clearly and *directly* as a man of science to a man of science – talking just as one does in normal life. His integrity seemed altogether plain; and now it was equally clear that a bond of friendship had developed between us. It meant that in areas in which I could not check, I felt I could rely on him. With this new matter I saw no difficulty – if Lang considered there was point in going to see David Young I was ready to do it without debate. I could always refer back to Dr. Lang. So I expressed my thanks for the suggestion, and said I would follow it out.

I thought time might permit of one further question from my list. I explained that it related to my meeting with Marjorie by the projective method of which I had told him. Lang gave me an encouraging look, and I remarked preparatory to my question that I liked the blue long-line dress she had been wearing at the time. There was a moment's silence as noticeably he turned his head to the right – where I had been having the instinctive feeling Marjorie was present. Then he said: "She is very pleased with it too," and added that he himself, having seen it, also thought it attractive. I continued that I was distinctly interested as to what *I* might have been wearing at the time – so far as my physical body was concerned I was in bed in my pyjamas. Again but more quickly and fully he looked to his right. "She says you were wearing a light suit – do you have a light-coloured suit?" But without waiting for this point to be settled he remarked apologetically: "She must go. She is saying good-bye, and waving to you. She gives you her love." I expressed mine, and he told me he had also to break off now. He shook me warmly if hurriedly by the hand, saying: "Arrange another meeting through George."

Collecting my notes I left the sensibly deserted consulting room, Michael then entering to see that his father had tea. George Chapman always wanted many cups of tea on coming out of trance.

At leisure I gave considerable reflection to the subject of the suit. It was quite true that I had a light-coloured suit. Marjorie had accompanied me when I bought it. But I did not see the connection.

Initially the whole issue seemed mystifying. How did I come to be wearing a suit similar to my light-coloured suit? Expressing the question like this (the way clearly Lang wanted me to) led to some speculative trains of thought.

One basic idea which I relied on strongly was that, in transferring my consciousness to my psychical body, I had most certainly entered Marjorie's world. Then, there was Lang's statement on how Marjorie had built her cottage. By conscious design she had formed the cottage by imposing her will upon the matter of her world. Perhaps, although unconsciously, I had been able to impose the power of my mind to organize the matter of this same world when, during that short time, I was present in it. Was this the truth about the light suit which Marjorie saw me wearing?.

If it was, then – so it seemed – I had gained at first hand some new insight into the character of the next world. More than that the creation of my suit, trivial in itself, might be an illuminating example of what I had learned from Lang concerning mind and matter: that, while matter exists in its own right, it is a function of mind (existing separately) to impart form to matter.

I had little opportunity to take these things further with Lang himself. It will become evident, and very fully, that facilities for communication with Marjorie came to be greatly extended. What Dr. Lang was saying about David Young is a pointer in that direction; and with trance mediumship eventually becoming available to me I was able to revert in close discussion with Marjorie to the wearing of the light suit. In this discussion she stated that what I was pleased in this precise context to call speculative was in reality not that at all. Sensing my thought on occasions like that on reflection on the suit, she often endeavoured to diffuse her own thinking into mine – to enable me to gather the answers to problems I was trying to think through. My 'speculation' on the suit happened to be the truth. It was the truth for the reason she had just given – and I had for a fact spontaneously created a replica of the light-coloured suit we both remembered choosing when buying it.

Chapter Eight

VISIT TO A SENSITIVE

Now that Marjorie had brought off her surprise at Aylesbury, and I knew about the cottage, she amplified the news in response to my interest.

She gave me visual impressions – both of the building itself and of its environs. I saw that the countryside included the rolling hills and woodlands she had shown me in the view looking down from her flying machine.

The cottage stood at the top of some local high ground. In front of the cottage and partly to form a valley the ground fell away sharply for perhaps two hundred feet. At the foot ran a pathway; and woods climbed the hillside beyond. Behind the cottage were large lawns. These stretched down to a lake about a quarter of a mile distant. You could walk down to the lake by a slightly curving path with the lawns spreading widely on either side. At the back of the lake I could see a wood, and a stream running through it.

The cottage was built of stone like Cotswold stone – and it was a thatched cottage. Between it and the lawns Marjorie had laid out a patio area. I did not gain any particularly clear impression of the interior of the cottage; but I learned that the rooms if few were large – and that bearing in mind a frequent experience when we had together been in search of some delightful old cottage for our home, I would not bump my head on the beams!

All of this information I received in two short sessions on successive evenings. The impressions mostly were vivid and definite; and as I gained them it was with the sense of knowledge Marjorie especially wanted me to have. I could feel her pleasure.

A fortnight after this Marjorie gave me information of a completely different kind. It was about my mother. She had died two years before Marjorie's fatal accident, and had been in hospital for several months. Most evenings I would visit her in hospital. Her condition appeared to remain very much the same. Talking to her the evening before she died, she had patted my hand fondly, telling me she must say a final good-bye. (Probably and rightly she felt I would only think it fanciful if she told me how she knew she must say this. Her reason for saying it – so I eventually discovered – was that during the previous night she had both seen and spoken to my father, who had died nearly twenty years before. He had assured her he would be coming the next night to take her away and take care of her. That was the reason also for the special quiet happiness I remembered clearly on her face as I talked to her.) Next morning a call from the hospital informed me she had died during the night. If I had been asked what were my views at that time on an afterlife, I would have said that *I did not know*. It was in fact the answer I gave to a friend who asked me whether I expected to see my mother again; and I still maintain that it is difficult in the normal course of events for the careful, reflective mind to give any other answer – at the level of *knowledge*, and of strictest honesty. In this present information Marjorie was telling me my mother was helping her in her medical work. As patients recuperated, and on Marjorie's suggestion, my mother would have them to stay with her and my father while their health continued to improve.

I had arranged the meeting with David Young as Dr. Lang wanted. It was at David Young's home in Reading; and near the end of April, 1976 – just one day after this news of my mother.

Lang had spoken of David Young as "a young friend" of his – but I was aware that Lang's use of the adjective *young* could cover a wide span of years: I was not necessarily expecting Mr. Young would by any means be a young man.

Meeting with him, however, this was so. He spoke quickly, almost briskly. I told him I had asked for the appointment on Dr. Lang's recommendation, and he but slightly inclined his head in recognition as I said this. I was about to give him a brief explanation in regard to Marjorie, but he hastily interrupted: "Don't tell me anything. I know Dr. Lang. At the moment I know nothing of you – but let me tell you a few things first, so that you can check on them."

I was acquainted only too well with the problem of the brevity of time, and it seemed that this proposal would markedly curtail the value of the meeting. To avert this possibility, I remarked that in the light of Dr. Lang's recommendation I was entirely happy to take his abilities for granted. He was insistent, however, and to avoid more waste of time I thought it best to take things his way.

"First of all," he said, "you are clairvoyant yourself." I agreed – to the extent it was a sensitivity that was only slight. "London comes into my mind. You used to live in South London," he continued. I said he was correct; and then he added: "I can see Clapham Common – but you lived further over than that." I told him it was in Streatham. Then he said something that particularly captured my attention: "Your mother's house was off the High Road." He had clearly pin-pointed where I had lived in Streatham; and he had told me the house was my mother's. This was true. He went on: "If I turned off the High Road to get to your mother's house I would have to go over the railway arch." His use of the word *arch* even more strongly attracted my interest. *I* would have said only that I must go over the *bridge*: if you were walking along the road it would appear to you that you came to a bridge which you must go over – just that and nothing more. As far as the railway or the arch of the bridge over it were concerned, you would never see them; because of the high side walls of the bridge. If on the other hand you were looking down on the scene, the railway and the arch over it carrying the road would be the things that would catch your eye. I wondered if there was anything in this – if it offered a clue to the way David Young was gaining his knowledge. Was he, perhaps, using a projective technique, as in the Stanford work (Chapter 5)?

He continued with two further comments on my earlier surroundings. "I can see," he said, "a large green area not far from your mother's house." I identified this to him as Streatham Common; and again noted that it was as though he had projected his consciousness to gain an aerial view. His next comment was: "And as you turn off from the High Road for your mother' house there is nearby a fire station." I told him that was right. With the confirmation he handed the conversation over to me, saying: "Now you talk a little, if you find that convincing."

I assured him it was most interesting – but that he had not surprised me. What I wanted to express was what Dr. Lang had stated that he (David Young) would be able to give me a further impression of my fiancée, Marjorie. Marjorie, I explained, had died as the result of a car crash in 1971. For sometime before her death we had operated a communication link in terms of thoughts and sensations. In these same terms she had been able to communicate with me within half a day of her death. I described briefly how, when I was at last able to realize she was making contact with me, I had sent a message back to her – and I mentioned its remarkable effect.

He amplified my statement with his comment: "Marjorie did not die in the car." I told him that this was so: she had died about midday at Battle Hospital, Reading, shortly after the ambulance brought her in. I had been awaiting the arrival of the ambulance – because the Government Establishment for which she worked informed me that she would be taken to this hospital. He said: "I can think of two Government Establishments . . . Harwell . . . but it was not Harwell. Alder . . . Aldermaston was where she worked." I told him this also was right.

He turned to me: "There were two deaths" – and he repeated this. Perhaps my expression was blank on the first occasion. I had not closely associated my mother's death with Marjorie's; but it came into my mind that it was my mother's death which he was including. I remarked: "My mother had died a little earlier." "Yes," he emphasized, "there was your mother's death."

His next statement I should perhaps have anticipated: "Your mother is here with Marjorie. Your mother is very fond of you. She is so glad you are here. She gives you her love. You did not really know your father." Responding to this comment on my father I said: "Perhaps not – but I always thought of him as a very good father." To that David Young immediately rejoined: "Oh yes, but you were much closer to your mother." Then he added: "Your mother wants you to learn she has found a wonderful friend in Marjorie. She never truly got to know her before. She is very fond of her."

My thoughts turned to unhappy differences between my father and mother, and I asked for news of my father. "Your father and mother," he told me, "are now very happy together – earlier a breach had built up between them."

Then he went on: "Marjorie is cracking jokes with me. She is very gay, and full of life." I assured him that this was good character description of Marjorie. He continued, trying to describe her physically, and finding difficulty over the colour of her hair. "She is not a blond," was his comment, "because her hair is darker than that." I said I thought at times it had shown a copper tint. He felt that best described how she now appeared to him.

I noticed in the last minute or so he had changed to calling her Margaret. I was puzzled; but not entirely puzzled. Often Dr. Lang had spoken of her as Margaret. I had thought it was just a lapse on his part. David Young's change now stimulated my curiosity, and I raised the point with him. He simply answered: "Well, that is what she calls herself now!" It seemed I must take up this matter at a later date.

David Young was continuing: "She is asking how Philip is." Momentarily this did not register with me. I knew no one called Philip. Perhaps he had misheard *Philip* for *Phyllis*, I suggested. He corrected the name to Phyllis, and I informed him that Phyllis had been a close friend of Marjorie at Aldermaston. Marjorie was, however, not waiting for an answer. I had – as I have set down – given her all my news of Phyllis at the very start of our evening exchanges; and Marjorie, I deduced, by not waiting was just confirming to me that she had received it and taken note of it.

She hurried on to say that at the moment she gathered there was a need for a tape recorder. My response was that I hoped to have one to hand in the very near future.

"You need this for a book you are writing," David Young interposed. I agreed and pointed out that other people unfortunately often found my hand writing hard to decipher. Recording on tape, the problem of a first draft in typescript would be much easier. Marjorie went into some details about the book. Then there was David Young's inspiriting remark: "She says she has been wanting you to write it for years – you are not to hurry to finish it."

The conversation changed to the house in which I was now living; and I should explain it was the house on which Marjorie and I had originally jointly decided. David Young stated that it made him think of Pangbourne. I told him it was not far from Pangbourne – and I said that, as it now was, I felt sure Marjorie would like it. This was responded to by a characteristic shaft of Marjorie's dry humour: "Dust my photograph more often!" The photograph was an excellent and framed colour likeness of her, and I had told her of it.

Marjorie continued with a very definite demonstration that she had received, and noted carefully, what I passed on to her. She mentioned a young friend of mine by name – both by Christian name and surname: a colleague with whom I was hardly acquainted at the time of her death. I know that I never mentioned him to her while she was alive. He had been encountering certain personal problems of late – but was handling them well. Marjorie knew of these problems, because I had discussed them with her. "He is a very steady and promising young man," was her comment, "but he is working too hard." I found in due course that Marjorie had cause for her caution.

There was some conversation relating very much to Marjorie's concern about me; but the subject changed suddenly – I was not at first quite certain where to. It happened when David Young stated: "You have been doing a lot of tests and checking." I should have thought of my recent telepathic checks with Lang; but, somehow, my mind turned to the early tests on our communicating link, when Marjorie was alive. I referred to them; and I said that when Marjorie and I noticed we had this link we wanted to find out all we could about it. To these remarks, David Young responded: "Yes – but you have been doing a lot of checking with Dr. Lang." I agreed this was very true. Then – thinking of detail checks not made with Lang on Marjorie's flying machine – I suggested that, as we were talking about checking, it would be good to check some things now with Marjorie about her flying machine.

I did not enlighten David Young as to what kind of machine it was. It was my impression from Marjorie, I said, that it possessed a blown skirt – was that so? The answer came back: "She says when it lands you must think of it like

73

a hovercraft" – a statement in full confirmation of my impression.

I thought of the interesting question also of the speed of the craft. I said I knew it could travel very fast – and I mentioned the figure of five thousand miles per hour, a low figure but one I had gathered from Marjorie: had I got it right? "She says it can go very much faster," David Young answered. "Five thousand miles per hour is only an example." I received a direct impression from Marjorie that it was a very poor example.

Not having been able to talk to Lang either about the basis of the power unit I wondered if I could collect some clue to the source of the jet thrust. It was really expecting too much at this point to get very far; but I learned quite clearly that a magnetic principle was important in the release of the thrust efflux of particles – it was on the fringes of modern physics.

The conversation thus far had been an enlarging experience. But it had jumped around from one topic to another, as conversations very often do. I hoped it could be brought round to one or two topics in a way which even in so short a session would prove enlightening – in a fundamental sense – on Marjorie's world. A criticism of the (by no means small) psychical literature, I knew, had been made that it concerns itself only little with the nature of the next existence – and that certainly nothing scientific has been gathered. There, it was even argued nothing is to be gathered. The next-world might appear to be a material world; but that was only an illusion – just as material objects in a dream are not made of matter but give only the illusion they are. Dr. Lang and Marjorie had never said anything to make me think the matter of their world is less real than ours. I wanted to get the issue exposed in a clear light. That as I saw it could only mean finding out if physical principles similar to those of our world hold in the next. Here a *reductio ad absurdum* line of argument seemed at hand to settle the issue. If the understanding of the next-world matter should be identical in character with that of our own, then our matter being real so must next-world matter. And to suppose next-world matter illusory as in a dream automatically reduced to saying that our matter is likewise an illusion: a clear nonsense.

It was reasonable enough that conversations across the interface with the next-world should mostly be on personal matters. With Marjorie and myself, both having scientific minds, the prospect for knowledge I felt was a golden one, to be seized on; and I had expectations that our present talk would be clarifying.

Marjorie was in fact able to help. The very first question it seemed to me must be whether the kind of matter which Marjorie now experienced is atomic. The answer given by John Dalton at the start of the 19th century to a similar question lies amongst the foundations of the scientific understanding of matter as we know it in our own experience. Originally the same thought processes had been entered upon by the ancient Greeks. If you consider any sample of matter of a particular kind and divide it and continue to divide it, will you eventually come to a point at which the particles no longer admit of further division? – at least if they are to remain particles of the same substance. If the answer is that you do, then the matter is called *atomic*, recognizing the then further indivisibility. The particles of matter at which you have thus arrived – as we know in science that you must – are called *atoms*.

With such thoughts as a starting point, I said to David Young that I would like to put to Marjorie a few questions on the subject of matter that were basic – and I had in mind questions on the fundamental physics of the material world of Marjorie's present existence. "Firstly, is the matter with which she is now directly acquainted atomic?" The answer came immediately, and excitingly: "Yes." Then, categorically, she insisted: "*All* matter is atomic."

With this comprehensive assertion my mind transferred from what had started as a brilliant conception of the ancient Greeks to an equally striking conception – a related conception – of modern science. "Present-day physicists," I continued, "are inclined to think that energy is a more fundamental aspect of physical reality than matter – that in some sense material particles express local and specific condensations of a more basic entity, energy. Would Marjorie like to comment on this hunch – and, of course, also in regard to her own world?" The reply was an authoritative: "*It is not a hunch – it is a fact.*" David Young spoke the words with force. The stress she laid, I reflected slowly, was indeed appropriate . . . if energy was a basic common factor between our two physical worlds.

Marjorie, though, was continuing to emphasize her point – and by a rather original and pictorial treatment of the subject. Certainly I had never thought of it in such terms. You can, if you like, she was saying, look on matter by analogy with a tree. A tree has roots, branches and leaves. Setting aside its roots, you can influence it in many ways: by wind, moisture, sunshine – they all have their modifying effect; and you can change it, too, by cutting off its branches – by lopping or by pruning. If, however, you cut off its roots you will destroy the tree. Energy is to matter as roots are to a tree. You can change matter in many ways – but if you remove its energy then matter will cease to exist. With this graphic imagery Marjorie confirmed the truth of the present outlook in physics. It is one that traces back to Einstein's outstanding pronouncement of 1905 on the equivalence of energy and mass (mass being looked on as the measure of the amount of matter a body contains).

Events had been realizing my expectations; and I hoped it would be possible to take the question of physical principles even further. The physics of our own kind of matter is now well known to follow the pattern of quantum mechanics. With what Marjorie had just been saying there were obvious and strong signs that in central principle next-world matter did this also.

I tried to put a question to ascertain the point shortly before the session ended – not successfully though. My failure was partly because I felt, on grounds I will explain at the end of the chapter, that there was a need for David Young to understand what I was saying; and partly because time was running out so quickly. A positive answer would have fully cleared up the issue of the reality of next-world matter: whether such matter was just dreamlike or whether it was real matter. To say that this material world of next-existence persons is illusory would then (as I have argued) be tantamount to saying that ours is so also. But David Young could make nothing of quantum mechanics as I tried to capture its ideas in a few sentences. It seemed evident I would have to abandon this present attempt. While in the end I was able to clear up the issue it was not until much later – but it will become plain that the science of next-world matter is on the same broad lines as our own. This will be seen in Chapter 16. Next-world matter is precisely as real as the matter we know here.

It looked as though yet one extra question could be fitted in. I turned for this question to a certain more special but still broad issue of principles – these principles going in their origins much further back in the history of science than quantum theory. It had the advantage, besides being simpler, of confirming the far greater permanence of material objects in the next-world: the permanence which, as I have noted, Marjorie had already given me the thought impression.

The period of scientific history I had in mind was that of the mid 19th century. Energy was by that time better understood and it was realized that heat is a manifestation of it. Principles then became evident which enabled the functioning to be correctly grasped of engines, like steam locomotives, that converted heat into useful work. These principles were the so-called and famous laws of thermodynamics: still important physics though seen now with a deeper insight than when they were formulated in 1850. Their relevance to questions of the material character of the next-world lies with their description in extremely broad terms of how matter *behaves*.

The description is twofold: as given in the rather diversely directed *first* and *second* laws. The first in a way sets the stage. It lays down a general constraint imposed on matter by energy when it comes to what behaviour – as a physical change – can possibly occur and what cannot. It has nothing decisive to say however on a change that has just taken place being retraced: on whether it could then be reversed naturally and without special contrivance. Such a question lies in the province of the second-law. In 1850 it was thought – as a matter of principle – that some changes were totally beyond the possibility of natural uncontrived reversal. While deeper physical insight came to see this as an over-strong statement, the hard-core truth remains that matter as we know it tends to discard form imparted to it, often very easily, and without significant likelihood of the original form being regained except by external intervention. A child playing on the beach makes a sandcastle. Before long the forces of nature acting on their own wipe out completely the form created by the child; and it is a forlorn hope to expect the form will return of nature's accord. The example illustrates the widespread and essentially one-way process of decay or degeneration of the orderly into the disordered that is constantly taking place in our world. This most distinctive process is very much the business of the second law of thermodynamics; and the prominence that attaches to the operation of the law is greatly characteristic of our existence. It is difficult to see that in any atomic world the second law could not apply. With next-world matter of course the operation of the law could conceivably be masked by the fact of a great lack of prominence. The important question concerning the behaviour of next-world matter seemed to be the extent to which operation of the law might in this way be disguised.

David Young I thought took the gist of my attempt to introduce and frame such a question; and I did not need to wait even a moment for Marjorie to give her answer. It was a succinct: "We do not have to contend, as you do in your world, with a kind of matter that is always so strongly tending to disorder."

With this great difference I left the subject – but it was possible to return to it in talks with Marjorie in other circumstances. These talks were highly clarifying. Marjorie fully confirmed the operation of the second law in the next-world context; on the other hand she went into details – which I shall give in Chapter 16, *Physics* – that explain the great difference holding in regard to the law as between the one world and the other. There is, she made plain, no fundamental

76

difference in the mechanisms of the atoms; but there is an enormous difference on the score of scale. It is this difference – expressed in the relatively minute next-world atoms – that is responsible for the great disparity of behaviour which Marjorie had asserted through David Young. The difference favours to a fantastic degree the forces of cohesion in the next-world order of existence – and when this is worked out it is seen that it correspondingly favours strongly the permanence of form.

In our world – because, perhaps, we are so constantly engaged in the battle against the forces of decay – we seldom appreciate these decay forces for their worth. They are nature's levellers. They have a most important role – they pave the way for new forms by demolition of the old: this is the mode of our world in a constant flux of change. What we find so irksome is the fact that such very necessary forces carrying nature forward through its varying phases and breaking down spent forms can work against us when we fabricate material things, because we are creative. We show such creative skill constantly; but, inevitably, the forces of disorder set about their natural tasks and may even obliterate, in the course of time, what we have constructed and built. In the next-world order there exists a factor not effectually present in ours; the direct power of mind to control matter and bring about change in its form. As I understand it, this factor virtually removes the need for a levelling action built into the behaviour of matter.

The forty-five minutes which David Young had said he could allow for the meeting were almost up; but the approach to their conclusion brought a twist to events which explained exactly why I failed in getting over my point on quantum mechanics.

Dr. Lang's assurance that telephathically Marjorie was very sensitive to me did not give me *total* assurance concerning such communication between us. I had experienced the difficulties I have gone into when she attempted to inform me about her flying machine. Perhaps here I greatly overrated what after all were initial difficulties – yet the fact remains that I was not sure the same difficulties might not occur with Marjorie when *I* was trying to convey to *her* subject matter which equally was scientific. In comparison with myself David Young obviously had great clairvoyant ability. That fact made me look to him on this transference problem, as I conceived it. Consequently I supported his keenness to understand the scientific points I wanted to make – imagining that where my thought might not get across his would.

The truth – as I was about to learn – was that my thought did not fail at all to transfer to Marjorie, even on issues of science. However the attempt to give David Young an understanding of quantum mechanics – with matter ordinarily manifesting itself in stable quantum states – only became lost in a morass. It did not register with him; and, so I have ascertained, Marjorie for herself could not see just what point I was hoping eventually to make. She intervened to save more wastage of time. It was probably something, she suggested, that could be left for the time being. Just at the end of the meeting I, entirely unwittingly, gave her the opportunity to correct me over my mistaken ideas on communication with her at the scientific level.

These ideas very much on my mind, I even remarked to David Young that although I was telepathically sensitive to Marjorie – the checking with Dr. Lang which he had mentioned showed this to be true – I knew I tended to run into trouble in the field of science; possibly Marjorie did also. I looked on this, I said, as a question of some importance, since Marjorie was attaching significance to scientific communication between us.

It may have been that at this point she began to realize why it was I had entered upon the fruitless attempt to enlighten David Young on quantum theory. But – at least that I should no longer remain in *any* state of misapprehension she broke in with a pungency of expression she reserved only for occasions that might especially merit it. "Tell him," she impressed on David Young, "that I *always* hear him well – and *remind* him that I am a scientist by training." The message was clear – I should have directed my quantum point simply to Marjorie, regardless of David Young. David Young undisguisedly a little shaken declared: "She has a dry sense of humour!" I said that *I knew*.

Then he remarked: "She is saying that she wants to know when you are going to Greece . . . or does she mean Egypt . . . no, she means Greece . . . that's it when are you going to Greece?" For the moment I was at a loss. I had no such plans. Then – possibly by Marjorie's direct prompting – I thought of her remark of the early days: that, when we met, Greek had met Greek. I told David Young that this reference to Greece must be only another way of saying the same thing She was giving our present exchanges an official stamp of authenticity. David Young took the point – and Marjorie added nothing in correction.

We had used up the time. David Young remarked that forty-five minutes was his maximum. "Marjorie wants you to know that you are always in her thoughts," he stated. I said my love was with her. "She knows, she knows," he exclaimed. "She is waving good-bye."

Chapter Nine

A NEW EXPERIENCE IN HEALING

Chas was among several good friends I made from my early interest in motor sport. He ran a small works specializing in the design and construction of competition cars. I was interested in the stability problems of such vehicles. As difficulties of this kind presented themselves to Chas, I would turn to their analysis, and we would go into them together. Usually this led to a clearer insight – and sometimes to a useful practical solution.

Marjorie with her own appreciation of motor cars had been introduced to these activities; and she met Chas; but I did not meet his wife Iris until three years after Marjorie's death. Chas and Iris then came on a visit one weekend. Not long after, and because they were interested, I told them of Doreen's remarkable recovery after her treatment by Dr. Lang at Bath.

Towards the end of 1975, Chas was exploring other business possibilities. At first these did not work out with lasting prospects; but there were developments and he became extremely busy on that account. I knew it was a phase demanding a large effort from him. What I did not know was that, at this same time, Iris had become ill – and it was raising acute difficulties.

On a Saturday evening close to the end of April, 1976, these circumstances forced themselves on me suddenly and urgently. The telephone rang. It was Chas, and his voice was I thought tense. "Iris wants to speak to you," he said shortly. He handed the telephone straight to her. "I am on the bottle again, John," she began, "and I do not know what to do about it." This opening surprised me because I knew a little about her. Fifteen years earlier she had shown alcoholic tendencies. They had developed after some parties; but she had fought the tendencies and mastered them – rigidly practising the alcoholic's only safe rule: to avoid alcohol at all times. Her present overwhelming worry with this new outbreak was the stability of their marriage. She could see the marriage breaking up; and she felt herself quite unable to cope with what was happening.

It was not easy talking to her. Her brain was functioning indifferently – and, it seemed inevitably, the conversation ran in eddies of repetition. I tried to discover what had brought on her present condition. It must, I felt, be a weighty matter to have broken through her defenses – and I was inclined to believe her when she told me how. Alcoholics run easily to fantasy, but what she said was that an intense pain had developed in her stomach – and pain-killing drugs had given her little relief. If she had a drink then the pain was held at bay for several hours. It sounded as though she must have a stomach ulcer; and I asked what was her medical advice. She had been to her doctor, she replied – but she had only been given treatment for her alcoholic condition. That, she confessed, she had not been following out. Bearing in mind she was an alcoholic, coupled with the benefits of release from pain offered by drink, I felt I understood why. Sympathetically with her doctor, I felt also I could understand the prescribed treatment – assuming thats, as almost certainly was the case, she had gone to see him in a condition like her present.

I gathered she had not eaten anything for a week – she was quite unable to keep down any solid food. At this point it was clear in my own mind that one or other of two courses must be taken – and soon. Either she must enter hospital, possibly for an operation; or, failing that, Dr. Lang must be brought in. The first was going to be daunting: Iris had an intense aversion to operations – the difficulties of persuading her must be very great. The second entailed a problem of time. Here, I should explain, my thoughts were running solely in terms of Iris's attendance at Aylesbury.

I have already remarked upon George Chapman's long waiting lists. Iris might have to wait many weeks. My next meeting with Dr. Lang, booked for Wednesday, 5th May, now came into mind. The date was about ten days distant – perhaps not too long to wait. I was thinking that part of the session could be given up to Iris's treatment. I asked Iris if I could speak again to Chas. She passed the phone back to him; and he listened to my proposal. On the strength of what I had earlier told him of Doreen he agreed that Iris should be treated on the lines along which I was thinking. He would certainly drive her over to Aylesbury. Put to Iris she said she would see Dr. Lang. In that event I said I would write at once to George Chapman – but I remarked that I anticipated no quick reply. Dr. Lang had recently extended his activities to France, Italy and Germany; and George Chapman was, these days, spending much of his time on the Continent.

The course of events did not exactly follow my proposed plan. A week passed and the next weekend arrived without response to my letter. That was rather as I had expected. But I was hoping for some communication by the following Monday. None came. On very comprehensible grounds George Chapman wanted to minimize telephone calls. Michael had said to me how difficult it was to find any time at all for themselves, and for relaxation. It seemed, nevertheless, that I must ring through on the Tuesday evening if I had heard nothing by then.

Unexpectedly however, on the Tuesday and just as I was leaving my office to go to lunch Iris came on the phone. She was ringing, she said, because she was so ill – *she had been so ill in the night*. As she spoke, I noticed how very different her voice was. It was weak; but it was clear – and like her normal voice. It made me think that Dr. Lang had been attending her. Had she, I asked her, noticed anything special in the night? – had she too perhaps been sick? Yes, she answered, she had certainly been sick. She had brought up a lot of matter, a lot of muck as she expressed it, black muck; and she had been aware of many loud clicks. I said it was obvious that Dr. Lang had been at work on her – and that she could consider herself well on the way to recovery.

She went on that the pain in her stomach had vanished; and that she had not wanted a drink that morning. "Tell me," I said, "have you received a letter from George Chapman?" She informed me she had – a letter had come that morning. In it, George Chapman wrote that he would not give her an appointment at

Aylesbury: she would receive 'distant healing' instead. "That makes it plain," was my comment. "I will ask Dr. Lang about you when I talk with him tomorrow."

The next day at Aylesbury, Dr. Lang smiled in recognition when I referred to Iris. I was quite correct he said – he had attended her in the early hours of Tuesday morning. She was suffering from a stomach ulcer. This had formed so that it was blocking off the flow of gastric juices. He wanted me to instruct her to drink large quantities of water – litres a day; and to restrict herself, for the present, to a purely vegetarian diet. This message I duly passed on to her.

For the remaining week, Iris continued to bring up matter at night, but less and less; and she began to regain her appetite. It seemed that her recovery was complete, or virtually so, especially as she was able to return to a normal diet.

But at this juncture I approach the real issue of this chapter. Events assumed a fresh slant; and a thought – one that looked very obvious in retrospect – occurred to me which had been elusory hitherto. It worked out remarkably when I put it into action; and this came as an entirely new experience for me in the sphere of healing.

On Monday, 24th May, I telephoned to check how Iris was – and I found that there was a new difficulty. The trouble was oedema. She was, she said extensively swollen. Tablets she had been given by her doctor to clear up the accumulation of fluid were not succeeding; and she was getting worse.

It was disquieting that the medical treatment was having so little effect. Almost certainly her recent heavy alcohol intake had triggered off the condition. It was well possible that loss of kidney function held serious consequences. Basic moves to put things right were very much needed.

I thought of a letter to George Chapman. That would I felt sure bring help as before. But the help might nevertheless be long in coming. On the last occasion delay had been more than a week – the letter presumably having to await George Chapman at Aylesbury. My mind carried through some quick steps of logic which I had not taken before and I saw a simple and new way of proceeding. With my visit to David Young it had become evident that however abstruse the subject I could nevertheless communicate it of myself to Marjorie – with clarity and certainty. I was positive, therefore, that I could directly inform Marjorie of what had now happened with Iris. Marjorie would have no trouble in passing on the details, with a request for his help, to Dr. Lang. Explaining the idea to Iris she agreed that I should carry it out – she would await the outcome.

I turned to Marjorie, and acquainted her with events. Next morning when I woke my first question to her was whether Dr. Lang had been able to look in on Iris. He had not, I understood – but he *would* be visiting Iris as I had requested. Wednesday morning I asked again – and the reply was the same. On the Thursday morning it was different. Dr. Lang had treated Iris. While of course I was deeply interested to learn how she was now, I did not in fact ring through that day, but left it to the next. "What is the news?" I then enquired. Iris answered with delight: she was back to normal – and all yesterday the swelling had been steadily going down.

I felt there had been achieved – if no more than in my own personal world – something of the nature of a breakthrough. Consistent with Marjorie's forcible words at the David Young meeting, and so palpably to hand ever since that meeting. I was slow to realize it. But now it stood out a momentous principle; and the pattern, having been established with Iris, was again and again repeated.

Normally the patients concerned did not make any request of themselves. For one thing, and a major reason, people brought up in the present climate of thinking tend to 'know' that events such as I have just been describing cannot happen. It was appropriate to act first; and afterwards and with a few individuals to explain at leisure.

The very first instance of like treatment after that of Iris was with a friend active professionally in the scientific field. He had gone into hospital for a minor operation; but in hospital he had picked up an infection of the operative wound. I heard of this when I came to telephone him at his home. Listening to his voice it was clear how sick he was – it was evident before ever he mentioned the infection. The hospital, he said, had brought all antibiotic measures to bear without checking the trouble. I observed like difficulties when, not long after my mother's death, and as the result of an accident, I myself had spent some time in hospital. Many patients in the ward had operative and other wounds that had become infected and failed to heal despite the use of antibiotics. In these circumstances the only resort was to a serum derived from the specific infection of the wound: procedure which was rather slow and wretched. It was this technique that the hospital was about to try in my friend's case.

I conveyed this news to Marjorie, asking that Dr. Lang should do whatever he could to cure the trouble. Letting a couple of days pass, I again telephoned my friend. His voice was brighter. "I felt much better in myself yesterday," he said, "and there is an improvement in my wound."

When we had the opportunity to meet, I told him of the main background facts – the main facts of this narrative – and then of my request on his account *via* Marjorie. Perhaps from his close acquaintance with the developments of nuclear physics – where facts have proved themselves unlike those of the familiar everyday world (and to the embarrassment of popular ideas) – he was less inclined than most to discount the strange simply for the reason that it was strange. He accepted my good faith – and took seriously the events and explorations I had been outlining to him. Rather like my friend Bob, he felt that what had been discovered should now stand as a basis for further discovery. I was not surprised he should put it to me that one or two of his friends might be proper subjects for Dr. Lang's medical attention.

So far as the infected wound was concerned, the hospital did not find it necessary to use the proposed serum treatment. In scarcely a fortnight the wound had soundly healed. Dr. Lang made two further visits, the fact and benefits of which were markedly apparent to his patient. With the first there was another major improvement in the condition of the wound; and with the second a great improvement in general well being.

Marjorie had in fact been present when Dr. Lang was operating on the wound. In a second talk that – not long after – I had with her through David Young she gave me an outline description of the patient – his age, correct (as I found on subsequent enquiry) to a year, height, general appearance, even his main mental characteristics. I did not know him during Marjorie's lifetime; and I am sure that Marjorie did not. At my next meeting with Dr. Lang, I told him of Marjorie's thumb-nail sketch. "Oh," he laughed, "she's a young woman. She would notice these things. I was just a doctor working on the wound."

Reviewing the many occasions on which Dr. Lang was able to operate on or treat patients brought to his notice because I transferred details of their illness to Marjorie, there is this to add: more often than not major improvement was quick and maintained; but some patients required continuing treatment; and a minority were little benefitted.

It was not difficult to see how in collaborating with Marjorie in this way I was taking part in the same basic process which operated when for instance, as I described in Chapter 3, Marjorie's mother was treated by 'distant healing'. I had initially to write to George Chapman; but then the key step was that he, so I ascertained, gave the information to Dr. Lang. In a very minor way Marjorie and I had set up a parallel but like communication link with Dr. Lang to the same end.

The new developments took my mind back to various reflections on 'distant healing' when I first encountered it. With George Chapman the words had seemed a misnomer. The terminology sprang from an idea that the 'healer' must always be centrally active in the healing. I felt this did not fit the facts in the instance of George Chapman. It is true that he required to know the address of the patient. But, significantly, he was entirely happy to operate the service free: as though – contrasted with his trance healing – his time and special expertise was not involved. It was Dr. Lang, I felt, and as it proved to be, who really needed the address information.

Next there was the puzzling question of how Lang found the patient's location. It seemed that in locating the patient's address Lang must be functioning in an environment that was scarcely interactive with his own world (if it was not so very slightly interactive, it was hard to see why Lang's world was not much more obvious to us). I knew rather more now; but remained far from clear.

I told Lang of this when the opportunity came; and he assured me that patient location and identification can often be demanding. He took identification first. In my communications to Marjorie, and when I personally knew the patient, they had been greatly assisted – because through my thinking of the patient (as I conveyed the details and the request) Marjorie had been able to gain visual images of the patient. She invariably came on the missions which I had asked for, and with these visual impressions she had little trouble in finding the patient. It was not necessarily so simple when, in some of my requests, I had no visual impression to give – for the reason that I did not know (but had only been told of) the patient.

In regard to finding the address of the patient, I understood that it *is* possible clearly to see our kind of matter by the radiations from it – though exactly how Lang did not try to explain. His assistant Hughie, acting usually as navigator, had the task of locating addresses. When locality information was poor they could find themselves "engaged in laborious street by street searching."

The growth of knowledge – true to an historic pattern – often throws up issues seemingly to run in opposite directions. I noted in the Introduction a standpoint believed to arise from science, and thought to allow no niche for psychical events in a rational scheme of things. This example – with the expanding horizons of knowledge and of science in particular – where issues have arisen that to appearance are inversely directed is looked at in Appendix I. What becomes evident there is how each may be seen in the light of a deeper understanding –

and that correspondingly it is a mistake to sweep one issue under the carpet to avoid conflict with the other; because seen more clearly there is no conflict. The present chapter is not an exception to the pattern of emergent conflict as knowledge increases.

Concerning the developments of this chapter, it must seem obvious that the kind of healing described is an unqualified good. Yet I met about the same time – quite forcibly as it was put to me – a view on the way life should be conducted which ran reversely and was argued as a matter of moral principle. While I felt, instinctively, this view could not be right I also felt it important to perceive exactly why. The principle argued was that *all* procedures in healing which place certain patients in a greatly favourable position compared with others must be basically unethical: such procedures must be a 'social injustice' and 'unfair' to all those left on the sidelines. The argument not only affects the healing of this chapter but all healing in like circumstances. As just put it seems to possess weight and present a genuine conflict.

The contradiction once again stems from unjustifiably simple forms of thinking – which if accepted lead one to look on some situations in an altogether false moral light. This is made plain in detail in Appendix II.

America's most influential philosopher of current times, Willard Van Orman Quine of Harvard, noted for his studies in the logic of knowledge, has argued that the web of knowledge is a seamless thing. Knowledge is various and can be astonishingly strange – its fabric is not split into irreconcilable fragments.

Chapter Ten

FURTHER EXPLORATION AND INSIGHT INTO MEDIUMSHIP

This chapter is far ranging; and certain of its events took me another highly important step forward: I had a meeting with Marjorie which – most valuably – gave me basic understanding of the mechanism of clairvoyance.

Obviously, and apparent from my first meeting with David Young and its muddle over quantum mechanics, I had reflected far too little upon mediumship. It was now a main concern with Marjorie to rectify this omission. Of course my visits to Aylesbury were to a medium; but I had not looked on them as *going to a medium*. The fact of the actual experience was that there I was meeting and conversing simply and solely with Dr. Lang. Moreover this experience – apart from an introduction to various conceptions which lay beyond my then established thinking patterns – was distinguished by its natural character. This natural quality – an anodyne to thought about it – is characteristic of such full-trance mediumship. With David Young's clairvoyance I became forced to think about what was going on at the meeting – how Marjorie was always in fact receiving my expressed thought directly, and precisely, and David Young was immediately relaying her responses to me. But my reflections went scarcely further than that. I did not make any real attempt to consider the logistics by which this format of activity took place. Inner workings still lay over my mental horizon.

What – this failure notwithstanding – I had done was to give the mediumship I had experienced to date some very general review. Naturally thinking from a scientific standpoint, it was clear I had come so far along a path of progressive and coherent development that I was experiencing the sense of security which in science tends to go with all developing knowledge of that character. The position was one that could be expressed in purely philosophic terms: the principle of non-contradiction, so far as was evident, had been operating without fail. This principle, and not merely at any scientific level, is one which lies as the ultimate test of truth in every build-up of knowledge. However the broad critique only confirmed there was solid ground for continued enquiry.

That I had every intention, and was in fact able, to pursue. The continued exploration – if most importantly directed to mediumship – also embraced a variety of other major subjects.

It was made possible by a series of sessions arranged over the nine months following upon my first meeting with David Young. In large degree I shall not try to give any verbatim or highly detailed account of these meetings – but I will attempt to trace more significant subjects as they arose or developed in the course of the meetings. The meetings took place specifically as follows:

(i)   at Aylesbury, on the 5th May, 1976, with Dr. Lang;

(ii)   at Reading, on the 1st September, 1976, with David Young;

(iii)   at Aylesbury, on the 8th September, 1976, with Dr. Lang; and

(iv)   at Aylesbury, on the 19th January, 1977, with Dr. Lang.

In these sessions I discovered more about the ways and pattern of Marjorie's new life. My ideas were re-inforced concerning the general physical nature of her world. From what she put to me on mediumship I gained insight in particular into the telepathic communication that had developed greatly between us with Dr. Lang's encouragement. Then, there was discussion – instructive concerning the electrical body – of a proposed but unsuccessful endeavour to deploy magnetic recording methods: a plan aimed at setting up between Marjorie and myself a further channel of communication. Looking at all of these subjects I will start with a facet of the first of them – concerning custom in Marjorie's new world that carried some import personal to me.

There was at the first meeting with David Young a question of Marjorie's name – which seemed to be a question of her *present* name. Dr. Lang as I noted had frequently called her Margaret instead of Marjorie; and I had tended to regard the variation as accidental – until David Young also began to refer to her as Margaret. At that point my curiosity though roused had only partially been satisfied. "Well, that is what she calls herself now!" was David Young's sole explanation.

With the meeting of the 5th May, and talking to Lang, I explicitly asked how it came about that Marjorie was now called Margaret. It was, he said, simply because Marjorie at the commencement of her new life had come under his general care; and that in his opinion *Margaret* was a better sounding name than *Marjorie*. Therefore he renamed her Margaret. I commented that I shared his opinion as a matter of detached judgement; but that from my biased position I tended to be unaware of any improvement in euphony. Nevertheless, and with the meeting *via* David Young of the 1st September, I gathered that Marjorie herself approved the change.

The subject had come up almost at the outset of that session. To show just how it arose I go to the very beginning of this second meeting *via* David Young – a start which holds, incidentally, some interest on its own account in relation to David Young's clairvoyance and to clairvoyance in general.

My arrival was five minutes early, and I had this time to wait. Marjorie, I knew, was there too. Punctually, David Young walked into the room; and – from the friendliness that developed in the course of our first meeting – I anticipated a cordial greeting as I held out my hand to him. Yet he looked at me blankly as though he had never seen me before. "You don't recall the occasion of our last meeting?" I began – as much even by statement as question. "No," he answered. To stimulate his memory, I mentioned Marjorie's name, and Dr. Lang's, and I referred to the book – in which he had seemed so interested before – but he still looked blank. "No, I do not remember," he said.

This long-term amnesia associated with the clairvoyantly altered state of consciousness is a characteristic I became familiar with in other mediums; but just then I could not help remarking – silently – to Marjorie that David Young did not recall us at all. Perhaps he overheard this remark – in any event he was immediately saying: "Let us take it my way – just let things come. Let me feel your hand for one moment."

We sat down, and he took my hand in his very briefly as he closed his eyes. In another second or so he spoke: "There is a lady. She is serious, and studious – but she is also vivacious." "That," I commented, "fits Marjorie." Instantly he corrected me with the single word: "Margaret!"

I explained to him how interesting I found this; and how Dr. Lang had renamed her. Almost at once he was speaking again: "She is saying that she used to be called Marjorie." Then he continued after a very slight pause: "She says that people even called her *Marge!*" From the way he relayed this last statement, I could not miss Marjorie's own view of the variant. All the time I had known her she had patiently never complained; but it stood out now the new name had its merits.

The next development at this meeting – which had broken suddenly into life from a poor beginning – led straight to one of the major subjects of this chapter: the general physical character of Marjorie's Universe.

When we discussed this at the previous meeting with David Young, *I* had raised the subject. Now it was Marjorie – and pointedly: enigmatically it must have seemed to David Young. "Tell him," she said as she addressed David Young, "I was delighted that he made more of the last interview *upon reflection* than he did at the time. He was much more impressed when he was thinking of it afterwards." While David Young was reporting her it came to me exactly what she was meaning: it was her tree analogy of matter – which, it is true, I only came to consider most apt and striking on later reflection. Indeed the same image of a tree formed in my mind as when she spoke on the earlier occasion. Not unexpectedly, an obviously puzzled David Young exclaimed that he was getting the impression of a tree. I tried to enlighten him, but with little success; and I thought it better to continue the conversation with Marjorie.

I wanted her to know she was entirely correct that my appreciation of her analogy increased with further thought – and I said so. At first sight, the analogy for some reason had seemed a distant one. Marjorie plainly sensed the incompleteness then of my mental response; and was undoubtedly disappointed. Given time, however, I *was* properly impressed. In a highly pictorial way she had been saying that one must think of matter as rooted in energy – it is a manifestation of the presence of energy. For present-day physics a particle is seen to have its form, its quantum description distinguishing it from particles of different character; but much rests with its energy. Losing this it tends to contract out of existence. When its energy is reduced to zero it ceases for instance to exert gravitational attraction – the rest of the world can no longer feel its presence in that fashion. Take away, as Marjorie was saying, the energy of matter and in the practical result there will no longer be matter – just as a tree will not survive as a living thing if you remove its roots.

I seized the opportunity to make doubly sure of something I thought I had learned at the time. I explained that a matter of first principle which I had concluded from our earlier talk was that her Universe, bearing a material aspect in exactly the same way as does ours here, is an expression in this respect of precisely the same entity as is our own: energy. "She says that is right," reported

David Young, adding: "And then she says the question is *what is energy?*" I remarked how I considered that a *very good question*; but we did not proceed far with it – except that Marjorie stated, profoundly as Appendix V makes clear, that energy has its special creative function. While I was contemplating the rudimentary truth of this last statement, Marjorie was going on to round off the whole subject in broad terms and affirm that *her Universe ran very much on parallel lines with ours – you could if you wished call it a parauniverse: a very good term for it.* I was delighted with this clarification and confirmation; but David Young commented, almost complained, that he had "not followed any of this." Since Marjorie switched at once to an entirely different subject, I was relieved of any need to explain to him.

With the switch, Marjorie embarked directly upon another of the main subjects I have listed: the subject in which the practical outcome – of a communications channel between us – was never achieved; but where nevertheless the subject itself seemed to be enlightening in regard to the electrical body of the individual. The subject was one that developed in the course of the meetings, and I had in fact raised it at the first of them; but I turn to it at the point of Marjorie's present switch of the conversation.

She dived into the heart of the matter by asking: "And what about the phenomenon?" This characteristically sprightly enquiry caught me in two minds: partly I believed I knew exactly what she meant because, as I felt, I had picked it up straight from her – but, then, there seemed nothing in the question to confirm what had entered my mind. In order to be entirely certain I asked for a clue. Marjorie gave it. It was: "Tape recorders!" And it handed me complete confirmation; but to explain why I have to refer to the meeting with Dr. Lang of the 5th May.

At that meeting I asked Lang whether any technique existed by which Marjorie might be able to control the modulator circuit of a tape recorder. I knew of reports of communication, related in nature, in which messages were said to be conveyed by magnetic tape; and if indeed it had been accomplished (which I did not know) I was keen to learn more of it – with obvious practical application in view. I put the question in the context of the modulator circuit, because I wondered whether there was any way by which Marjorie could establish directly – even if weakly – electrical effects that would control the modulator and so influence the tape. On these specific lines, Lang was not particularly hopeful; but he was certain that on other lines which he had in mind a recording could be made. The modulator would then be influenced in the normal way *via* the microphone of the recorder.

I should get in touch with a Mr. Leslie Flint (Michael Chapman, he stated, would be able to give me Mr. Flint's address). Mr. Flint had the ability to materialize a voice box which Marjorie would find possible to use. Her voice could then be recorded on tape by a strictly standard use of the recorder.

I did, in fact, write to Mr. Flint, and I received a friendly reply; but without gaining any definite promise. Shortly after, I learned that Mr. Flint had decided to give up his wide practice of these activities – which he had continued for many years – making them available in future only to his close friends.

So my answer to Marjorie's enquiry on the *phenomenon* was on these lines. David Young at once gave Marjorie's comment. She wanted me, he said, to try a scientific experiment. I must operate the recorder simply by running the tape through in my presence – and it should be in a very quiet room. I promised I would do the experiment; and, as the idea seemed quite clear, I did not stop to discuss it.

It turned out that the experiment when we tried it – early in the morning of the following Sunday – was a complete failure. I told Lang of this a few days after at my meeting with him of the 8th September. He remarked that possibly it would help if he related a story about George Chapman when he was in France two years earlier.

A French interpreter was with him in his room busy putting some notes on tape. George himself was having a drink of champagne and just sitting relaxed. He had half an hour to wait before going down to dinner. The interpreter talked into the recorder for some ten minutes, and then went out of the room forgetting to switch the recorder off. The machine ran on to the end of the tape; and when the interpreter came back to it he was astonished to find his notes on the tape obliterated by a strong voice, totally unknown to him, which continued for the whole of the rest of the tape.

Lang did not disclose what was on the tape; except to say that it was a message from a personality living in his own existence. This communicator had used George's physical energies to make the recording. George Chapman's physical energies, Lang emphasized, were outstandingly great; and the communicator had harnessed them to influence the magnetic state of the tape and thus convey his message.

So far as I was concerned, Lang thought it was worth trying again. I had good physical energies. In what we had already attempted, I had been wrong to concentrate – as I had – upon what was happening. He suggested a drink, to assist relaxation; and then that I should sink into a comfortable chair by the side of the recorder, forgetting myself in some interesting book – say a book on adventure. It was quite possible that Marjorie would succeed in magnetically modulating the tape if we tried on these lines.

Despite several attempts, in the last of which I laid my hand over the recorder, nothing was achieved. In placing my hand in this way, I reasoned that the physical energies of which Lang spoke were those of the electrical system forming the electrical body. As I naturally assumed – and Lang subsequently confirmed – the system is constituted by a collection of electrically charged particles that are free to move. Flow of charge is the essential idea. Given that, then it is no more than elementary physics how the motion of electric charge entails the production of a magnetic field. I had read of experiments in which children participating caused the deflection of the needle of a magnetic compass by bringing their hand near the compass and willing the deflection. If these were valid experiments it was obvious that the children were controlling charge motion of the electrical-body system to generate magnetic deflecting fields. The generation of a magnetic field in this way must have been how George Chapman unwittingly influenced the magnetic tape when his interpreter's notes were obliterated. With our tape experiment any magnetic field that I might produce would operate with greater effect upon the tape in circumstances of closer proximity – hence my hand resting over the recorder.

The experimental account is not complete without including a further attempt – also ineffectual – made with the aid of Iris whose treatment by Dr. Lang I described in the previous chapter. In this attempt, the idea was that Iris taking my place should generate the necessary magnetic fields under Marjorie's control. The substitution was prompted by a remarkable sensitivity Iris had since shown in treatment by Dr. Lang when she had some other medical trouble. She had seen Dr. Lang on his night visit – even heard his words of encouragement. Besides this, when Marjorie had looked in on her, to check on her progress, Iris was visually aware of the fact. These events, indicative of her psychical sensitivity, were surprising to her. Thinking of the tape experiment it was possible such ability might prove of advantage. I explained to Iris what needed to be done; and she was agreeable to help. She gave me a day, and a time, that would be convenient; and I then informed Marjorie.

The result, although a failure, was not entirely null. Iris's report contained an unexpected feature – she had been forced to give up the experiment. My proposal to achieve maximum effect, was that she should let her hand lie close to the recorder – just as I had done. She had found, in following this out, that she was affected by pains in her arm between wrist and elbow. These were so disturbing she felt she had to abandon the programme when only fifteen minutes into the experiment. Playing the tape through there were other than expectable background sounds present on it. But they were undecipherable. And I had to be content with the emergent more complete view of the electrical body.

I revert to the subject of the pattern, the ways, of the next-life; and turn again to the meeting with David Young. This second meeting with David Young held most interesting developments of a family nature.

In the first place Marjorie, explaining that she was thinking of her mother, told me she had brought along her father. He spoke – rather formally but quite characteristically, so I found out – and he asked if I would be so kind as to bear a message to his wife; which message he gave and I promised to convey. This family message directed my mind to members of my own family in Marjorie's world. I was interested to know how many she might have met. I knew that Marjorie had built up her friendship with my mother. Putting my question, Marjorie was slow to answer. The fact that people are apt to change their customary names did not help – and this shortly became clear. Marjorie's first response, and very true to her manner, was just the exclamation: "It's a large place, dearie!"

Thinking that with more time to reflect she might come up with something positive, I turned off to the non-family subject of Dr. Milne, whom I referred to on my first meeting with Dr. Lang, and when I remarked that he had only recently died. Marjorie had known Dr. Milne as our family doctor, and had liked him; and she knew of his active life in general practice – maintained long after his retirement from the Moorfields Hospital. The question as to whether she had met with Dr. Milne since his death brought an immediate: "Yes." To this David Young added that she was smiling, and saying that he still looks very old. "Something is making me think of Scotland," David Young went on. I told him that Dr. Milne, who was ninety-three when he died, was truly a Scot.

That satisfied David Young; and almost at once he announced: "She is going back to your family. She is mentioning Ann, or Annie – and then Elizabeth." With this pronouncement it was I who was now in difficulties. I recalled a distant cousin of the name of Annie; but at the same time gained the impression that I

90

was on the wrong track. As to "Elizabeth", my mind was first of all a blank – but an aunt called Florence came into my thoughts; and I remembered that she had a second name Elizabeth. So she must, I concluded, also have adopted the practice of name changing. As I was reflecting, David Young informed me that Marjorie would look into these things "for another time".

Talking the subject over with my sister, we considered I was right over "Elizabeth"; but my sister ventured strongly that "Ann" or "Annie" must be our mother's mother, whose names were Mary Ann.

Curiously, on the other hand, as Marjorie spoke to David Young of "Ann", I felt she meant some – by appearance – comparatively youthful person: this came over to me beyond any question. But I only knew my maternal grandmother when I was a child, and to me she always seemed *very old*. It was confusing. Some remarks, however, of Dr. Lang at our meeting of the 8th September seemed to resolve the subject. There is apparently a natural if gradual tendency for the body that is used in the next existence – while initially conforming to the body characteristics of the life here – to assume a form very like that of the physical body in this life at the age, approximately, of twenty-five years. Children grow up to this bodily appearance, and those starting with an older appearance can be expected in the course of time to revert to its youthfulness. The rule is a general one; and it is subject to exceptions. If a person has reason not to wish for so young an appearance, then it comes about that he or she takes on an appearance which is appropriately older. Assuming my sister right – and I feel that she was – in the identification of our grandmother, it looked that (despite the elderly features which along with her Victorian manner had impressed me when I knew her) she had not opted to depart from the general rule. I reflected also that if Marjorie had met my grandmother when visiting my mother then this meeting ground was not unlikely; for – as I and my sister knew quite well – our mother had always been very close to her mother.

The David Young session continued on the topic of the pattern of the next-life. Marjorie however now looked to the distant horizons of man – to the far future as seen for the life of which she was now a part. It was dazzling as she expressed it; and in its concept. With the lengthy passage of time the human psyche develops gradually but in an incredible contrast: the present dependence upon a material world lessens and lessens; until the psyche soars on its own and enters upon an entirely new universe of existence – totally beyond the physical. Man – in a common individual experience – has to discover this in the working out of his evolution. But Marjorie – because of the short time available in the session – wanted to leave her statement there. This was in order to take up a subject of great immediate importance. Therefore the session held no opportunity to discover more from her about the far-future reshaping of life. With later opportunity however, and with a different medium, Marjorie stated that her present phase of existence is one which normally runs on for thousands of years before the further transition comes about. This phase could last for ten thousand years – more, or less, and resting with the individual. In the pure-psyche life it was always possible at will to create a body to participate temporarily in her present material world.

But, continuing further the David Young meeting, Marjorie turned with one of her lively sallies to what she now particularly had to say. It was a prelude to initiate thought processes in my mind that would build up some understanding in principle of the mechanisms present in mediumship. "Tell him," she impressed upon David Young, "that *I* want to give *him* something to think about." As David Young relayed her words, I understood exactly the force of her emphasis.

Marjorie had known my fascination for problems – for searching them out and then trying to resolve them: gnawing at them, like a dog with a bone, was how she described it. In this atmosphere, it was difficult for her to escape the challenge of these problems herself – she was now alluding to the way that I had made her think; and was taking, obviously, her delight in a balancing of the score.

I had the feeling that what she was going to put to me would not only be especially interesting but would also provide me with some homework.

Without pausing she was asking me to describe and explain to her a laser: "what it was like – and how it operated". The request fired my imagination and curiosity – in Marjorie's lifetime I had never to my recollection discussed with her any of the technicalities of lasers.

I began an answer. To be specific I said I would think of a solid-state laser; and it could be a ruby-crystal laser. You had to think of a wave, I explained, which was of the nature of a wave of light travelling back and forth through the structure of the crystal. The wave was forced to do this because of the presence of reflecting mirrorlike surfaces at the ends of the crystal. The wave ran to one end of the crystal, but there it was directed back by the mirror, and so caused to travel in turn to the other end of the crystal – only to be directed back again in the same way.

But this traversing of the crystal by the wave did not, of itself, give you a functioning laser. The energies of the atoms forming the crystal structure needed in the first place to be raised above normal – at least this must be true of some of the atoms; and the wave must be of a nature sympathetic to this elevation of their energy. As I was making these statements, David Young (with I am quite certain no scientific knowledge of this kind) was nodding his head and giving verbal agreement in an encouraging way. I continued that if there was such sympathy between the wave and the elevated energy state of the crystal structure, then the atoms of the crystal could hand over to the wave, as it swept through them, the energy they were holding above the normal. With this transfer of energy, operating everywhere along the path of the wave in the crystal, the energy of the wave becomes steadily increased. You could say that as the wave impinged upon each excess-energy atom it stimulated the atom into radiating a wavelet that merged into the main wave, so augmenting the intensity of the wave. This form of statement elucidates the acronym LASER – in significance of *light amplification by stimulated emission of radiation*. As my explanation reached this point I was gaining an impression that I had not said enough. Marjorie moreover threw in a question: "Would I not say that in some sense a thought was energy?" Perhaps, she suggested, we could talk about it again.

Time had run out; and as I was looking back on this laser conundrum – wondering just what I ought to make of it – I also reflected that the whole session had seemed to last but a couple of minutes. Surely – I questioned at the back of my mind – David Young could spare more time. David Young answered my unexpressed thought. "I know it has seemed only like two minutes," he stated, "yet in fact it is forty. It is all I can give. I am leaving for Canada in a few minutes." Marjorie, he told me, was saying she looked forward to meeting me again at Aylesbury a week hence. Her love was with me – in the meantime she wanted *me* to do some thinking. As he laid the stress of her emphasis, I felt I saw both her smile and the sparkle in her eye!

I did my thinking. It was plain Marjorie was asking me to equate the operative laser crystal with the mind-brain combination of the medium receiving a thought. The wave traversing the crystal represented the thought. Was this going to work out though? Something was not right. In the laser, and as I had described it, the crystal was giving energy to the wave; but with the case of the medium things were the other way round. There, it was the thought that imparted something – rather than gained something.

I recalled my impression when explaining the laser: that my description was incomplete. Had the session not closed I could have gone further. The process could be reversed. The wave can give up energy to specific atoms of the crystal – if the crystal structure is of the sympathetic nature enabling it to interact like this. It stood out clearly that here was the mode of operation which Marjorie was wanting me to contemplate.

Just as the impinging wave in this mode selectively transfers energy to excite certain atoms of the crystal, so a thought impinging upon a medium selectively interacts with, for example, linguistic elements present in the medium's mind-brain structure to excite these elements. The impinging thought – in this linguistic instance – must selectively excite, and so bring into action, the components of a sentence. But the elements excited could be those of a visual image – which elements, taken together, are again counterpart to the thought.

The elements which are stimulated, and this way made active, could result no more than in the medium becoming aware of the sentence, or the image – like with my telepathic impressions received from Marjorie; but the basic process could also be variously expressed. The medium might relate what had become known to him – in the fashion for instance of David Young. Beyond that, as automatic writing, the medium could be directly controlled in a particular function by the received thought. The possibilities for the expression of the thought once it had interacted through selective excitement of the counterpart elements in the medium, I could see were several. Much later – on the lines of Appendix V – I perceived the logic and significance of Marjorie's connection of thought with energy.

It was my intention to put Marjorie's laser analogy and its interpretation to Lang, when I met him again at Aylesbury on the 8th September. This meeting was unfortunately curtailed by circumstances, and I was forced to wait until the meeting of the 19th January before I could take up the subject. Then, I explained to him what it seemed Marjorie wished me to understand about mediumship: that a thought, as a special form of energy, is able automatically and selectively to excite mental data of a basic kind held available in store in the mental apparatus of the medium (basic data of a kind that is built up in store with every one of us) to cause the formation of a received counterpart to the thought. With this formation it is possible for the content of the thought to become present to the consciousness of the medium. In the end result the avenues for the influence of the thought must be many; but, so I said, the essence of the matter seemed to lie in the selective excitation. Lang affirmed that my statement was what Marjorie meant me to understand. And he said he liked her analogy: it was a good one.

I remarked that the utilizing of a medium on such lines seemed to be a rather different form of control compared with his own control of George Chapman. Lang's reply went back to his first long talk with me (Chapter 4) – he restated that if the use of the medium's senses is sought then displacement of the psychical body of the medium is essential. With this displacement in his use of George Chapman, his own (psychical) body replaces George's psychical body. George's mind then ceases to be involved with his surroundings. Lang emphasized this point. His medium's mind is no longer present. This contrasts with the form of mediumship that Marjorie was concerned with, where the presence of the mind of the medium is vital.

It took him, Lang added interestingly, four years to learn how to achieve his present use of George's physical body. He did not then amplify this statement, but I was to discover that, in taking over George Chapman's physical body, Lang's utilization of the physical mechanisms which in this way become available to him ranges far beyond the simple employment of George's senses. Lang's power to heal his patients is greatly enhanced when he can call upon the physical energies of his medium.

The meetings which provided the subject matter of this chapter extended over other topics. These centred upon a more complete understanding of human life; and it is convenient to leave them to Chapter 12.

Chapter Eleven

MARJORIE *VIA* MRS. YOUNG

Dr. Lang's idea to turn to David Young held promise – which was soon to waver.

There was in truth a mass of things which Marjorie wished to tell me. Her start with David Young had shown excellent potential. Lang, I believe, was conscious that with the even more extended schedules he wanted to operate through George Chapman he must relieve George wherever possible. The physical toll – in this special form of mediumship – was severe. But if my sessions with Lang were to have halted at this point – which happily they did not – every indication existed of Marjorie's capacity through David Young to continue with the widening of my intellectual field of view. Then however the visit to Canada – planned to be comparatively short – which David Young spoke of at the second meeting with him became greatly stretched. And there seemed no immediate prospect of his return to this country.

That fact was evident early in 1977, and I intended to raise it with Lang at a meeting fixed for late April. I thought it a distinct pity that this obviously fruitful line of advance should come to an end, and when it had just been set in motion; but Lang might have his own ideas on trying some other medium. The April meeting did not come about – for purely incidental reasons – and the earliest date George Chapman could propose for deferred talks was in August

Since the time was slipping by unproductively – from the standpoint of an improved venue of communication with Marjorie – and since I felt sufficiently confident, knowing something now about mediumship, I decided to push forward on my own initiative. If any new mediumship was at all of the quality of David Young's, it must yield positive results – and there was very definite ground for wanting it. My own sensitivity was laboriously slow in operation; and even if it were to improve – in particular with scientific questions, which with time it did and fulfilling an important function – there was always the great desirability of checking by an independent channel. Dr. Lang was willing and most helpful on this account; but I could see the practice easily choking up the meetings with him – they should be free as far as possible for things that were more strategic. All such thoughts were in my mind – not least the very true generosity of George Chapman in offering his time and energies as he did. They all influenced me when I made an approach to Mrs. Millicent Young.

No relation of David Young she also, conveniently for me, lived in Reading. What I knew about her was that she had some sensitivities, and that Marjorie – putting the idea of Mrs. Young's mediumship to her – encouraged my hopes that it could take us forward. The prospects in fact were borne out.

I was in touch with Mrs. Young by letter in the first place. I mentioned the kind of session that David Young had been able to give, and I told her of the special aim I had – the writing of this book. She replied quickly, but somewhat uncertainly. She was, she wrote, by no means sure that she could match David Young; and she had little time available. Since she stated that she was willing to try, I felt it was worth speaking with her on the telephone. The conversation enheartened me in two respects. While she was not assured of *seeing* Marjorie, like David Young, she was certain that she would be able to *hear* her. Then, although I had told her nothing of the nature of Marjorie's death, and it was altogether improbable she would have known anything of it in the ordinary way, she volunteered: "She died in a car crash, didn't she! – she hit something very hard." I felt Millicent Young had sensitivities which could prove helpful; and I asked for a meeting. She said she could give me an hour on the afternoon of 15th July, 1977.

There were six weeks to wait; and, on occasions, I talked over with Marjorie in the evening periods the possibilities of this new meeting. I suggested that it might make a good use of Millicent Young's clairaudient ability if she, Marjorie, dictated an account of say one day of her present existence – a typical day. I could take it down as she gave it – it would be greatly informative. Marjorie made it clear that this was not feasible – it would be too much to expect. She wanted the meeting as much as I did – and its success; but, so I understood her, we would have to take it as it came. Marjorie insisted I must understand that the capabilities of differing mediums can be widely diverse. The session itself strongly underlined this; and while the thought of it induced doubts in my mind they were dispelled when I woke up on the day. Marjorie was optimistic; and I gained, too, the impression that she wished me to take the ring I had given her – it would act as an aid for Mrs. Young.

As I drove to Reading, I was aware that Marjorie was accompanying me. Meeting Mrs. Young, she looked to be an energetic woman in her early sixties. Before the session itself we spent about twenty minutes in general talk. This was mainly because she wanted to outline her training as a medium. She knew of David Young from the early training classes that they had both attended. There, she emphasized, it had been evident how widely sensitivities varied from person to person. She was certainly clairaudient herself. The onset of this receptivity was always preceded by a click in her left ear; then she would experience tingling sensations in her neck and shoulder on that side. The voice that she heard at these times was audible in the same way that voices ordinarily are heard. Her more normal activities, however, were in gaining impressions when objects were handed to her. She also had it seemed some kind of diagnostic ability with the physical disorders from which a person might be suffering. While it was not at once clear how she customarily practised this activity, she shortly gave – in the session itself – a remarkable indication of it.

She made one or two polite enquiries about the book – as to how many chapters I had written for instance; but I was not particularly informative, and I suggested that the value of her mediumship would be the greater if matters were kept that way. She was quite happy with this remark; and then she partially drew the curtains to reduce the light level in the room.

I handed her Marjorie's ring, and she sat down on an upright chair placing the ring on her finger. She seemed to find pleasure in the ring, and she said she was glad I had thought of bringing it. Then she added that she had been brought up in the Church of England, and that she would like to offer a short prayer for the success of the meeting – which she wished for as much as I.

She sat still, inclined slightly forward on her chair after the prayer and with eyes closed. In a few seconds she was speaking with a quiet voice. "She is a lovely person," she began. "There was not much hope, was there! It was such a bash. Her hair is not particularly light, is it! She has a good, and upright, figure – and she was younger than you. She is speaking to me and telling me: 'We were most deeply attached – more than average. We were together so much in thought – I could almost read his thoughts'"

Millicent Young opened her eyes, and turned to me. She now looked huddled and in pain as she exclaimed: "I can only put it this way – I am going through hell on earth. I hurt everywhere. My face feels bruised, badly bruised – to the point that a woman holds fear for her looks. My right shoulder seems crushed. Everywhere I am crushed – dreadfully crushed. I cannot feel my legs. They seem to have serious injuries; and my pelvis is badly damaged, all of that region is damaged." In this poignant statement, I recognised as she was making it a close description of Marjorie's injuries – of which I knew from the hospital report. The pain seemed to have passed when Millicent Young spoke again. She ventured that had Marjorie lived she would have been seriously crippled. This remark tallied exactly with the medical opinion. Then Millicent Young said that she thought Marjorie survived only a few hours. I confirmed it and gave the information that Marjorie died in Battle Hospital on the morning of the accident. At the mention of Battle Hospital Millicent Young expressed strong interest, stating that her son had joined the staff of the hospital in 1973.

The variety in the character of events during the session to this point will be very clear: the clairvoyant start mixed with simple impressions; then with rapid switch the clairaudience; a diagnostic phase; and at the end further simple impressions. It was true of the whole of the meeting. First one of Millicent Young's special sensitivities would be to the fore, and then another. No one sensitivity was ever maintained for very long; and I understood Marjorie's lack of enthusiasm when – obviously calling for a long-sustained spell of clairaudience by her medium – I proposed she should relate the various detailed events that went to make a typical day for her. Knowing the characteristics however of Mrs. Young's mediumship, Marjorie had decided she would be able – in the fashion of playing it by ear – to harness and bring them all together in a useful whole. This was the basis of the confidence I found in her on waking that morning.

Marjorie was speaking again. "She is saying," announced Millicent Young, "that the tall lady doctor tried hard to save her life." With this statement several thoughts leapt to mind. Marjorie was referring to some of the few things she was able to remember of the time of the accident. I knew from one of the staff when the ambulance brought her into Battle Hospital that Marjorie was conscious at this point. It was "the tall lady doctor" who came eventually to tell me of the failure of her efforts. She was certainly taller than Marjorie and more slightly built – she would have appeared to Marjorie just as Marjorie had now described her. Millicent Young's next announcement underlined what Marjorie had just been saying on the fight to save her life: "She adds that she is well aware of the skill of the doctor."

I connected this remark, when I returned to think about it, with information Lang conveyed at my meeting with him on the 19th January, 1977. It was that Marjorie had given up her rescue work (her attendance on accident victims of this present existence) and was devoting her full energies to medical studies and her training as a doctor. Lang said that the execution of her work gave him much pleasure – he looked on her as brilliant. Bearing in mind this information, Marjorie's assessment of the doctor's skill was, I felt sure, not to be treated lightly: it was made from knowledge. She was well qualified to go into the medical facts; and, as I came to learn, this was just what she had done – she had gone over the details with the next-world hospital staff sent at the time to attend her.

In this reflection I remembered the misgivings I had experienced after Marjorie's death: that the hospitals in general were not so well organized as they might be to deal with such emergencies. They were thoughts I am certain Marjorie – in her awareness of my mind – had not failed to notice. What Marjorie was telling me, and with authority, at this point of the meeting was I need have had no such fears. Here I note that Millicent Young repeated the assurance: "She wants you to know that she is very aware of the skill of the doctor."

Millicent Young continued: "She says, also, that as her mind goes back to events just following that time they come to her in an almost unreal way – it is as though she was watching an old film." The suggestion of unreality in these happenings appealed to me as most true. That was exactly how events had forced themselves upon me. For months after Marjorie's death they possessed an artificial atmosphere – such as it was life happened, and I was watching it do so, but I did not feel I was really present in it. Marjorie's analogy of the old film far from escaped me – viewing old film I have so often experienced that same uneasy impression of illusion and the artificial.

Marjorie changed to a new subject. "She has special memories of a tall, fine-built man coming towards her – and looking after her," said Millicent Young. I had told Mrs. Young in my letter that, although my own sensitivities were not great, I had gained some impressions myself; and I broke in here to say that what she was relating formed part of an early impression of my own. The "tall, fine-built man" was Marjorie's father. Millicent Young did not respond, except to incline her head. She went on: "Her father had predeceased her much earlier. The trouble was mainly his lungs." I interrupted again to remark that this was tuberculosis; and she commented: "Yes – but there was other trouble; though the lungs were the main trouble."

She stated that his name was William – and I remarked that she was not correct. Her reply was that she always had difficulty in getting names right. I did not offer my help; but without any doubt Marjorie noted the error. Later on, Mrs. Young looked at me and said quite out of context: "Marjorie is asking you to state who Wilfred is." I answered: "Oh, that is Marjorie's father" – and I took it Marjorie had been thinking that another attempt in altogether different circumstances might well yield success.

With my answer, Millicent Young enquired if Marjorie's father had been athletic – presumably because that impression was forming in her mind. I told her

I understood it was a strong characteristic of his: he was enthusiastic over rowing and tennis – and very interested in sport in general.

Taking the development of the meeting in its actual sequence however, Marjorie was plainly intent to cover more of the ground of her early new life experience. Mrs. Young told me it was shortly decided that Marjorie should enter a convalescent home: "to build her up". Immediately there were signs of astonishment from Millicent Young. She was gaining vivid impressions. "It was such an extensive place, this convalescent home, or hospital," she exclaimed; and: "made of bricks and mortar!" The fact seemed totally to surprise her (though I noted that it fitted with my own early impressions). There were medical people everywhere. The place was teeming with nurses. She herself seemed to be in one of the corridors; and the nurses were wearing uniforms, "such as we are familiar with."

Next she announced she was experiencing tingling sensations from head to foot; moreover Marjorie was saying that she had sensations like these when she received treatment in the hospital. It was a form of beam treatment that irradiated the whole of the patient.

Marjorie made the interesting comment that in the ward she had entered there was a girl opposite her who was having therapy for mental trouble. Hearing this, the impression formed in my mind that the scale of the hospital was huge, as Millicent Young had seen, because the treatment given aimed at the whole wide spectrum of patient maladjustment – of body *and* of mind.

When, a few weeks on, I was speaking with Dr. Lang at Aylesbury I questioned him about the irradiative treatment; and he confirmed its use in Marjorie's case. He told me the primary remedial basis of the hospital is relaxation therapy. The objective is a general integration of the patient – in regard to each patient's individual powers. The relaxation therapy is supplemented by special treatment where necessary; and this was true with Marjorie.

I interpose also, but in rather greater retrospect, some observations by Marjorie when I reverted again to the subject of such hospitals or convalescent homes. It was in conversation with her by way of another medium (functioning clairvoyantly). I wanted to know better the significance of these medical institutions. Predominantly they are concerned, Marjorie then told me, with difficulties induced by the transition from this to the next life. The experience of the transition can loom a very big matter in the minds of some individuals. Speaking generally, a big experience always tends to make individuals withdraw into themselves. This is why bad experiences can produce major psychological disturbances. The transition to the next life, though it may be free of trauma, can set up a withdrawal state in some. It does so especially in those who have never experienced the transition before – people whose life on earth just left behind them was their first life here. People suffering from serious withdrawal make up roughly sixty per cent of the patients in hospitals like that to which Marjorie introduced Mrs. Young so realistically. Because the total transition flux is great even a small proportion of these withdrawal cases brings about the need for numerous such hospitals. For the withdrawal patients the hospitals serve very much the role of a rest home. Conditions of simple relaxation, as Dr. Lang had said, are basic to the therapy.

"Time is advancing," Millicent Young was now saying, "and Marjorie is attending concerts." I saw Marjorie's classical taste present in the composers Mrs. Young mentioned: Mozart, Liszt and Chopin. The recitals had been a great delight to her, Mrs. Young added. Nevertheless, in spite of these pleasures, Marjorie's thoughts were again and again returning to the life she had left behind.

The last statement tied in with my own experiences. For instance on many occasions during those early days and when I was at home busy, say, in writing a letter I would become aware of the perfume of which Marjorie had been fond. At first when I observed these effects, I tried to trace them to a physical source – only to find immediately they had vanished. This was always so – hence my conclusion that it was purely a matter of thought; and very probably by intention on Marjorie's part.

For this reason alone it came as no surprising news to me to hear from Mrs. Young that in regard to events on earth Marjorie had engaged upon specific lessons to avail her, without actually making a visit to earth, of some perception of particular things which held a deep interest for her. Millicent Young repeated this – Marjorie perhaps thinking her news, because of its peculiar nature, might not have fully registered with a first telling. Mrs. Young added a statement that once again cast Marjorie in characteristic light, enthusiastic and thorough going: for these lessons she had been to one of the foremost instructors.

Marjorie recalled her first attempts to put his tuition into practice. "It was as though she was trying to penetrate grey mists." This statement seemed to be supplemented by an impression coming to me in which I was acutely aware of the kind of visual difficulty one experiences from the intervening mistiness of the atmosphere as one looks down, even on a fine day, from an aircraft flying at altitude.

At first sight Marjorie's instruction might appear dubious news. There is a body of opinion which thinks that *any* talk of the nature of such news must be 'unscientific' and contrary also to 'commonsense'. But Marjorie's projective perception is clearly related to the projective methods of acquiring knowledge studied by the Stanford Research Institute (Chapter 5); and it is an important consideration how one of the philosophic and psychological realizations of this present time is that in the most ordinary of contexts we have little idea of the way exactly we know what we know. There is no simple touchstone – such as popularly-conceived science. It is most powerfully evident that the understanding of our world presents our minds with a task where the greatest demand is placed upon human capacity for fundamental conception. Even the down-to-earth subject of physics bears, these days, the nuances of the esoteric. Oversimplicity of view in which the difficulties are disguised or pass unheeded is a trap for the unwary.

Marjorie went on to say that her thoughts were turning to the stage when she was no longer affected by the shock of the accident. This was not just a relief – her new found health was a satisfying and delightful fresh experience. "Now," exclaimed Millicent Young, "she is joking with me – she is saying that she doesn't possess any wings! She is saying, too, that there is no 'eternal rest'. That's a fallacy! You are still much as you were – but more beautiful! You are able to do more easily the things previously that you wanted to do – there aren't the 'thistles and nettles' to make it difficult."

Two of Marjorie's last remarks call for comment. The one flowing, in its analogy, from her deep love of a garden and of living things – just like her tree analogy in regard to matter and energy at the first David Young meeting – runs in very true vein. But saying that she was more beautiful lay entirely out of character. She did not naturally spend much effort in her lifetime on her looks, though she could look very good – which she knew gave me genuine pleasure. The days however were full and she felt the pressure of other claims upon her. Knowing this background I knew exactly and at once the force of this out-of-character remark. She was referring to an issue which had been on her conscience; and she knew that I would take the point. It was most unlikely she would have turned to it with David Young as medium – although unquestionably outgiving Marjorie was also reserved. Mrs. Young on the other hand was a woman – and the fact presented a greater freedom for expression. I doubt if Mrs. Young as she relayed Marjorie's remark had much idea of what she was actually conveying.

Marjorie expanded the subject she had touched on when explaining it was now much easier to do the things she wanted to do: "So much works by thought. By thought you can make a garden into a paradise. The aim is to develop yourself in mind – to endeavour to improve your mental powers all the time. In that way you build yourself up." This I gathered was an idea which even in her world did not operate easily. "There are many people," and Mrs. Young recited Marjorie's words incisively, "not succeeding particularly well, because their minds function so much after the fashion of their life on earth. They are preoccupied with that kind of life – and their cravings run the same way. You needed to understand that new opportunities are now presented to you; and that you should seize upon them." Unquestionably earnest, revealing and vital words. But Mrs. Young was reporting: "She saw that she must do this and she knows that she has been developing as a result – not that this," and Mrs. Young laid emphasis, "made any difference at all to 'our relationship'. That remained exactly the same." Mrs. Young stressed: "She particularly wants you to know that." Marjorie stopped and there was a pause.

With the pause, Millicent Young removed the ring I had handed to her, stating – correctly – that it had not belonged in my family but that I had bought it. She described the circumstances of its choice. Marjorie was with me, she said; and she could see us casting our eyes over a display. Then *simultaneously* we became attracted by the opal stone of the ring we decided on. I confirmed the accuracy of this account; and at that point Marjorie broke in with an exclamation of her very great pleasure in the ring.

As Millicent Young was looking at the ring again, and seeming to like it, Marjorie followed up with: "Next time, tell him to bring the brooch that is like it. It's in the small box he uses to keep my jewellery."

Millicent Young holding her relaying mode continued: "She says she loved the ring so much that she expressed her delight in it to a very good friend of hers – who found much pleasure in it too." This lady, Millicent Young stated was older than Marjorie; and she went on to give a description of the lady, both in appearance and character. I asked Millicent Young if she knew the lady's name, because, from the description of her, I had identified her as Marjorie's friend Phyllis; but Millicent Young (perhaps having difficulty in gathering the name from Marjorie) said that she did not – although she knew that the lady was living. This was true of course of Phyllis; and Phyllis, when I told her of the episode remembered how Marjorie had made a special point of showing her the ring.

Leaving the digression of the ring, Marjorie returned to the subject of her present life – to speak of her feelings about it; and of the attitude of mind to which she had come about her fatal accident. Millicent Young was obviously listening to her. "Marjorie says," she began, "that 'our sense of sorrow' is easing now. She is deeply grateful that she is not a cripple – as she would have been had she lived. She now has a sense of completeness which is a deep pleasure. She has accepted what has happened; and she is taking life in her stride." Millicent Young stopped for a moment; and then remarked: "Marjorie is giving me a visual impression of the kind of supporting frame, she would have needed to use to get about as a cripple, if she had survived."

In these further statements Marjorie was expressing little of what I was not already aware. Concerning the accident it was all a matter long mutual between us – for which reason she could speak as easily and freely as she did. I knew too that she was most certainly taking life in her stride – and it would have been news uncharacteristic of her had it been other. These confirmations were simply part of the operation of the general principle of checking through a diverse channel.

I was, though, interested that Marjorie spoke of her "completeness" in describing her present sense of well-being. It was a term Lang had used once or twice when referring to the goal of personality. By a state of completeness he ordinarily meant not the goal itself but any well-developed state *en route* to this goal: a state in which one's potentialities are highly developed and well integrated. Emphasizing that it was not a final state, it was rather a basis for even further development – and the realization of new ability. This goes back to Lang's early enunciation of the continual development of the psyche. Speaking with him, it is clear he does not look upon existence as having any necessary limits. Illogical as this might seem from the standpoint of the still influential science-based thinking of the 19th century, developments in logic of the present century, considered in Appendix I, see existence as necessarily hierarchical without limit. I know that when speaking of her developing mental powers and her completeness Marjorie had in prospect just such never-ending horizons.

Mrs. Young's visual impression of the supporting frame seemed to take her on a new digression – one concerning the accident. I found this phase of the meeting fascinating because of a puzzle it appeared to present.

Mrs. Young's first comment amplified her remark on the telephone. "She hit a tree," was what she now stated. Over the telephone she had informed me only that "she hit something very hard." The more precise statement was entirely correct, and I said so. Next, she turned to me with the pronouncement – almost the exclamation: "There was nothing wrong with the car." I told her that that also was correct. The confidence of her statement particularly attracted my attention. But Mrs. Young had more to tell me – and the more surprisingly the more I thought about it: "There was another car involved. I can see it clearly coming down the road in the opposite direction. There is a man driving it. He is the only person in the car. I can see him better now – he is clean shaven, and has short hair: not long and down on his shoulders like some men wear their hair these days. Marjorie took avoiding action." I note that the details of this further statement were all known to me, having learned them at the inquest.

Mrs. Young had even more to say; and one reason I was so interested in her reconstruction was that I had the impression, listening to her, of a change in the overall situation: Marjorie was not now the motivating source of events. She also was passively listening just as I was. This impression became confirmed at my next meeting with Dr. Lang and Marjorie at Aylesbury. How then did Mrs. Young gain her knowledge of the details? Marjorie, on account of the amnesia induced by the accident, had no recollection of them. Furthermore, and importantly I felt, although I knew them I had not been thinking of any detail prior to Mrs. Young actually announcing it.

There is an extreme viewpoint not to be passed over which – because of the basic assumptions it makes – finds it inconceivable for Mrs. Young ever to have such knowledge except by ordinary enquiry; such as looking up beforehand what had been published on the accident. (The assumptions are of a kind to which in due course Marjorie applied certain practical tests vitally sapping their validity. I describe the tests in Chapters 14 and 16, *Physics*). But concerning publication I was in fact well aware of the reporting in the local press at the time – what I saw fell far short in detail. To cover every aspect I did actually put it to Mrs. Young that some people most certainly would say that – with fraudulent intent – she had been making private-eye investigations of her own before we had the session. She simply told me I must believe her when she said she knew nothing of Marjorie except for the slight information I had given her and what – which was very much more – she had learned through her sensitivities. How they operated she had no idea.

The considerations of the last paragraph I include for completeness; but I felt there was very much more point in asking Mrs. Young just why she had sounded so confident when she stated there was nothing wrong with the car. She answered that she was a driver herself – she had at that point the feeling she was sitting in the driving seat and going through the motions of driving the car. Everything was working as it should.

This and the whole question of Mrs. Young's knowledge in detail of the events of the time of the accident – in addition to Marjorie's purely listening role – I took up specifically with Dr. Lang. His first comment was that Mrs. Young had been tapping into next-world knowledge of what happened.

It was not entirely clear what Lang was here expressing to me. I wondered how it related, if it did, to the "records" which Hughie had spoken of (Chapter 7) when Lang just before touched on my past lives and Marjorie's. These "records" had been *looked up* according to Hughie. I said I was not even at all sure what I was to understand by such a statement. As to the "records", Dr. Lang told me he did not want there to be false ideas of massive computer-type data banks holding great tracts of information on past events. It was nothing like that – but it was far from easy to convey intelligible conceptions on the subject. Highly developed minds could if they wished achieve direct access to past events: that was the truth – but he did not feel he could usefully go into how the access operated. (I discovered in due course that Lang employs his own powers of direct access to past events when treating some of his patients. When there is a psychological element to illness, patient history may be an important factor. Later still I talked with Marjorie on the subject. She agreed it is one of great difficulty for understanding; but she felt that modern physics is able to cast some light where it has shown that physical energy can act in a non-local way to bridge between widely separated particles – given special circumstances – as though there was no intervening space. With the present subject one could think yet again in non-local terms – in relation to the energy of mind bridging across a time interval).

But on the point I had raised specifically concerning Mrs. Young, Lang was explicit she had not been using direct access – nor was she able to. There are always next-world persons, he said, taking account of events of this world. It was possible for Mrs. Young to share in their remembering of these events. That was what she had been doing with her digression on the accident. Marjorie was not the only next-world person present at our meeting. She had brought along another such person – now a close friend – who had been well aware of the events of the accident, as a witness. This lady keenly remembered these things as the accident came up in the conversation – and they were transferred to Mrs. Young's highly impressionable mind.

Lang pointed out that in principle, and if Millicent Young's mind had not latched onto the source that it did, then supposing I had concentrated on one fact and another that I had learned of the accident she might well have picked up like impressions from my own mind. That of course would have served very little purpose; and it was important when putting questions with a medium who works simply by received impressions to ask – as a matter of rule – only those questions where you yourself really know nothing of the answers. Obviously the weight to be attached to an answer must be the weight to be attributed to the source when it has been traced.

I broke the rule Lang had given, as it turned out, in the very next part of the Mrs. Young session. What prompted me was the striking phenomenon, in the accident digression, of Mrs. Young showing, by all appearance, the ability to bridge across time. Not realizing then the true nature of this apparent ability, I had wondered what similar ability she might show in bridging across space. Taking a drastic step – as I thought it might be – in this direction, I referred to Marjorie's present home, her cottage; and I asked Mrs. Young what account she might be able to give in particular of its surroundings.

She proved able to relate much of what I have described in Chapter 8; and beyond this to give fresh details. She referred to a stream – of which I was aware – at the foot of the steep slope in front of the cottage. The stream, I knew, ran through a valley to the left as one looks down into it from in front of the cottage. At the end of its course and far to the left the stream swept finally into a large lake. Mrs. Young commented that, as the stream found its way down to the lake, it reminded her of Welsh scenery – there were waterfalls and large boulders. These waterfalls were a thing I did not know of.

To take matters further, I asked Mrs. Young to give her attention to the landscape more directly in front of the cottage. Slightly to the right I knew there was a curving viaduct running across to the hillside opposite. It was constructed of many sandstone pillars topped by arches and a roadway. On the roadway I had seen Marjorie driving off with Pickles in a jeep-like vehicle to go for a walk by the large lake. Dr. Lang had confirmed the jeep.

I told nothing to Mrs. Young, only asking her if she could see a bridge spanning the valley just to the fore of the cottage. She objected at once that she did not think *bridge* was a good word. There was, she said, a road across to the hillside opposite; and it was true that there was access under the road, if you were in the valley; but she would not call the structure carrying the road a bridge. While she did not venture that it was a viaduct, it was clear that she must have been gaining an accurate impression.

In principle – and as I was already realizing with my questioning of Mrs. Young – this particular impression could have derived from my own mind. But Millicent Young had seen the waterfalls of which I was unaware; so it was likely that none of her total impression could derive from me. Marjorie, when I came back to the matter *via* another medium, told me she knew she was picturing the scene around the cottage with much pleasure when I started my line of questioning. Mrs. Young would undoubtedly have gathered her knowledge from this picturing. Marjorie was positive that Mrs. Young would not have been able to achieve her knowledge by any direct access across space – though she would fully have expected it with David Young. His description of the bridge over the railway in Streatham at the outset of our first meeting with him was by the direct access I had suspected.

Millicent Young's tendency to change from one mode of sensitivity to another, I also learned in due course from Marjorie, arose from tiring. To change from first one to then another mode allowed recuperation and a regaining of sensitivity of the mode temporarily taken out of use. With the lengthy period just spent on impressions, Marjorie probably felt her medium had rested the clairaudient mode sufficiently long.

Staying with the subject of her home, she now stated that she frequently entertained there – this was one of the ways in which life remained the same. But, with some emphasis, she said she wanted – in contrast with her former life – to give much more time on her own for reflecting, and thinking and learning. She attached much greater importance to having time to herself.

Then she continued by asking Millicent Young to tell me that the summer-house – of which she knew I was aware and which was situated on the hillside opposite the cottage – was a favourite retreat of hers. From there she had a good view of the large lake; and she usually went to this retreat when she wanted to be closest to me. *It was there the idea that I should write the book came to her.*

Since we were still talking about Marjorie's home surroundings I turned to certain rose beds which I had seen, in my visual impressions from her, she had laid out behind the cottage – where the lawns ran up to it. I remarked how some very strange roses appeared to be growing in these beds. My impression was that they were blue with orange-gold leaves. Marjorie neither confirmed nor denied such unusual roses – she simply declared that in her world I must expect to find all sorts of exotic plants which we do not have on earth. It will be evident in Chapter 14 that my chance remark about these roses gave Marjorie the opportunity to put to practical test purely psychological conceptions of psychical events (Chapter 1).

I thought also of the pets that Marjorie appeared to possess at the cottage. This seemed to be the opportunity to verify that they included my black half-Persian cat Chi – on whose accidental death I had commented to Lang. I had never obtained any independent check on Chi; so I made the enquiry. The answer came at once and characteristically: "Yes, bless you – and I have many pets!" Some, Marjorie added, were budgerigars. The last news did not surprise me. I had gathered many impressions of an aviary by the cottage. Then there was more confirmatory news: "Marjorie is saying that the little white dog which was run over – and had a quick ending – follows her dutifully on long walks, and is very fond of her." This of course was Pickles. When I told my sister, she remarked it was so true of him – unlike her other dogs he was always ready to follow at heel. Millicent Young went on to say that Marjorie was informing her she also has a white Persian cat. Of this pet I had no prior knowledge.

Marjorie had a total surprise for me. I heard first that Millicent Young was receiving a visual impression of another pet – of a dog with a golden coat; and then that she knew the breed but she couldn't remember the name for it. I must think of a dog with long floppy ears – like those of a red setter; only the dog was much smaller than a red setter. In my mind I had now a strong and clear impression of a golden cocker spaniel – one that I possessed in the years before, and running into, the period of the Second World War. I stated to Millicent Young: "The dog is a golden cocker." She smiled – that, she said, was exactly the name she was trying to find for it. Then – and entirely true of this particular dog – she told me that it was a very gentle dog and that it had suffered a lot of trouble with its ears. It did not meet with an accident nor die of old age – but it had to be put down I remembered how with the war, and as food rationing made it increasingly difficult to feed him properly, he had developed acutely troublesome ear canker – for which very little could be done. He had to be put down.

When after the meeting I had the time to review its details I noted that this communication from Marjorie conveyed something further upon the subject of animal postexistence. Both my father and my mother had been most fond of the dog. If they had predeceased him, then, on what I had learned, he would have found his way directly to them – yet my father did not die for another ten years; nor my mother until much later still. It seemed likely that with my father's death he had found my father; or my father possibly succeeded in locating him.

Marjorie had organized another surprise. It was very different; and it showed she had not forgotten that, with the second of our David Young meetings, she had promised to look into the question of members of my family. We were now almost at the end of the hour promised for the session; and Millicent Young was silent for a moment. Then she stated that she had an impression of a little old lady. She smiled as she announced that the little old lady was most Victorian – almost like Queen Victoria herself! As Mrs. Young repeated this last statement, the image of the little old lady was forming in my own mind. She was all in black except for a pattern of white flowers arranged round her hat; and I saw that she was regarding me with a kindly smile on her very round face. It was my other grandmother – not my mother's mother, of whom I came to think Marjorie had spoken at the David Young meeting, but the grandmother I knew as a child on my father's side: by his father's second marriage. She had always been fond of my sister and myself.

Millicent Young now remarked that the old lady was smiling. Then the impression seemed too much for Mrs. Young's restraint. She exclaimed that the old lady really had no height, no height at all . . . and it was true . . . she simply had no waist! I agreed with Millicent Young that it was all true. It was exactly my grandmother. Continuing Millicent Young stated, quite correctly, that my grandmother was in her eighties when she died. "She lives now in a large house in the country." "That," said my sister, when I came to tell her, "sounds quite

106

likely – after all she was the daughter of a mayor of Bournemouth."

Millicent Young had exceeded the stated hour – she must bring the session, she said, to a close. I thanked her, and I assured her it had been an absorbingly interesting experience.

Coming at the time to look back on the meeting there seemed much in it to be followed up and understood better: this very clearly so. At large also – with the whole study I was embarked upon – the same looked true. In the context of such thoughts and despite them it stood out equally that, having come as far as I had, I was at grips with reality in this sphere beyond the usually experienced and the normally accepted. With the meeting it could perhaps be said I had served my apprenticeship.

PART II

Chapter Twelve

MORE ON HUMAN LIFE – AND A RECOLLECTION

A proper study of a subject demands some fair acquaintance with its raw data. In this present research there was at the very beginning my mental transfer experience with Marjorie in her lifetime – to be followed by the extension of this experience with her death. Then, also, I had become deeply involved at first hand with mediumship of widely differing forms; and I had besides special psychical experiences at a personal level. There was Marjorie's physical appearance to me in which I had been the medium – and there was my projective experience. Given the raw data of a subject – and given raw data like this – it is always important to come by a basis of understanding. In its absence explorative efforts are like trying to navigate without a chart.

It was not difficult to see that any light of understanding must be unavailable from science – if by science was meant classical physics. Whether modern physics might hold out some clear view of the inner workings of my experiences I really did not know – though this was something on which in due course Marjorie would be busy in explanation. What I did know was that Dr. Lang had presented me with certain broad ideas of a fundamental nature; and that these – most usefully – had aided me in my successful projection endeavours. But I understood these ideas in only a very general way; and I was at a stage where I wanted to make progress, if I could, by discovering how they worked out in much closer detail.

There were respects in which Lang's basic conceptions were not fully clear – and one at least that was puzzling. I shall come to it shortly. It concerns the electrical body.

Concentrating on what I understood however it was plain why Lang had furnished me with a general understanding of human existence – and had lost no time in coming to it. From what he had to say I could perceive the nature of a human being as sufficient *of itself* to enable life to continue naturally, despite physical death. I saw, too, as I looked back that in this nature I had a working basis by which I could piece together (in projection for instance) facts I had encountered; and I noticed that the element of mystery pervading the whole study was already receding. This alone was good encouragement for review and critical recapitulation.

The issue possibly standing out the most strongly – if implicitly – in Lang's approach was his entire rejection of the view in which a human being is accounted for solely by his physical characteristics. I give stress to the point because it is basic with any subject that no real progress in understanding can ever be made without right and *adequate* conceptions at the start.

This principle, in fact, is the moral of the great difference between the physical science of the 19th century and that of the 20th. With the end of the 19th century, scientific circles were shaken by the now historic contradictions then being encountered. The contradictions besides internal were contradictions between physical theory on the one hand and the facts concerning matter and radiation on the other. As the 20th century came into being, new assumptions about physical reality – those of quantum mechanics – were adopted that removed the impasse; and they led on to vast developments. It is also a matter of history that these new assumptions, glimpsed at in the closing of the 19th century, were strongly (even polemically) resisted as first they made their impact. To most of the great scientific minds of that era the presuppositions of the time appealed very much more than the postulates to be substituted in the interests of progress. Presupposition in regard to the nature of human life falls as an exact parallel.

Today, the hypothesis that here largely appeals is the one that (eventually at least) a human being will be fully understood through the study of his physical make-up. In this – the Lang approach inevitably asserts – is a hope as destined to failure as the classical hopes of the 19th century physicists. If real advances are to be made then there must be a change of view as momentous as the changes terminating 19th century science. From his present position, with its expansion of knowledge, this was what Lang was saying; and from all I had been experiencing I felt that it must be accepted.

Lang's starting principles are easily set down. Firstly the apparatus of consciousness is not purely physical in nature. It belongs, finally, to the radically differing dimension of mind and the psychical. Then when we speak of the individual we are to see the consciousness of the individual in the individual psyche (Chapter 4). The physical body acts essentially as a sense channel and vehicle for the psyche – so that the psyche can participate in the events of the physical world (Chapter 3).

Against these initial ideas Lang had introduced two further factors – for the reason, of no little interest, that of themselves the psyche and the physical body are incapable of any full account of the facts of experience. Distinct from the speculations of the ancient Greeks the psyche alone, on the death of the physical body, is unable to provide the kind of continuity of conscious existence that the individual actually experiences. This continuity is achieved by the presence, immediately to hand, of what might be called a duplicate body (Chapter 4): one, as I went on to learn, formed of the matter of the world that the individual enters on death. Besides this psychical body, it was necessary to contemplate the presence also of the special intermediating nervous system that constitutes the electrical body (Chapter 4). This special system could be said to provide an answer (in part at least) to the long standing philosophical problem of how mind can influence matter and reciprocally be influenced by it. It has value, Lang asserted, only for life as we know it here – in the continued existence, and with the strong sensitivity to mind of the matter of the next world, the psyche is able to use the psychical body without any such intermediary. The intermediary is therefore abandoned and disbanded on physical death.

With reflective analysis this conception of the electrical body – always far from

112

clear – seemed to attract special problems. I had presumably to imagine a concourse of electrically charged particles. Whatever their density, if the electrical charge should happen to be of the same kind throughout then the particles must be subject to mutual repulsion – under which the system must tend to disperse, if not explode. It was still puzzling if the charges should be some positive and some negative.

When to gain more definite ideas I came back to him on the subject, Lang affirmed that the electrical charges carried by the particles were both negative and positive. The particles were thus subject to attractions as well as repulsions; and these forces were in mutual balance. On the other hand in my mind this was not an end to the difficulties; and I enquired if the particles were those known to physicists as electrons and positions. Lang assured me this was so. I felt then that the difficulties entailed in the nature of the system were compounded rather than eased.

Since it seemed that a resolution of the theoretical problems now apparent must be more time consuming than the talks I was able to have with Lang could easily allow, I set the matter on one side for further reflection. The outstanding trouble was that the electron and the positron are not renowned for their qualities as stablemates. If they come into close mutual proximity they are apt to annihilate one another. One moment they are an electron and a positron – one ten millionth of a second later they may have interacted leaving behind nothing except a light-like flash of energy. On the face of it the lifelong permanence of the electrical body was not possible: how did this body come to be so stable?

Of course in the history of science a mystery of this kind is no stranger. There was, for instance, the penetrating research of Lord Rutherford early in the century which revealed the electrical structure of the atom – and at the same time revealed it in a form that apparently ensured its rapid self-destruction: in a millionth of a second or less – judging by the well established and much respected laws of electromagnetism. Such mysteries have a way of becoming resolved with the lapse of time. This in fact applied to my present problem.

On further talks with him, Lang pointed to a crucial consideration; and with Marjorie's help later in detail I arrived eventually at some clear insight into the physical processes of the electrical body. They are set out in Appendix III. Lang's primary clue was that the sea of electrons and positrons that forms the electrical body does not exist on its own. If it did, then its lifetime *would* be negligible. The vitally important fact was the close relationship it sustains with the psyche presence. Appendix III sets down how a relationship of sufficient closeness can make all the difference between instability and self-annihilation on the one hand and permanence on the other. The permanence is a state conditional on the psyche. The state is the result of an inhibited instability; and it is for this reason that the electrical body automatically disintegrates with death. When, finally, the psyche no longer requires the electrical body, the psyche gradually withdraws its previous inhibiting control and the instability correspondingly takes effect.

This study in depth of the electrical body is of major significance for more than one reason. It shows how Lang's various assertions concerning this body are to be seen consistent when subjected to analysis in the terms of modern physics. Had they been flights of fancy that result could never reasonably have been expected – it is a clearest indication I was in contact with a mind speaking from knowledge.

Then again it shows that these fringe-of-knowledge matters are now capable of rational understanding.

The present problem became amenable to such understanding when Louis de Broglie advanced his entirely new conception of physical reality in 1924. This was a watershed in science. Physics recast took on the totally different modern form; and it is not so much true that a rational understanding of the electrical body problem has emerged in scientific terms as that – for reasons altogether unrelated – the form of physics has been compelled to change and in the result it now offers a rational solution to this problem.

Although the study of the problem ran on protractedly far beyond that generally of the main series of issues looked at in this chapter – of which series it is just a part – I have summarized it here, first and foremost, with its conclusions because of the positive and illuminating character of its outcome. It supports weightily the whole effort I was now starting to make – to see the conceptions Lang had put to me more clearly in nature, in significance and in rational resolution. The way this effort got into motion is the special consideration of the present chapter – it goes back to the topics noted at the end of Chapter 10 as those topics of the meetings there covered which were more conveniently left to the present point. The topics formed part of the Aylesbury talks of the 8th September, 1976, and the 19th January, 1977.

One subject – taken up in the first of these two meetings – related to personal continuity and in part to Lang's basic view of the individual psyche as the ultimate ground of continuity in the individual. He had laid down that the psyche stems from a psychical parentage – a primal act of birth in the next world, before ever the individual enters this. That being so it must follow, incidentally, but inevitably, that there are two answers to the question: How old are you? *An* answer is the one which, in the Western world, has almost invariably been regarded as the only possible answer: the age of your present physical body. The second, clearly, must be the age of your psyche – always greater and, depending upon reincarnation existences, perhaps greater by far than present bodily age. Then Lang had spoken of the other continuity factor: the psychical body, which – by taking on the former role of the physical body – ensures the continuity of physical experience *on much the same pattern* when we die. While answering main questions of continuity with death Lang's exposition, thus far given, nevertheless left particular questions unanswered. What time span is to be set on the element of the psychical body? Where does such a body come from? With reincarnation, does the psyche acquire a new psychical body each time – just as it gains a new physical body? What were the answers to these questions?

Late in the meeting of 8th September, 1976, I came round to them. As a start I put it to Lang: What is the origin of the psychical body? His reply cleared up all my questions with the simple and simplifying statement: "You owe your psychical body to your psychical parents – just as you owe to them your psyche. Your psyche and your psychical body are of the same age." He continued by saying: "Your psychical body always tends to mould your physical body to the same pattern – its own pattern. In all your physical existence you have – as a consequence – *tended* to look the same."

I knew that the remainder of the session must be brief, and I thought it appropriate to round things off for the moment by taking up one further topic.

114

This was in pursuit of the origin of the electrical body. "That," Lang remarked firstly, and only as I had become aware, "belongs really to the material of your physical world." Then, directly answering my question, he said: "You owe it to your physical parentage."

Taking up our conversation again on the 19th January, and reverting once more to the subject of the complex human make-up, I put to Lang a question which might seem second-rank; but it was with a prime and strategic aim of testing out how well I had been grasping ideas. My question in principle ran like this: having told me of the elements that including and besides the physical body go to make up a human being, in particular the element of the psychical body, what is it that holds them all together?

I posed the question in very specific terms. I asked him to suppose that I was driving my car, rather too fast, on a wet motorway in exceptionally windy conditions. Imagine, I said, a violent gust which caused me to lose control; and imagine that I ran into the massive support structure of a bridge across the motorway. The motion of my physical body would be arrested almost as suddenly as the motion of the car – that, in any event, I asked him to assume. What happens now to the psychical body? This has its basis, as I understood, in physical energy in the same fundamental way as does the matter of the physical body. Therefore, just as the physical body possesses inertia, and so must tend to continue its motion, my psychical body equally must possess inertia and thus equally tend to go on: what exactly happens?

Lang seemed to like the question – if I was to judge by the smile on his face. "Yes," he said, "the psychical body will go on. It will be wrenched free and for a short time it will continue in the same direction; but then it also will be suddenly stopped – by the link between it and the physical body." His medical interest prompted him to add: "It will be greatly shocked as a result." This rider bore closely on Marjorie's need for treatment for shock; but in regard to my question I felt, with Lang's confirmatory response, that I was gaining a better insight into the human framework.

I commented on the breaking free of the psychical body with the impact: that normally it must be bound to the physical body by some equilibrium system of forces – existing purely between the two bodies. "Oh yes, it is," Lang answered immediately.

This confirmation added to the confidence of my understanding. I could see my ideas coming logically together. A first and natural reaction on introduction to the fact of the psychical body is to regard its difference from the physical body as radical. The extent of this difference is undoubtedly enhanced by the invisibility of the psychical body – but one has always to keep proper perspective. Free electrons in a vacuum tube, or again X-ray photons that might be generated by them, are equally invisible. But this is no ground for holding such entities so radically different as to separate them from the physical order. Equally one has to be wary of over emphasizing the difference between the psychical and the physical body. There is no total difference. If there was, there could be no equilibrium system of forces (forces identified in due course as van der Waals forces) between the two: things that are *totally* different can share nothing *in common*. The two bodies have in fact a definite kinship in a single material order to which they both conform – if such a material order is viewed more widely than is customary at present (Chapter 16, *Physics*). This undoubtedly is why it is possible for a linkage as stated by Dr. Lang (Chapter 4) to exist between them.

Consistent with these rational conceptions and from information I went on to gather, I can provide some amplification and explanation concerning the character and activity of the linkage. The additional information derives for the most part from talks that were specially arranged with Marjorie. Lang entered further upon the subject of the link in conversation with him later in 1977; and it was then that I understood the link conveys supporting energy for the psychical body from the physical. Marjorie supplemented this by saying that the energy transfer takes place in the form of radiation – so that the link could be said to be a radiation guide. There are two matter-radiation interfaces: one at each end of the link. At the physical body end there is emission into the guide, from the interface, of radiation of a kind belonging to the next-world order: radiation of the category of the matter of the psychical body. At the psychical body end this radiation is converted at the interface into matter of the same category. The matter is utilized in support of the psychical body.

The linkage runs from the back of the head of the psychical body to the solar plexus of the physical body. In appearance the link is of a bluish hue.

Marjorie explained what happens if the link should break. The reason Lang had said that breakage of the link must lead to death (Chapter 5) is this: in the conditions of the heavy loss of radiative energy that results the physical body is steadily reduced, over a matter of days, to a state of total exhaustion. Death is from this cause.

Lang's comments on the forces holding together the physical and psychical bodies did not fully answer the question I had had in mind on the point. There was the electrical body: how was that held in place? Eventually – and the account is given in the appendices – I discovered that the electrical body is bound by intensely strong forces to a physical manifestation of the psyche: a manifestation which can be termed the *psyche presence* (Appendix III). And the psyche presence is held in turn by relatively light, but sufficiently strong forces (of a van der Waals character) to the psychical body (Appendix IIIA). This it finally appeared, in the fashion of a chain of coupling, is the mode in which the whole human organism is held together in a unit.

But now that I had established with Lang the kind of conformity between the psychical and the physical bodies which the hypothetical motorway accident educed, I wondered whether it was possible to extend my understanding of the psychical body still further; and I postulated another specific situation.

Let us consider reincarnation, I suggested, and contemplate the actual associative act of reincarnation. There exists on the one hand the psychical body of the human being about to enter once more into the life here – on the other there is the physical body of the selected child chosen in order to effect the new entry. The first of these two bodies, we must suppose, is initially of full stature. The second of the two is inevitably only of the stature of an infant. I questioned Lang: what ensues with reincarnation? Is one to contemplate an incompatibility of size between the two bodies until the child has grown up? – or is there some adjustment, rapidly made perhaps?

Lang reminded me that he had told me of the moulding influence of the psychical body upon the physical. The psychical body, he explained now, not only constrains the physical body, but it is constrained by that body – so that it moulds itself to the infant's physical body. With the association and reincarnation completed, there is no size incompatibility.

Not long after, talking with Lang again on the same subject, he told me that the change in which the psychical body is caused to conform in size to the physical occurs under the control of the psyche. The power of the psyche is brought into play appropriately to discard atoms of the psychical body until the size adjustment is made. Lang said that, while the ability to perform the needed adjustment is fully adequate, there are – as a theoretical matter – definite limits set on the possible reduction of size. The psychical body could not be reduced to the state of the embryonic ball – for which reason association at conception is an impossibility. As the child grows, he continued, there is the sympathetic tendency for the psychical body to grow also, to maintain a strict conformity of size. Growth of the psychical body is by cell division in a way closely similar to that taking place with the physical body. The build-up of the psychical body, he stated, requires the support of the physical *via* the link. In this regard – and for its medical interest – he contributed the remark that some people lead lives (of excess) which largely vitiate or starve the needed support. It reacts also on the psyche. They become persons in need of immediate hospital treatment when they pass to the next life (*confirming* Marjorie's statement given in Chapter 6 concerning the permissive society).

Returning, however, to the conversations of the 19th January I wanted then to hear more on the details of association, whether indeed on first entry into this existence or with a reincarnation. I asked the question: how exactly is the association brought about? Is it something perhaps requiring outside help? Lang shook his head – any idea of that kind was, he assured me, far from the truth. The act of association is not only one essentially of volition but it is also essentially *automatic*. The infant is selected; and the association takes place naturally; and without assistance. This, he reaffirmed, is normally *at birth*.

Reasserting as Lang had in his last statement that the human embryo and foetus are capable of being seen in a light in which – as a matter of principle – a human being is not, my mind ran back to his first categoric dictum on the timing of association (Chapter 4). What had seemed categoric to me was undoubtedly an expression of common fact for him. In talking of course, as he came to, of the embryonic ball he gave a rational argument in support of his position. It is likely that this argument is not one of a nature to be appreciated by those who – purely dogmatically, as it seems – maintain the embryo to be of the status of a person from the point of fertilization. On hearing this present categoric statement on the moment of association, I felt I should ask Lang whether, setting aside any technical type of consideration, he might be able to present in support a rational argument of a general kind.

He was very ready to meet this form of question. He asked simply and directly what purpose could possibly be served by any early association in the womb, or by any association in the womb at all. People tended not to think in terms of purpose. But it was nevertheless important for understanding – quite widely so.

He turned to illustration to show the scope of his meaning and in regard to association. People failed to realize for instance the fact – of which he had told me in first conversations – that with young children the degree of association is often slight; because little is to be achieved at this stage. "Think," he commented, and taking a very maternal example, "of the mother cuddling and shaking the child. This is of little interest to the psyche itself." It does virtually nothing to heighten the degree of association. Then to underline the character of his form of argument he referred to the subject of grossly deformed children cared for and maintained in hospital. Such children, he stated, *could* be *so greatly* deformed that it is possible to set no value *whatever* upon association. In such fringe instances, therefore, association does not take place. "These particular cases," he was emphatic, "are only biological mechanisms."

The proposition that there is no conflux – or contingence – between the psychic element and the physical, unless a purpose is to be served by it, ranked in Lang's mind as a main principle. It became greatly interesting to find a foremost contemporary philosopher, Sir Karl Popper, arguing powerfully in support of such an attitude. This was before the World Philosophy Congress at Brighton in 1988 – and giving his lecture entitled *The Allure of the Open Future*. Explanation purely in terms of the actions and reactions of machines has been altogether dominating in human thinking, as Popper concedes. But from about 1927 physicists began no longer to believe that the world "was a huge clockwork." It was in contrast increasingly evident from that time that modern physics lends no aid to such a belief. There are tendencies, probabilities, *propensities* as Popper calls them in the physical world: that is the essential character of the physical world. It is a world which has led to the emergence of life – and life itself bears the same character. "It is not," he states, "the kicks from the back, from the past, that *impel* us, but the attractions, the lure of the future and its attractive possibilities that *entice* us: that is what keeps life – and, indeed, the world – unfolding." I encountered this teleological outlook again with Lang, and almost immediately when I turned to a question of evolution.

Up to the present when speaking of evolution, Lang's interest had centred upon the individual psyche and how it develops. Of course this development required a certain framework within which to take place – a certain format of the human organism: with not only psyche and physical body but psychical body and electrical body present also. Was this format unique to humans? It seemed to me it must be possible to trace it back through man's progenitors. But how far? Was it to be considered that in the process of biological evolution a point could be found before which the format was non-existent? Then there was the separate consideration that, after such a point, presumably evolution of the participating psychic element occurred to match the biological evolution.

Lang seemed to go along with these thoughts as I expressed them, and taking my last point first he agreed: there was such a matching parallelism. "But, he continued, "the parallel does not exist at the lower levels." By this statement he meant, as he explained, that in the nature of things the psychic element only enters upon the scene, to participate in common evolutionary progression, when the evolutionary developments of matter for their part have reached a requisite pitch: that level at which the confluence of the psychic and material *can usefully accommodate a purpose.*

In answer to the question as to just what point one must look to find the confluence starting, Lang turned to the stage of the primordial single-cell animal forms of life. Hard as it maybe to imagine, there with these animal forms, so he asserted, it is that thought first became present – in nearly vanishing degree. That is the stage at which being starts to transcend pure mechanism. But no psychic presence attaches to plant life. (I went over this ground with Marjorie, when the opportunity arose in mediumistic talks with her, and she had a most interesting point. The psychic element she maintained entered upon the scene in the first instance to increase the otherwise purely physical probabilities of the formation of both animal and plant single-cell structures. This formation, left only to physical activity, would have been altogether too tardy.)

Still following my aim of understanding in more depth and detail, I changed to a very different subject. It related to memory – and to an idea which had been forming in my mind. If the processes of memory trace ultimately to the psyche (Chapter 4) and so are able to operate continuously through the life transition taking place at death, and if we have no difficulty therefore in remembering after death events of the life we have now completed on earth, was it not possible that our powers of memory in the next life extend also to any *antecedent* existence on earth? I thought it likely; and I expressed this anticipation to Lang – indeed I suggested that in the next life the memory of the individual would range over *all* his life spans: in this and the next existence. Lang I could see was agreeing as I made the point. "Yes," he said, "*that is exactly so*." Then adverting particularly and very practically to lives just completed he added: "And after their death and return to the next life people often realize that they have not achieved the kind of thing that they had set out to do here – or other people remind them that they were going to do so-and-so, and they hadn't!"

Lang's last remarks made me think of the writing of this book – because they brought to mind an impression which had been forcing itself upon me of late. This impression was that a plan to write a book had formed a prime reason in deciding Marjorie and myself to launch ourselves once again upon this present kind of life. Then I remembered something that my sister, Grace had passed on to me when I told her of the request or instruction I had received *via* Dr. Lang from Marjorie to commence this present writing. "That is odd!" Grace had exclaimed. "You know, when Marjorie was talking with me only three days before her death – during that weekend you both came up and spent with me – she said that she was going to make you write a book." The two things looked connected; and I thought it might be worth enquiring of Lang about them. The question proved well-founded. "There was an original plan," he said, "and according to it you and Marjorie were to collaborate in a psychic research; and then you were jointly to publish your results in a book. Marjorie's accident, as you know, was not anticipated. However, Marjorie has since come to the conclusion that the accident needn't cause the total abandonment of the plan. Although you were left, you could still carry it out – even if differently." I did not comment upon this reply; but *clearly Marjorie had recollected the plan.*

The meeting shortly came to its close; and the conversation was no longer closely related to the pattern of human life. It was concerned instead with the background to life in this present existence; and very much with the origins of the physical evolution that led to an environment in which biological evolution could begin. Lang's remarks were so far-reaching and unanticipated I cannot fail to include them.

Everyone, these days, is acquainted with the idea of our spaceship Earth, a speck in the ocean of the cosmos. Circulating around the sun, it is carried with the sun upon its journey through our local galaxy of stars, the Milky Way. Since 1924, and from the work of the great American astrononomer Edwin Hubble, we know also of other galaxies, distantly separated from one another and lying in the vastness of space far beyond our own. Like ours, they are cart-wheeling formations of stars and interstellar gas; and – difficult to conceive – they count in tens of thousands of millions. In any one of them there may be hundreds of thousands of millions of stars. Each is so extensive light can take 100,000 years to traverse it. Their totality – an astounding conception – we term the physical Universe.

As to why the Universe is what we now perceive it to be is a question to which wide-ranging study has been given; with much debate and controversy.

One view placed great weight on the fact that the entire system of galaxies *appears* to be flying apart. The literal expansion of the system in an enormous dilation was early regarded (1929) as an explanation of the facts; and it is one now thought – on powerful evidence – to be the truth. If it is the truth then the physical Universe has to be seen as an *exploding universe*. At one time it must have been intensely compact – so compact that the mind again finds it difficult to conceive. To speak of pin-point magnitude would almost for certain be totally to overstate the size within which it was once condensed. That time must be little different from 15,000 million years ago; and not greatly more remote than the origin of our own planetary system in the Milky Way – just 5000 million years ago. The figures may give some conception of the violence with which the matter of the Universe has been rushing away from its point-like beginning. In this light, and with the fantastic initial eruption, the view has come to be known as the 'big bang' theory. It undoubtedly gives the physical setting in which mankind has made his home.

But what might Lang have to say about such an account?

I was most conscious of the fact that Lang's primary field is medicine; yet he had always come across to me as a man well informed on issues outside his own special interest. The limiting effect of 'watertight compartments' in the scientific knowledge of today is a drawback imposed upon scientific research by the natural bounds to human capacity. Lang belonged to a world – I had the impression – in which such bounds on knowledge were less severe. For these reasons I considered it far from pointless to gain his reactions on the subject.

Our session had already been a long one, and I could feel very distinctly that for George Chapman's sake Lang was now anxious soon to bring it to an end; yet he attended carefully while I gave him a thumbnail sketch of big-bang ideas.

As I spoke I became increasingly aware that his thought was divergent from mine; but he allowed me to continue without interruption. The divergence arose in fact from the difference of meaning the words *physical Universe* held for each of us. For him, as I was quickly to discover, they meant something infinite in extent and which had no beginning in time – yet I plainly was declaring the physical Universe to be finite in size and to have an origin hardly more than 15,000 million years ago.

My outline completed, there was a tense moment of pause.

"Oh, there have been many 'explosions'!" came his opening – and to me, at that point, entirely unexpected – remark. Yes, it was he said true – the galactic system of which I had been speaking did indeed arise out of such an explosion; but the formation of that system – which I had been calling the physical Universe – was only a recent happening in the physical Universe as he understood it. "The physical Universe has always been there," he impressed upon me, "and happenings such as you have specially described have occurred throughout it from time to time." The physical Universe as viewed in his circles was "just a vast, always present, store of energy – that bursts out on occasions in these gigantic explosions."

Cosmologists first wrestling with the problems presented theoretically by the big-bang explosion and guided by relativity ideas were inclined to suppose that, along with the world of matter, space and time also came into being only with the first instants of the eruption: before that time, if such language can be used and however the explosion might have occurred, space and time and matter were all non-existent – or at least without scientific significance. It was an outlook colouring my own mind when I was talking to Lang.

The supposition made by the outlook does not admit of the resources present in modern quantum mechanics to explain the eruption. It is not possible on a footing of logic and rational argument to explain anything in terms of an effectively altogether null (preceding) situation. But quantum mechanics, certainly in principle, and eschewing any such banishments of space and time, is able to assign a finite occurrence probability – extremely small – to the eruption. With the quantum view the eruption probability naturally entails like eruptions at other times, if utterly remote, in the past. Theoreticians of the last few years have been seriously turning to a quantum view of the big-bang explosion.

In regard to what Lang had to say, it appears that those circles in his world of which he spoke were decided in favour of a view akin to, perhaps even identical with, the quantum view rather than the earlier purely relativistic outlook which at the time influenced my own ideas.

However precisely this may be, it is a greatly significant fact that – just as with the quantum testing of Lang's statements on the electrical body – his pronouncements on the big-bang origin of the physical Universe have come in due course to find support. At the time he made these pronouncements, and as compared with the then-current scientific opinion, he could well have been accused of fantasizing. Assessed nevertheless by a science incomparably better fashioned for the grasping of reality than any earlier science, the story is different: modern quantum mechanics does not find his thinking at fault – rather, deeply penetrating into the character of the cosmos.

The two tests, the first lying with the electrical body and now this test concerning the big-bang, give a stamp of validity that must extend to what else Lang had to communicate. And they both similarly signal confidence in the line of progress by understanding which I was now hopefully following. There is – equally significant – Popper's major support of Lang's teleological outlook on the world.

Chapter Thirteen

THE NEXT-LIFE IN A SHARPER FOCUS

My new mood was highly motivating; and I was wanting to discover more of the fashion of things as Marjorie experienced them now.

In many respects it was, I knew, much the same as here. This I understood was particularly true of first appearances. The similarity was so marked it could in special circumstances be the cause of extreme confusion. Someone awaking to consciousness in the new environs after death might refuse even to believe he had died; rather he would insist it must be that he was transferred to another hospital. To persuade him of the actuality of events it might be necessary to ask some relative or friend whose death he remembered to come and visit him.

But the matter of which this different world was formed, whilst real matter, was of another kind; and that, I was also aware, introduced in the experience of it certain major differences. It was a kind of matter, for one thing, distinctly sensitive to the influence of mind – I had only to think of Marjorie's construction of her cottage (Chapter 7). There was besides a peculiar freedom from decay processes (Chapter 8). I suspected the next-life of sustaining many special differences; and my imagination played upon the possibilities. Just to be specific and to illustrate how my thought was running, I wondered whether you could, when you were out for a walk in the country, feel the breeze blowing on your face.

Therefore it was the detailed possibilities I especially wanted to hear of now; and questions flowing in this fresh direction were multiplying. Marjorie helped me to explore the new avenue; and I found that divergencies from our own experience could be far more marked in special respects than I had imagined. It seemed that the kind of departure in this instance or that could be so great as to verge on the incredible.

On the other hand to sit back and review such instances from a scientific stand-point suggested that the remarkably strange ought – realistically – to be anticipated. The incredibility of a situation is often a matter of first impression and reaction. When circumstances are looked at with more depth of thought it is possible for incredulity to dissolve away. This mode of resolution was in fact to prove a recurring one in other avenues of exploration beyond that of the present chapter; and Marjorie repeatedly directed my thinking with issues that fascinatingly were made clear by the rational concepts of modern science.

For the developments of the present chapter, I am indebted – in the first place and very materially – to the sensitivities once again of Mrs. Millicent Young.

The 7th October, 1977, was the date of a second meeting with her; and, speaking with Marjorie in preparation for it, I went over with her some very specific questions having one main aim: that the story of her new life could take on more of the actual and vivid character she herself experiences in living it from moment to moment.

The meeting commenced much later than the set time. This was due partly to unexpected traffic difficulties; and I mention circumstances otherwise trivial only because – more as a happily successful experiment – I was able through Marjorie to inform Mrs. Young that I was in fact on my way, although temporarily held up.

When finally I arrived, Mrs. Young first wanted to tell me of another scientist who had come to her since my first meeting with her. He had explained to her the significance of what she had been conveying to him. She went on to show me a letter she had received from him that set out the meaning of statements which she had made to him but which had been far from clear to her. Marjorie accepted, I believe with interest, the further hold up of our proceedings.

Starting our meeting, Mrs. Young commented – with a flash of clairvoyance – on Marjorie's lovely smile and her good carriage. Then quite correctly she said: "Marjorie was a person who always carried herself well on a special occasion." However Marjorie broke in quickly and clairaudiently on Mrs. Young; and to get to the real business of the meeting.

She wanted me to know one important thing before she took up my specific questions. It was that, while she was giving considerable time to studies, these studies were by no means tied to medicine. She amplified her statement by giving Millicent Young visual impressions of scientific laboratories, and equipment and experiments – and saying that she had been attending lectures by men of distinction in the sciences: "People," commented Millicent Young as she turned significantly to me, "that you would know of." I could not fail to note how putting things this way Marjorie avoided the attempt to transmit names that Millicent Young certainly would not know; and so might be expected not to be able to grasp and convey. Of more importance, I saw that the news of scientific lectures linked up with earlier scientific statements by Marjorie. My thoughts reverted to the first meeting with David Young, when she had authoritatively remarked on the general character of matter: *all* matter – whether it is the matter we are familiar with here or whether it belongs to Marjorie's order of existence – is to be seen rooted in energy. In what she was now saying about lectures she was preparing me and looking ahead to what she would later be telling me on the clarification flowing from modern science.

Marjorie however, and entirely naturally, wanted to add information about her medical training (something very important to her). It was to let me know it embraced not only the physical side but also the psychological. In this field she had gained much practical experience – often of a sad and depressing kind. She was referring to her endeavours with would-be suicides in this life, when she had been deputed to attend on them. The anxiety from which they were suffering usually defeated her. I well appreciated this last statement – since I clearly remembered with our message communications during Marjorie's lifetime the way that anxiety could defeat us, and prevent our minds from bridging the gap. Suicide cases, she emphasized, "are so surrounded with their troubles it was as though there existed an impenetrable barrier enveloping them." If they could only attain some degree of calm, she could reach their consciousness – but normally "it was too difficult to stop them."

With the physical side of medicine, she was these days attending at operating theatres – to observe and learn; and Millicent Young interjected she was receiving from Marjorie the visual impressions of surgical work. Marjorie stated that, although they amount to a small proportion only, there are many people who 'come through' with a specific need of surgical treatment. Here she was – necessarily – referring to the psychical body; and her observation reinforced Dr. Lang's comment: the belief that the psychical body is inherently perfect and free of defect is erroneous.

Now that she had given me her special personal news and, eminently, this initial scientific news – foreshadowing major developments in understanding which she would communicate to me – Marjorie came to the subject I had particularly asked her to go into at this meeting: a more detailed look at the characteristics of living in her world.

She began saying that, because of her many activities, she was often away from her home – which she loved very much. Mrs. Young's reporting here was in fact indirect. She changed at this juncture to quote Marjorie's actual words: "At times I return to my home. I love to sit by the water: the water I have told you of." Marjorie made Millicent Young repeat these last few words; and when Mrs. Young restated them I had an impression of the lake at the far end of the valley that lay in front of Marjorie's cottage. As the impression formed Marjorie exclaimed: "It's so peaceful – and I am showing it to your medium. I so enjoy dipping my toes in the water. These visits to the lake are always most happy – its a delightful, lovely place."

The words were graphic. With the impression they took me intimately into Marjorie's world, and paved the way for my questions. I had often experienced a like communication: that, when – usually taking Pickles for company – Marjorie came to the lake, she walked by its edge. Saying that Marjorie walked I mean quite literally that she walked – *like we do*.

If this was the case, then just as we are held to the ground on which we tread by the Earth's gravitational pull so Marjorie must, I reasoned, be constrained – as she walks – by a like force. I plunged into the subject without introduction. "Do you experience the force of gravity?" I asked. Her reply was affirmative; "but it is in a milder way than with you," she added. "The Earth's strong gravity by comparison is so tiring. We don't have to contend with that kind of weightiness – we don't experience the pressure of gravity as you do: *but we don't float around!* The proper answer is that we experience gravity to some extent. We walk – but we walk with a lightness of step."

The context in the conversation of the lake and of walking seemed right for referring to atmospheric conditions. I had wondered, as I have said, if Marjorie's present world was one in which you could experience the wind against your face. I put the basic question: "Do you have an atmosphere?" "Yes," Marjorie answered, "we do – and it is not unlike yours." Then, very interestingly, she commented: "It's one that we breathe." She followed up with the medical statement: "But we don't have the lung troubles and breathing troubles that you experience on earth." Going back to the atmosphere itself, but speaking of the conditions that prevail, she was again most interesting: "We have rain at times –

but much sunshine." The sunshine, she said, is of an atmospheric kind.

In talk with Dr. Lang shortly afterwards, I mentioned the rain. He smiled. "People get mistaken ideas," he said, "– it is not a fairyland world: you can get drenched in it!" He confirmed the atmospheric character of the light.

These glimpses of a real world different from our own remained acutely with me. They were fascinating; and some years later I was able actually to see for myself the peaceful shadowless sunshine in a countryside setting of fields and copses. That was in a brief experience of a projective kind. With that experience stimulating my interest I eventually came back to Marjorie, to hear more of these intriguing slants upon her world. I told her how they continued to rouse my curiosity; and I asked her if she would take them into still greater detail.

She did. This was through a medium that I shall explain shortly was proposed by Dr. Lang.

What she spoke on first was the sunshine. It did not differ greatly from our own in character, apart from not being produced by a distant luminous object like our sun. The spectrum of the light was much like the continuous spectrum of our own sunlight. But it was the background radiations of her Universe which excited the atmosphere and caused it to radiate in turn so as to illuminate the surroundings. Since this was the mode of operation they do not experience day and night as we do in our world. There is no nightime drop in luminous intensity.

They breathed the atmosphere in her world because their bodies had a need for the element – she called it simply oxygen – corresponding to what we call oxygen. It was not the vital need that exists with us. They do not die without oxygen; but they become eventually very weak. For a day's visit to Earth they could exist on the oxygen storage in their bodies; but on a longer stay – if that was necessary – they would bring an oxygen supply with them. Additional to its oxygen constituent their atmosphere has a widely varied chemical composition broadly akin to our own.

She referred to respiratory infections. That opened up a whole subject. There are infections in her world tending to disturb the physical organism just as in ours. Their defences against infection were though much more effective than we are accustomed to: their collection of immune mechanisms is much better. It is not particularly dissimilar in principle – to be very specific their bodies produce the 'pathfinder' T-cells which, much as ours do seek out intruder bodies and call up assistance to overwhelm the invader.

To revert to the conversation with Marjorie *via* Millicent Young my thought now was in a different direction: one nevertheless that relates to what I had just been learning about the atmosphere. I was thinking of how Marjorie had often given me impressions of birds which flew in the grounds of her home just apparently as birds fly here. If – as she had been saying – her world had an atmosphere like ours; and if besides – as it is with us – all material bodies experience the common tug of gravitation; then, it seemed only reasonable, when a bird flies over her cottage or swoops over her lawns it must do so in accordance with mechanical principles just like those by which in our world the motion of a wing through the atmosphere contrives to balance the force of gravity. So did such a bird in fact fly in the same way as our own? I tried this question; and I saw it as a good one. The answer must dispose of all those ideas about a further existence which assign to it only ethereal and dreamlike qualities (Chapter 8). It must do so in a most effective and dramatic way. But even before I had completed the question I was sensing Marjorie's thought: from all she had told me to this point it was needless really to ask it – I could see that winged flight in her world must, inevitably, follow a mechanics similar to our own. When she answered through Mrs. Young it was in level tones: "Yes – much the same!" I dropped the subject.

However apart from confirming my ideas Marjorie was glad, she said, I had raised it: it had taken her mind to the many birds she kept and of her pleasure in them. With a reiteration of her pleasure I was left in no doubt that Marjorie still found the same delights: "They are such a joy to watch – they are beautiful!"

There were some comments on animals, and the pleasure she took in them too. The last statement, she was at pains to make clear, included even animals we should class as wild. "In our world," she assured me, "you can safely play with a leopard!" To this contrast with our world she added: "It will leap about – but it will not bite you."

She continued with some animal news for me very personally. She had brought my cat Chi with her. As to his name, she made no attempt. She just gave Millicent Young a visual impression of his appearance – for her to describe to me. But as so often happened in such circumstances, I picked up the impression simultaneously; and, to dot the i's and cross the t's, Millicent Young stated exactly the injuries which Chi had suffered when he was run over and killed. Then, unexpectedly, Marjorie remarked that Chi had grown while he had been with her. This I thought a strange comment. He was not a kitten when he met his fatal accident – he had been fully grown for five years. Presumably this was another of those contrasts with our world.

Marjorie went on to give me the answer to a question which had remained in my mind since, on the previous occasion with Millicent Young, I first received news of my cocker spaniel. I knew then that an animal which forms during its lifetime a strong attachment at the human level seeks at once, upon its death, to renew the attachment. This clearly it can do if, in the next existence, the loved human being is already there present. What happened when, as with my cocker, the animal itself is the first to die? That was my question. "Such domestic pets," Marjorie explained, "are cared for in specially allocated areas – from which it is possible, when the time comes, for their owners to claim them."

I returned to the subject of flight, but in a rather different connection – I was thinking of what I might learn on the recreational activities of the next-life. I suggested this: if birds could fly in the same kind of way that birds do on earth, then it was not silly to think of glider flying as a possible form of sport – just as it was a sport with us. Even if it seemed an odd question, the answer I conjectured might be revealing. No, it was not silly to suggest it, Marjorie replied. Such flying was perfectly feasible. She did not do it herself – and she did not know of anyone who did. It was really a matter of inclination. She was certain there must be some people who would be strongly attracted by it; and that being so these people would, in fact, practise it.

A topic I particularly wished to take up was that of travel as Marjorie now experienced it; and, hoping it might provide a useful starting point, I referred to the location of her home and that of her father's. I had an impression, of which I was very sure, that the separation between the two places was about 250 miles;

but wanting to check it I began: "How far is your cottage from your father's home?" Marjorie was half teasing: "Yes, well, I know you will want to have it in miles! – but," she became more serious, "we don't think that way. As I look on it, it is like the distance between two nearby villages. I do, quite often, use my flying machine in order to visit my father. The flight takes very little time – and you gain a great impression of speed." While Millicent Young was reporting this, the impression entered my mind of a time of flight of 30 seconds (corresponding over a distance of 250 miles to a speed roughly of 30,000 miles per hour) and I perceived the flashing past of objects down below on the ground – as I would from the cockpit. Next Marjorie made a statement which I had gathered from her before. *It concerned the great difficulty she felt in conveying to me exactly how time can be encountered in her world.*

There was a difficulty in this instance; and the difficulty lay in the extreme rapidity of events – that is to say with how, seated in her machine, she experienced the ground rushing by beneath her: she had both to be clearly aware of what was happening and be able to control the course that events took.

Earlier, when – in fact in the first Millicent Young meeting, though I did not record it in my account of Chapter 11 – she had tried to impress upon me the truth that in her world time can bear aspects with which we here are simply not accustomed, she had stressed a natural and far greater consciousness of the immense scale of time. It was a scale underlined by Dr. Lang's thinking when – at the end of the previous chapter – he had alluded to an antecedent sequence of big-bang universes. I quote Marjorie on the earlier occasion: "There are aeons of time in our world – you have to think of the everlasting!"

When she had been speaking like this, just as she was now, I found myself slipping into reflection. By allowing ourselves to be dominated by our customary experience we all too easily take on a frame of mind which is parochial. An outlook of that kind must necessarily make it difficult to accept the strange. That was the basis of the great difficulty Marjorie found in talking about time.

With leisure it was not difficult to follow up this standpoint in more detail. The mind has a natural and proper tendency to think of normal experience as rational; and from there it is inclined to go on by an assumed antithesis to class all else as irrational – and so unthinkable. This is a position which is altogether too sweeping. If only taking a step-by-step approach I want to detach from it Marjorie's communication on very rapidly succeeding events.

In the first place it seems one should cast around, searching for knowledge that while well authenticated is the less common and less restricted. Success in such a search must yield the freedom of wider horizons. Modern scientific knowledge, it is quickly apparent, can assist in an extension of outlook. In reflection like this, and as I know was so often happening now, Marjorie's mind was thinking with mine.

It is true the exceedingly fast succession of events which Marjorie handles in her flying – sensing them and reacting to them – might seem freakish to us, even in our age of supersonics. But physicists in the normal course of their work are these days accustomed to dealing with happenings that take place in a span of the order not only of millionths but of millionths of millionths of a second. When study is extended to the interior of the nucleus of the atom, there are encountered events which in their brevity run fantastically beyond this. In the world of the nuclear interior, specific events occur not in times of the nature of millionths of millionths of a second but in fractions of such times which are millionths of millionths over again! These considerations open up the arena greatly.

Admittedly physicists whose field is the atomic nucleus are not able to follow interior events directly – though they have awareness of them. Physicists however in more normal work, and concerned with less rapid events in repeating sequences, are easily able to achieve a form of direct awareness of fleeting changes: changes occurring in a millionth of a second – and in *very* much less. It is not by any means an awareness fully of the character of the normal senses; but it is an ability to observe such excessively rapid changes. As a sense mode it is one in which these changes can be looked at retrospectively in a way that does not overwhelm the senses. In all this, and in regard to the scale of time, parochial conceptions are left far behind.

An expansion of horizons is also possible in regard to the control of rapidly changing events. By extending human mental activity through the medium of modern computers it is feasible to stretch the bounds of human ability to master and control exceedingly rapid changes. Aircraft can be and are now flown, through such techniques, that make rapid-control demands far beyond the reaction capabilities of any pilot to meet naturally.

For the rational mind the incredulity of first reaction must weaken. It is not categorically unthinkable, because it is not beyond rational anticipation, that Marjorie – naturally equipped as one may assume her now to be – is able to distinguish and not only distinguish but cope with events occurring at a speed so rapid they lie far beyond our own powers of response.

Nevertheless – as Marjorie confessed at a meeting not long after at Aylesbury – the truth was something she had felt must be hard to convey convincingly. I note that eventually Marjorie was able to give a full scientific basis of resolution for the physiological problems of her flight experience: not only those in particular of speed of nervous response and reaction but also the problem of the ability to withstand the enormous accelerations (Chapter 16, *Physics*).

The argument from scientific knowledge is able to weaken and overcome the credibility gap other than in the context of the high-speed flight in which the argument arose. There is difficulty, for more popular types of thinking, in the idea that the next-world existence is lived out in the environs of real matter. I want to consider this difficulty; and show how it can usefully be looked at in the light of science.

In its approach the essence of the argument is this: that if an alleged fact seems to lie so far at variance with the ordinary tracts of our experience that it is hard to accept, then it should be considered whether there may not exist some other part of human experience – which has come to be accepted – where some similar strangeness is to be found. If such an other part should exist then it must follow that the difficulties are greatly reduced. That is the outline of the approach made by the argument.

The difficulties with a next-world matter which, as Dr. Lang and Marjorie had amply maintained, is truly material fall in two categories. It is for one thing, and I quote Lang in his early exposition of the psychical body (Chapter 4), a matter which is interpenetrating with ours. It is for another thing a matter which is hidden from our perception. In both cases there is a situation which is irreconcilable with the ordinarily conceived character of matter. Ordinary ideas of matter are based on our experience of ordinary solid bodies. Ordinary solid bodies do not interpenetrate; moreover they affect us strongly through our senses.

I aim to make it evident that ordinary conceptions are an inadequate basis for the proper understanding of matter; and that in this sense they are a misconception. Should they not be a misconception, there would certainly be good ground for the dreamlike view of next-world matter. If next-world matter is to be thought of in the highly limited terms that apply in our experience to ordinary solid bodies, then there is a particularly cogent question to be asked: why has this matter altogether escaped discovery? The embarrassment of the question is indeed avoided if the matter is held on the contrary to be an illusion of dreams. But I want to show that the new view of matter, which science today has found itself forced to take, enables one to look on next-world matter – precisely in the fashion that Dr. Lang and Marjorie have maintained – as real matter.

It is useful to think of a material particle of our own order of existence, and one which is now well known practically to physicists. While long suspected it proved highly elusive; and was far from easy to track down. This particle, called the neutrino, was first postulated in 1931; but it was not observed by the experimenters until 1956. It is one free of electric charge and found to travel with a speed that of or extremely close to the speed of light – and it reacts scarcely at all with other matter. Its motion through matter as dense as lead can continue unimpeded for as long as 3,500 years. Put another way, if ten thousand million such particles impinged upon the Earth along a diameter, all except one perhaps would emerge from the other side of the Earth – virtually as though the Earth had not been there. Within the normal ambit of experience, such interpenetration of matter by matter is utterly strange behaviour; but interpenetration and lack of interaction – and with that a lack of detectability – is in these neutrino terms, a fact of scientific experience. When such fact is contemplated, and accepted as it must be, the ideas of interpenetration and undetectability connected with Marjorie's material world lose their difficulty.

What is clearly demanded – with the facts concerning the neutrino – is the entire discarding of ordinary conceptions of matter, and in substitution a new understanding which accommodates the extremely strange facts known to modern experimental science. Modern quantum mechanics has the understanding of such facts. Unfortunately the new understanding is little grasped outside a small core of experts. On the grounds of quantum theory it would be a real difficulty if – holding their world truly material – the evidence of Dr. Lang and of Marjorie had been different: if it had been other than that for instance of interpenetration (Chapter 16, *A New World-View*).

By all accounts the experience of the next-world is vivid, very vivid. Lang, joking with me, remarked drily that if vividness is the test of reality then of our two worlds his was the 'more real'! One would certainly expect vividness of sense perception if next-world matter was real matter. Dreams rarely even approach to the vivid character of sense experience. The dream theory of next-world matter, here also, fails to attract.

Summarizing, it seemed that *Marjorie's world is not such a strange world and yet it is a world in which the element of difference, commonly not marked, can at times stand out most remarkably.* That appeared to be the substance of what,

129

overall, she felt she had to get across to me. She walked by the large lake much as we would; she enjoyed its water lapping around her feet; I was left in no doubt she enjoyed equally the breeze blowing on her face; but she had made me realize acutely, and for one thing, the extraordinary bodily comparison in nervous activity: she could take note of change and react to it effectively with a rapidity that was totally astonishing.

Conveying this kind of information, which Marjorie had done, I though it natural to follow up with some rather differently directed questions. They might be classed as inevitable. There was for example, the question that given this is so, then just where exactly is it happening – again, how even did such a world come about.

In answer to the first question, I thus far knew only – by mental impression – that in some sense the place which was now the centre of Marjorie's activities was 'near'. On the second, I knew still less.

The meeting had already largely run its course when I came to this new questioning; but there was time for Marjorie to make a start which provided a basis for later more complete ideas.

Questions of location and origin apart, I was so ignorant of what this world actually might be in which Marjorie now lived. It seemed good to take things up precisely here; and I put the question of expanse: how large was this habitat of hers compared with our Earth?

Marjorie's initial reaction was simply to state that it was greatly larger, but then – increasing my curiosity – she added it was so great that her own experience was inadequate of itself to give an answer. Reminding me of the fantastic speeds which she could attain in her flying machine, she stressed: "By your standards, you would say that we travel excessively – as well as unimaginably quickly. Even so, my own explorations of our world are but slight – I have hardly come to know it. As to the scale of Earth, it is insignificant in comparison." Although she did not then enlarge on the point, she affirmed categorically that her own habitat was but one like certain others associated with it.

On the question of its whereabouts, and with the session running out of time, she left me this clue: that, by using the exceedingly great speed of which her flying machine is capable, the journey to Earth never need take much time. When she said this, I had the marked feeling that she hesitated to reveal her actual speed of flight for fear I should not believe her. I was to find out that on such journeys she commonly flew at speeds approaching the speed of light!

I attempted to go more deeply with questions on habitat when I had the opportunity of further meetings with Marjorie. This was distinctly informative. There was a meeting with Marjorie using a different medium, who – as I noted earlier – was suggested by Dr. Lang: a Mr. William Elton. And after that I had a meeting with both Dr. Lang and Marjorie at Aylesbury. A physical background to the populated regions then emerged in a picture of a paracosmos entirely co-extensive and – as I have endeavoured to make more understandable – interpenetrating with our own cosmos.

Very largely, and I quote Marjorie at the Elton meeting, the matter of this paracosmos has followed the same evolutionary patterns with which we here are familiar. This has arisen, Marjorie stated, because their matter is endowed with a nature in many respects like that of our own. Consequently in their Universe they are fully acquainted with explosively expanding galactic systems and – less dramatically – the condensation of stars in the process of their formation. Such things take place just as they happen with us.

On such parallel behaviour I must enter a caveat. Marjorie explained on another occasion through Elton that despite similar physical principles, large differences in time scale follow from the very great difference in fundamental parameter value. She elaborated on this in the context of the sequence of big-bang universes to which – in Chapter 12 – Lang had referred. Every such universe erupts out of the void only to disappear finally into the void, leaving no trace of itself. That, she said, is the fate to be seen for our own Universe – in some exceedingly far distant time. Compared with its life yet to run, its present age is triflingly small. But the life-span of our Universe is like a clock tick in relation to the unimaginably great lapse of time between consecutive big-bang eruptions of our cosmos. The life-span of the physical Universe in which she lives was, she stated, very great indeed compared with such an unimaginably great time lapse – its duration included far more than one only of the big-bang universes of our cosmos: it was vastly vast. This illustrated particularly what she had meant when she spoke of the far greater consciousness in her world of the scale of time.

Taking up again however the first Elton conversation, Marjorie pointed out that a big difference must be reckoned with on lines that I already knew well in relation to mind. Their matter has its special sensitivity to the powers of mind; and mind has always been present organizing specific tracts of matter in a course of evolution altogether different from that which occurs when matter follows its own inherent dictates. These specific tracts – distributed on a universal scale – are the inhabited tracts: utterly vast, every one of them, and including local centres of habitation – just as her own habitat was one such centre of a group.

To an extent, the organization of matter by mind is the work of the common individual. The forming of Marjorie's own cottage, and of its immediate environs, is an example. In a vital aspect, though, greater powers of mind have been active. "There never has been a time when human beings of some kind have not inhabited such tracts" was how Lang took up the subject at Aylesbury. "The development of some minds has therefore, over the aeons, been very great," he said. In direct consequence "their power is almost unbelievably large." To reinforce his point, he made an astonishing statement: "The annihilation of the Solar System by psychic power would be no difficult task." Accepting this statement, and in its light, the fact and character of the general organization of those vast tracts of which Marjorie had been speaking can better be appreciated.

I was naturally curious concerning the form of such tracts – the way in which they were constituted and set up. In illustration Lang spoke about the tract which included his own habitat. This tract he stated was a system always maintained in close and fixed station with the Solar System. When I enquired further, he said that the position thus preserved is one lying out of the plane of the Solar System. Still later, and talking with Marjorie once again through Mr. Elton, it became clear that a very specific stationing of the tract with respect to the Earth, despite the Earth continuing in its own constant orbital motion, is achieved by means of a counterpart gravitational orbiting motion. It was about a central artefact mass which corresponds in dynamic principle to our Sun. The scheme established a fixed distance to Earth from her habitat at all times. Marjorie could take her flying machine up to a speed of one fifth that of light without difficulty, and then the journey to Earth would occupy less than two minutes (so that the fixed distance of stationing must be – as Marjorie agreed – about four million miles). That was what Marjorie had had in mind when she told me her own habitat was 'near'.

When I asked her, she said that the other habitats of her group were in the same orbit as her own; and all were maintained in a fixed distribution over a small local segment of orbital arc. Each habitat, as I might anticipate on gravitational grounds, was constructed spherically in overall form.

I leave the subject of habitat. There was more that I wanted to see filled into the present picture of the next-world. I knew scarcely anything of the nature of next-world society. Much earlier (Chapter 4) I had understood that in this kind of society the range of human development extends over a large number of levels – but did society, I wondered now, possess a formal structure. If so, what was this structure – and then, was there any counterpart to those national groupings of communities which we call *states*. I raised these questions at the joint meeting with Dr. Lang and Marjorie.

Lang informed me that there commonly existed differing territories. To each there was "a chief of state". Like that there was similarity with us. On the other hand, the life of the individual in any such state was almost entirely autonomous. When Lang made this last statement it became clear why in his first conversations he had concentrated upon the levels of individual development. They are the essential characterization of his society: formal structure is only a minor feature. I understood when talking with Marjorie on a separate occasion – and checking with her on what I anticipated must be the case – the full range of individual development is to be found in any state.

To conclude the chapter I give the conversation which brought the meeting with Millicent Young to a close. It began with a point on Marjorie's mission here. On a visit to Earth, I asked her, did she find herself at any special, for example physical, disadvantage. "Not at all physically," she said, "but we find that we tire more quickly." This, she explained, arose from psychological factors – the psychological activity called for by the mission for instance. Also she found it hard not to become strongly aware of pervading mental attitudes – some of which were so narrow-minded, or so wrong-headed, that contemplation of the havoc following inevitably from them depressed her and lowered her vitality. She was now declaring herself to be subject to fatigue, and I could not fail to note it; but she reminded me that in her world – and as she had formerly impressed on me in thought transfer (Chapter 6) – natural tiredness arising out of effort is nothing like so great as we experience here. Once more it was interesting when she added: "Since fatigue exists in our world, therefore there is a natural rest period which we take for granted rather like you take day and night for granted."

Finally, switching completely from the subject, Marjorie dropped a remark about *seeing her*. What it was she was exactly conveying eluded me – and I could not find out because there the conversation terminated abruptly. Marjorie was simply not saying any more. One thing which came, impressionally I felt, into my mind upon later reflection was that she was keen I should understand – *in some detail* – how it was she had been able to appear to me physically in my bedroom.

Chapter Fourteen

ROSE AND DOG EPISODES

Marjorie's sudden and puzzling ending of the second meeting with Mrs. Young acted as a potent nudge. It marked the onset of a stream of development and ideas. The chapter looks at the start of this main flow of thought and progress: to how psychical events are to be viewed. Further on, it will be seen displaying powerfully the relevance of modern science to the psychical field. But the nudge was more especially to jolt me over some remarks by Dr. Lang, when we had met two months earlier at Aylesbury.

Lang then had briefly referred to the subjects of *materializations* and *transfigurations*. He spoke as though I was already of some acquaintance with them. This was true of materializations for the very good reason at least that I had seen Marjorie materialize close by my bed; and that moreover we had talked about it. As to transfigurations I was not sure I knew exactly what he meant; and I said so. He told me it was possible for a person in a trance state – usually a medium already practised in the demonstration of the phenomenon – to allow his features, principally his facial features, to become modified so as to conform strikingly with those of someone now living in the next existence. He did not go into details of the phenomenon; but it was clear he wanted me to learn more about it; and about materialization besides. Very helpfully he started to assist me with this learning.

First, he said, he wanted me to meet a Miss Jeanette Dunn. She could aid, he felt. Also he recommended a visit to Stanstead, in Essex.

This visit had as well another object in view; and again he considered that Miss Dunn could help. About the further object, he gave no particularly clear indication: it was in fact the prime material of this chapter.

What he told me was that there had been established at Stanstead Hall a college devoted to psychic studies. Mediums of proven ability were present at the college from time to time. Marjorie and I ought to go along and take advantage of whatever opportunities might be to hand. In regard to Miss Dunn, he had been speaking with her only that afternoon; and, as she was remaining to talk with George Chapman, I would be able to meet her when our present conversations were over.

This I did. I explained to her the general nature of my researches; and I added how Dr. Lang now believed they might be extended. She was willing to have further talk, and she explained that although she lived in the north of England there were occasions when she came to Stanstead Hall – because of her connections there. For this reason it was agreed we should meet again before long at Stanstead. I could then, we hoped, make some headway such as Dr. Lang had in mind – it was possible in particular that I should be able to utilize the facilities of mediumship associated with Stanstead Hall.

As it finally worked out, Marjorie employed these facillties in an important way; but up to the point of the nudge, and beyond following Dr. Lang's instructions to the extent I have been setting down, I had done no more; and certainly had given very little thought to the specific subjects he had raised. With that I had fallen below Marjorie's expectation and it qualified for the nudge. From there Marjorie took the initiative: towards a clearer insight on a wide front; and to show the great relevance of scientific understanding.

To mitigate further delay and just after some holidays I was in touch with Miss Dunn on the telephone. She suggested that we meet in a few days in the way proposed: the 20th October, 1977, was the actual date. We could then devote the bulk of the day to the aims we had discussed.

The day itself, I remember, was sunny; and I arrived midmorning. In the sun, and with its quietly extensive grounds, Stanstead Hall created a pleasing impression: a good background to the day's activities. We had some initial and exploratory talk. Miss Dunn told me she had witnessed materializations; and she described some of her experiences. She showed me the exhibit of a glove-like wax shape formed according to the evidence by a materialized hand dipping into melted wax to form a coating on it, and then dematerializing when the coating had hardened. We went as well to the college library to see photographs of materialized and materializing forms. I understood from her that there had been plans for a transfiguration medium to be present at the college just then – but this had been prevented at the last moment by a fatal accident in the medium's family.

Miss Dunn stated that she herself had various special sensitivities and that these ran also to transfiguration. She made no offer of a demonstration however of the phenomenon for that particular time; but I gathered she might be willing to attempt it on a future occasion. We went on to more widely ranging issues of the psychic field, and this took us past lunch.

It was after lunch that I encountered the principal developments of the day. But I particularly do not want to leave the conversation of the morning and its fascinating look at the materialization phenomenon without regarding this phenomenon from the perspective of what eventually I came to learn about it. This understanding constitutes a basic scientific explanation of the phenomenon; and is therefore supportive of it. The last remark – at this point in which Lang was inviting me seriously to consider the phenomenon – needs in fact very much to be made. With little recent evidence, the view has been expressed – no scientific explanation having been forthcoming – that the phenomenon is not a real phenomenon.

For myself I certainly had, speaking with Miss Dunn, no idea whatsoever as to how materializations happened; and if it were not for the fact of all that I had gathered since Marjorie's death, more especially by my immediate personal experience of her short materialization at my bedside, I am conscious I could well have inclined to the subject with the explain-it-away-if-possible attitude to which scientists are all too prone. It is a great temptation in circumstances notable for lack of a theoretical basis of understanding! Lord Cherwell is better recognized for his assistance to Winston Churchill in building up a scientific intelligence system during the Second World War than for the wide researches which earlier he had conducted in the field of heat. As chief scientific adviser to Churchill there was a memorable occasion when he proffered his views on the first aerial photograph of a notorious object. Seen in the photograph it was lying on the ground; but before long it became known as the German long-range ballistic V-2 missile. Churchill turned to him when it was proposed that the object must be of this nature. Cherwell denied any such possibility. It was probably some kind of torpedo, he asserted – there was no way he could envisage by which the Germans might successfully engineer any such ballistic device! Churchill was unimpressed.

As I conveyed, I did not remain lacking of understanding of materialization phenomena. Largely through Marjorie's instruction I became aware, during the next year, of the scientific pattern of activity which operates in the formation of materialized structures.

Such structures it was clear are made out of the kind of matter that is familiar to us. It is matter expelled from the body of a living person (referred to as the medium); moreover the structures are formed normally in the likeness of next-existence persons. The explanation I shall give of such structures in Chapter 16 will show that their creation is fully feasible in the light of the scientific discoveries of the present century. It will then also become clear that the medium involved in such happenings may be little more that an assenting and passive element in the proceedings – in which case while his natural abilities fit him for these events their actual control lies in the hands of next-existence scientific experts. These experts incidentally may utilize practical resources of a highly-developed kind.

All these ideas give significance to the various facets of the materialization process – such as those shown to me by Miss Dunn: they are swept out of mystery into the light of comprehension. However I leave the subject for the present to take up the events of the afternoon and the principal material of this chapter. The events centred around two episodes of a marked character. Travelling to Stanstead I had no knowledge of them at all. That was how it remained throughout my discussion with Miss Dunn. But not long after lunch I reminded her that earlier in the day she had promised to introduce me in the afternoon to a medium so that I could have a talk with Marjorie. Miss Dunn substantiated her promise immediately by making me an appointment with a Mrs. Gaye Muir: for the time of 3 p.m. – and for a period of half an hour. Miss Dunn had some business of her own, and I awaited my appointment.

There was no doubt of Mrs. Muir's competence as a clairvoyant and clairaudient. Without a word of introduction on my part she was aware immediately of Marjorie, whom she referred to as my wife. She told me my mother was present also; and that my mother wished me to know this. My father had come. He at once started to speak of a family matter – making clear to me that he was concerned over an unhappy family division. Mrs. Muir commented that he had in fact called it a *rift* – whereas for herself she inclined to name it a *division*. I found this an interesting detail, and I confirmed to her that *rift* was exactly the word my father would have chosen. My mother spoke. She was solicitous as it is in the nature of mothers – and Marjorie joined in with her on a matter of diet.

Next took place an episode which out of its real context would be bizarre. It was unquestionably outstanding – and the first of the two special episodes.

Mrs. Muir became puzzled – as though she was not seeing correctly; and she announced her diffidence over what she was about to say: what was occurring appeared to her so exceedingly odd. She was afraid that I would think it silly. "Your wife," she said, "is presenting you with a blue rose." I remarked how this certainly made sense to me. Although I did not enlighten Mrs. Muir, my mind had run – on hearing of the blue rose – to the first session with Mrs. Young (Chapter 11) and to the blue rose conversation then.

I was talking with Marjorie about her home surroundings; and I had mentioned an extraordinary visual impression: I had seen rose bushes set at the head of her sweeping lawns – and the rose blooms were blue! It so astonished me I was inclined to question the impression – and that was why I was referring to it. Marjorie, knowing well enough my doubting nature, endeavoured to inspire confidence in my sensitivity: I must be prepared to see such things!

It was a total surprise to be brought again, by Mrs. Muir, to those strange blue roses. But Marjorie's aim now was not to boost my confidence. It was to hand me a powerful and clarifying logic of events. This logic was to serve in critique of theorizing upon psychical happenings. It bears on the psychological compensation theory I considered in Chapter 1.

In that chapter I pointed to the major shortfall of this theory in important theoretical respects; and I noted in particular the heavy weather of fact it would have to ride out in order to survive. Marjorie's presentation of the blue rose focussed attention acutely upon this very point. If as required by the theory the events we are here concerned with are to find their explanation solely in terms of the functioning of my mind then, on the contrary, it seems palpably clear it was not my mind which was involved but the mind of Mrs. Muir.

That was the essential logic of events Marjorie was giving me *via* Mrs. Muir. It is certainly an aid in picturing the probabilities of interpretation. In the light of it, let us assume for the moment the truth of the non-survival hypothesis, and let us consider also the 'impressions of Marjorie' I experienced with and since her death.

Starting out thus, my very first impressions are undoubtedly by far best accounted for by the compensation hypothesis that is suggested by psychology. Then in the contingent situation shortly afterwards when Phyllis experienced an impression also, that impression might well be said to have resulted from transfer to Phyllis from myself – so that basically it could be seen as part of my own psychological activity in compensation. Perhaps all subsequent events – such for instance as the total impression of Marjorie coming to me *via* David Young – might be construed in exactly the same way. This would be plausible if, at the time, I was telepathically prompting David Young – unintentionally but nevertheless effectively – by my conscious thought processes. What of the many instances where, my conscious mental activity quite unrelated, I must most strongly suspect I did not prompt him? The blue-rose episode was contrived by

Marjorie to bring me face-to-face with just this type of circumstance. Could it still be possible that, without related conscious activity, I had been influencing Mrs. Muir?

Marjorie had planned a second special episode to throw light upon this question. I therefore continue to give the events of the session, and with Mrs. Muir remarking on my "grandmother on my father's side." My grandmother, she told me, was staying with Marjorie just then; and she had joined in the visit to Stanstead along with my father and mother. Mrs. Muir described her "short and rotund appearance." How my grandmother was dressed interested her: it was in a material like silk or satin and of a purple hue. With my relatives Marjorie had brought also a large dog.

This dog looked rather like an Alsatian; but its coat was entirely black and short – and Mrs. Muir stressed that it had ears which drooped or flopped round its head: a most unusual mongrel. Its name, she said, was Hunter. For myself, I could make nothing of this animal – I had never known or heard of a dog like it; but I noted down the details.

A few days later, talking with Marjorie's mother, I told her about my visit to Stanstead. Coming to the dog, I asked her if she perhaps could throw light on it. I had seen her starting to smile when I described the dog; and with my question she assured me at once that she could – it had belonged in her family; but its name was Rover, not Hunter.

The difference in names did not seem to worry her – she felt so sure of the animal itself. Knowing well the difficulties that mediums have with names, it did not trouble me either. After all, the concepts of *rover* and *hunter* are not markedly different. *Rover* is an old term for the sea robber in search of his plunder – a term, at root, not different at all from that of *hunter*: a tracker of his own kind of game. The discrepancy is scarcely so much a difficulty as an interesting commentary upon the mediumistic mechanism – on which Marjorie had cast light through David Young. (When a medium picks up a thought there are normally *many* linguistic elements of a corresponding sentence which are selected in the mind of the medium as the thought is incident. Should there be some ambiguity with any one of them, the context of the rest forms a helpful constraint which assists in accuracy. Any such help is minimal or non-existent when the thought centres simply upon a name).

To make further check concerning the dog, I took up the subject with Dr. Lang and Marjorie at my next meeting with them at Aylesbury. There – as I expected – I was told that the identification with Rover was correct. Dr. Lang also showed pleasure that I had not treated the episode of Rover as insignificant – it was no mere accident, he emphasized, that the dog had accompanied the party.

The force of the black-dog episode – and the heart of what it was planned to tell – is that Mrs. Muir was able to come by real and pertinent information without any transfer stimulus from me, conscious or unconscious. She had been acting entirely independently of me, and of my psychology. There has in consequence to exist a high probabillty that with the episode of the rose she was gathering her information in just the same independent way. And, most importantly, doubt must even be cast strongly upon the operation of the psychological hypothesis in my very first impressions. The only other hypothesis of any standing in the field is that Marjorie was then communicating to me exactly as she had long been accustomed to do before her death – death having no effect upon the basis of this communication.

The significance of the two episodes was transparent. Lang and Marjorie had aimed to make more clear the necessity for a natural – a realist – interpretation of psychic events. The two episodes plainly left the anti-realist position in very great doubt and confusion.

I could see how the present aims went back to a conversation with Dr. Lang, when he and I were discussing just how this book should be written. Marjorie had already given her ideas to me (Chapter 6). Lang supported them; and explicitly he and I both felt the account must be more than narrative alone. There must be present a substance of events carrying conviction of the reality of what was *prima facie* to be understood – intrinsically the book must refuse to be *explained away*. Therefore the account would need to include facts the logic of which was resistant to such 'explanation'. With the visit to Stanstead it was clear that Marjorie and Dr. Lang had been helping me with this part of my writing – and that particularly they were intent upon stressing the high natural improbability of the psychological compensation view.

In due course Marjorie came back to the anti-realist issue – no longer concerned with the psychological theory, but with other complexions of the issue. She took things up yet again on a basis of practical test. I will not now go into the details of the test – they are part of a new turn in developments which I give in Chapter 16, *Physics*; but it fits in well at this point to consider the generalities. The test bears on the question of how Mrs. Muir could know of the black dog *if the knowledge could not have been conveyed to her by persons no longer living.* It is possible – just conceivably possible – that with her extrasensory perceptions she might have been able, by a super use of them, to obtain the information say from the memory of Marjorie's mother. To base any theory on such a possibility is optimism in no trifling degree. There is recognition that no good evidence supports it; but it has been seriously argued that such a super use of extrasensory abilities is an explanatory hope and to be entertained. Mrs. Muir might have been able in this way to obtain information on the blue roses I had seen in my impressions – by gaining access to my memory store, or to my written notes on these roses. Marjorie's practical test aimed to evaluate such ideas.

It was with the help of a different medium, and in a very different and purely scientific context. She set me a lengthy calculation to carry out at my leisure, telling me at the same time the result I would obtain. Her predicted result was in fact the result which, going through the calculation, I arrived at when (some days later) I turned to it. The force of the logic here rests with the fact that the result to be calculated existed in the mind of no living person prior to Marjorie announcing it. It could be conveyed because her mind did in fact exist to convey it; but, to the point at which she conveyed it, it was not known to the mind of anyone living – so that with the anti-realist viewpoint even if the medium could have exercised super-extrasensory powers to collect the information the difficulty lies that there was no repository from which to collect it.

The test shows most powerfully that thought transfer from non-living persons is a real and impressively functioning thing. This cannot but underline and confirm what, with the rose and dog episodes, the logic of events distinctly points to: that adoption of the realist footing is the proper basis of interpretation of – and approach to – psychical events. The calculation test can be seen as significantly clinching the argument from this logic. The realist footing is indeed very much justified and as compared with the manifest uncertainties attaching to anti-realist suggestions. The anti-realist quest is a search in the wrong direction.

I return to the test more fully in Appendix IV – where I aim to review anti-realist ideas in a broad appraisal. An important issue is that, while fifty or more years ago there might have seemed good scientific reason to look to these ideas, modern science in its enormously increased accord with reality has no call for them. It is naturally equipped to relate to the realist view (Appendix I).

Chapter Fifteen

REINCARNATION

Enquiry and development flowed on – now because my visit to Stanstead left me, in one respect, in a state of major curiosity. Reincarnation – in the light of the visit – seemed a principle carrying a question mark. What new slant, looking into the question, might perhaps present itself? It made my mind restless.

At a very early stage Dr. Lang had introduced me to the principle: he spoke of the *fact* of reincarnation and he laid great emphasis on it. The return to the present kind of life was of the essence of human advancement. In our reaction to the discipline, the rough-and-tumble, the storm and stress we encounter here, the unfolding and the shaping and the build-up of the psyche becomes possible. Such schooling needs to be successively repeated. It takes long to be accomplished. Marjorie had given me the clear understanding that, with entry upon the next-life, there is a widespread tendency for people to remain *very much the same*. While the challenge to endeavour is certainly present – with great opportunities – so often people do not seek the challenge: life can be highly pleasing and they aim to keep it that way, static. Therefore it fails to be coloured by the progress of evolution. The challenge has deliberately to be looked for and found. In our world here, the challenge is hard to escape; and, so strong is the underlying primal urge to evolve and grow, people insufficiently developed for continuing life in the next-world naturally find themselves wrestling with this challenge again, and again, in a return-life. "Life is a battle": Lang had stated that categorically.

But in conversation with Miss Dunn at Stanstead, mentioning the subject in passing, I learned there were some grounds to think reincarnation might *not* be a fact. When I enquired into these grounds, Miss Dunn explained that reincarnation is denied by some next-world communicators. They have given their evidence, just as Dr. Lang had given his in his conversations with me; but to reverse effect. It seemed an odd situation, and it greatly roused my interest.

This was especially so since I had recently been studying an account of some hypnotically-induced past-life regressions of patients of a hypnotherapist, Arnall Bloxham. The regressions arose out of the normal practice of Bloxham's profession. They provided evidence which – in a fascinating way – had seemed to support Lang's statements. Miss Dunn suggested this might not be so. To appreciate better her remarks it is only proper first to look at the way Bloxham came to achieve these regressions; and to look also at their nature.

After serving in the Royal Navy during the First World War, Bloxham had commenced a career in hypnotherapy which was to continue for over forty years.

In the latter part of his career he amassed a library of tape recordings in each of which it seemed that the patient had been taken back under hypnosis into a past life.

Generally speaking he made a wide use of the hypnotic-regress technique to assist him in the treatment of his patients. This worked by causing the hypnotically altered state of patient consciousness to lead him through events far back in the life of the patient. Among experiences which the patient had long since forgotten he was thus able to track down the events lying at the root of the patient's disorder. With the help of the tape recording he had made of the regression, the identification of such events by the patient – now in a purely normal state of consciousness – was the first step of the treatment. Then there was the occasion when successful treatment could only be achieved by taking the patient to events of – apparently – a previous life.

This launched Bloxham on a study of seeming previous-life existence using the regression technique. One woman, retaining her anonymity under the name of *Jane Evans*, contributed to his studies by allowing him to regress her into six separate such previous earthly existences. A selection of former-life regressions of this kind, extending over a range of patients and taped by Bloxham, has been the subject of careful and detailed research.

In regard to Jane Evans and in the first of the six regressions (taken in their historical order) she is Livonia, the wife of a tutor in a Roman family living in the vicinity of York. As Livonia she mentions events of intrigue and rebellion that occurred in Roman Britain about the year A.D. 286. Next she is a Jewess, Rebecca, in York, who dies in the York Massacre just after the death of Henry II in 1189. After that she is an Arab servant in the medieval French household of Jacque Coeur, a most wealthy merchant who was financier and adviser to King Charles VII. With the downfall of Coeur in 1451, and the seizure of his property, she is saved by a poison draught (given her by her master) from the fate, inevitable at the hands of the King's soldiers, of an unprotected non-Christian. Subsequently, she is a servant to Catherine of Aragon (1485-1536) who became married to Prince Arthur of England, the Prince of Wales. In her next life she is a seamstress in London at the time of Queen Anne (1665-1714); and after that a nun in Maryland, U.S.A., dying in 1920.

As Jane Evans now she was born in 1939, and her schooling was but ordinary. At sixteen she left school for a secretarial course at a business college. Her scholastic attainments hold out no basis for explaining the wealth of detail (checked widely in elaborate researches) that she presented in her various regression accounts. The possibility she was simply creating fantasies must be judged by the fact that – checking at the level of detail – she was able when again submitting to hypnosis some five years later to produce accounts which gave the selfsame story as that originally taped.

Some chance corroboration is impressive. It is connected with her statement, made as Rebecca in York, that she and one of her children were murdered by the soldiers in the crypt of a church close by the castle. In the researches on the tape, it was not too difficult – with the aid of Rebecca's description – to identify the church as St. Mary's Castlegate. Upon the identification of the church, it appeared however that Rebecca was wrong about the crypt. Neither this church, nor indeed any of the other churches surviving from the period, had or showed trace of a crypt; or of any underground cell of any kind – apart from the Cathedral, which it seems Rebecca did not mean. Six months later – in September of 1975 – a discovery by a church workman engaged in renovations on St. Mary's revealed a vault (under the chancel of the church) with round stone arches of Norman or Romanesque style: evidence that under the hypnosis Jane Evans knew of the crypt *only* because, as Rebecca, she was there at the time.

A full account of the Bloxham tapes, and the researches on them, is given in a book by Jeffrey Iverson entitled *More Lives Than One?*, (Souvenir Press, 1976). Learning of the book, I had in fact told Dr. Lang of my intention to read it. His comment was that he knew of it, and that I would find it a most interesting and rewarding study. This proved the case; and it was with some surprise at Stanstead when citing the book – as supporting Lang on reincarnation – that I listened to Miss Dunn explain how the Bloxhan tapes could bear an interpretation different from reincarnation. The explanation was not insisted upon by Miss Dunn; yet she held it possible that the 'past-life regressions' which Bloxham had obtained were not what he took them to be, genuine regressions, but fakes produced by 'interlopers' – mischievous next-world persons, I gathered, like the 'playboys' Lang had warned me of when projecting to meet with Marjorie.

The whole subject needed further study and naturally I intended to seek Lang's view when next I had the opportunity. Meanwhile, through reading and reflection, I tried for any exploration which might be possible. Concerning the next-world communicators who denied the fact of reincarnation I could only speculate; but I managed to cover useful ground in regard to hypnotic regressions.

One or two books on the general subject of hypnosis to which I referred were concerned primarily with the practice of the subject. They threw little or no light on what might actually be taking place in the hypnotic state. To understand that was obviously important. It helped, I felt, to reflect on some experience I personally had had.

This was not as hypnotic subject – but in the active role of the hypnotist. It was with my father in fact as the hypnotic subject – in the few years before his death and when he was suffering a trying illness. Often sleep, which he greatly longed for, evaded him; and – perhaps with no special hope in mind – he had asked me if there was nothing I could do. I had never practised hypnotic suggestion before; but I was aware of the technique. It seemed worth trying – in order to give him some sleep; and I put it to him whether I had his full co-operation. He assured me that I had. So I made the attempt.

The result never ceased to astound and puzzle me. He was asleep within ten seconds – and he remained asleep for the period of one hour, according to the instruction that I had given him. Our family doctor approved of the treatment; and the device became one to which we resorted if it seemed necessary. It always functioned – if anything more easily each time; and I found myself confident that I could induce peaceful sleep within seconds.

Looking back now, the significant thing was the control I could exercise upon my father's state of consciousness – I could totally divert his awareness from everything which, through the channel of his physical body, had been streaming in upon his mind. As a switching of consciousness, it possessed something akin to my own switch of consciousness when (on two separate occasions now) I had – with projection of my psychical body – transferred my awareness to this other body to enable me to meet with and see Marjorie. Whereas in this latter respect I had switched my consciousness to the psychical body, with my father I had no more that switched his consciousness away from his physical body. I reflected upon David Young's clairvoyance, by way of contrast, as a further example of the control of consciousness. David Young it seemed could (through the exercise of his volition) divert his consciousness so as to see Marjorie in her world while still retaining the normal consciousness that makes use of the physical body. This was a rearrangement of consciousness of a more complex kind – inducing the characteristic twofold consciousness of the clairvoyant. Considering Bloxham's regressions, it was clear that the state of consciousness which, with regression, he induced in his patients was also twofold.

The evidence is that – like a clairvoyant – his patients remained conscious in the normal sense: they stayed aware of Bloxham and of their surroundings. Besides this there impinged upon their consciousness an influx from an entirely different quarter: not, as in David Young's twofold state, a stream of data gathered directly from the world of the next-life but, so it appeared, a controlled stream of data drawn from the memory storage of the patient himself. This controlled stream is formed by the mind of the patient into a reconstruction of earlier experiences.

It was also interestingly if incidentally apparent that such a reconstruction – although derived from stored memories – has to be distinguished sharply from the reconstructions of ordinary memory. Bloxham's patients relived, under his hypnosis, many terrifying experiences. In these experience they exhibited *all* the natural fear of a future that holds impending peril: fear that is fully real because what is going to happen remains unknown. In the normal remembering of events, one can recall times of fear; but equally, the quality of such memory being what it is, the recall may not inspire fear. One may know that fear is not supported because simultaneously one can see that the events then lying ahead do not bear it out. Bloxham's patients in their reconstructed lives could (quite clearly on the evidence) not look ahead – so they were not remembering in the ordinary sense of the term. After some fashion, the hypnotic influence was causing the data held in memory storage to be withdrawn only in the order of their actual time sequence. Like this the mind of the patient needed to interpret the data in a strict accord with the sequence of happenings that he once before experienced in real life. In those circumstances fear in recall takes on the quality of real fear.

But, to keep to the main subject, did these comparisons make it any more apparent how an 'interloper' might intervene in the hypnotic state? The answer has to be yes: not entirely clearly, most certainly, but definitely suggestive of a resolution in the light of the parallelism between the hypnotic state, as a twofold state, and the clairvoyant-type twofold state of consciousness shown by David Young. Mrs. Millicent Young can be cited usefully in exactly the same way. As she switched to the clairaudient state – and could then hear the voice of a next-world person in the perfectly normal auditory way – she experienced a click which signalled her extension of consciousness: the sudden change to an openness to next-world control of her aural mechanisms. It was possible that the parallelism of the hypnotic state extended to this kind of added sensitivity – and to susceptibility of control of the patient's speech mechanisms to next-world influence.

Was it though possible – beyond this – to see some marked likelihood of events happening in such a way? Lang had told me categorically that if he wished to take over the sense and motor system of a medium then he must substitute his own body for the medium's psychical body (Chapters 4 and 10): that was essential. I recalled certain events illustrating this necessity in most unconventional circumstances. A lady related to my friend Bob had developed pneumonia while staying with him and his wife Doreen in Trinidad. As this relative was thought to be dying, Dr. Lang was asked to attend and treat her. Lang was successful in his treatment; but, in the account he gave me later at Aylesbury, he stated that on arrival he found the patient so near to death that the psychical body was already starting to separate from the physical. Because he wished to speak to Bob, he removed the patient's psychical body entirely and substituted his own. He was then able to give Bob instructions concerning the further treatment of the patient. All of these considerations seemed to offer some understanding in the interloper issue.

If the psychical body of the patient should be displaced to any significant extent under the control of the hypnotist, then an interloper could presumably follow the procedure that was adopted by Lang in order to pass on his nursing instructions. So, if the hypnotic suggestion should tend on this fashion to make the patient vacate his physical body, even only slightly, the final result could be of the same kind as when a highly able medium like George Chapman voluntarily causes his psychical body to vacate his physical body, and so allows the use of the latter. The door, one might say, would have been unlocked, and set ajar, for the interloper to enter if he wished. I could not argue out the matter further – there existed, at least, this real possibility.

My first opportunity to speak with Lang at Aylesbury on these topics was the 18th January, 1978; and we were then able to go into the subject – following up the discussion at one or two succeeding meetings in particular respects. It seemed that I had been reflecting on the right lines; but the talks went further than the interloper problem and reviewed the whole question of the conditions in which regression and past-life regression could be regarded as reliable.

On the interloper matter, Lang agreed that under hypnosis there can exist some risk of the door becoming opened to the interloper – even if it is only just opened. There was, he stated, a similar risk when a person is heavily drunk: that condition can also induce some degree of separation of the psychical body from the physical. An interloper is, in such circumstances, able to gain control. It does not happen often; but it could happen – and as he had agreed it can happen under hypnosis.

Looking generally at the subject of hypnotic regression, he pointed out that there is always present the risk – a primary risk – that the patient is not regressing to past experience, rather he is merely creating a fantasy. The obtaining of a more or less exact repetition of the account by the patient when under hypnosis again at a later date is the right check – and it was applied by Bloxham with Jane Evans. Then he remarked – and this goes back to the interloper possibility – the fact of historic verification of the patient's story of a past life is not to be taken as proof that the patient was recounting events of his previous-life experience. An interloper could give an accurate and verifiable account of a previous life of his own. To verify that account historically is to show only that the interloper was recalling well the details of his own earlier life.

Lang saw this situation as likely with a recorded regression series I mentioned in example of good historical verification. The series gave ostensibly the accounts of differing past lives of a woman patient. In one life, which was verified, the subject of the life was not a woman, but a man. The change of sex might have been genuine – that is to say the life could have been lived by the patient despite as a man – but Lang took it as suspect: a true change would entail physiological and psychological incompatibilities (which cause disturbances – for which reason such a change is to be avoided). The verified male history he felt likely to be that of an interloper – and if he was right then the change of sex gave away the intrusion.

Intruder deception could always be detected if the hypnotist was able to collaborate with some next-world observer of the occasion – to whom of course the intrusion would be obvious. A collaborator like this could even take positive steps to prevent the intrusion.

Normally, and subject to check against fantasy, Lang was satisfied that the bulk of past-life regressions are genuine – a view that seems only reasonable, since otherwise hypnotic regression in psychotherapy could not constitute the distinctly reliable instrument which it is. The hypnotic conditions are the same irrespective of whether regression relates to earlier events of an individual's experience lying in his present life, or lying in some life before that. Concerning the Bloxham tapes Lang regarded them as good material providing in themselves strong support in favour of the truth of reincarnation.

Before leaving the subject of past-life regression by hypnosis, I note Lang's general comments on the phenomenon itself. "You can say," he summarized, "that the hypnotic suggestion *opens the mind to the life.*" This was not to imagine that the life was actually relived in the induced state – however much the experience was full of reality; nor to suppose that is was simply being remembered. In its own particular way it was an experience of the life – but essentially a reconstruction, rather than the real thing. Importantly, the activity of the will was absent.

It has seemed to me, since our talks, that one might look on hypnotic regression as a halfway house between *remembering* and *actually living.* There is one highly interesting and colourful fact which bears on this and stands out strongly from Bloxham's records. It is that his patients, when in past-life regression, would answer his questions on events of the life they were then re-experiencing with the personality and knowledge they possessed at the time. They had therefore – in contrast to remembering – merged into the past life to the marked degree that this demands.

As a philosophical point, and at the end of the talks, I remarked how the fact that suggestion under hypnosis is necessary in order to elicit the details of a past-life raised questions the answers to which might be illuminating on the purpose of reincarnation. It was clear he had chosen his words with particular care when he stated that "the hypnotic suggestion *opens* the mind to the life." Normally the memories of a past life are *closed off* from the mind. Why was this? So often the mere fact of recalling one's mistakes enables one to avoid making such mistakes again. If we remembered the errors we had made previous to our present existence, would that not be a great assistance in preventing repetition now?

"Yes," replied Lang, "but it is even better if you can reach the pitch of development in which you turn to the right thing to do naturally and instinctively – without having to refer back." I had suspected an answer like this; and it added to the developmental rationale of reincarnation.

I felt the whole study took one to the edge of major questions. I wondered whether any simple terms existed by which the amnesia we experience towards past-life events, amnesia which can be overcome by hypnosis, could be understood more completely: in the sense for instance of a *modus operandi*. When one has said that the hypnotic suggestion lifts the amnesia there remains the question: but *as a mechanism* exactly how?

On the evidence, the amnesia is not apparently absolute even ordinarily – without the aid of hypnosis many people, it seems to be the case, can recall events of high trauma in a previous life, though other events cannot be brought back. Was it possible to gain an idea of how the channel between consciousness and the data storage of events by the psyche is selectively operated, so as to offer some reasoned and fundamental account? There was no chance to follow this up with Lang; but, in mediumistic conversation, I was able to consider the question with Marjorie. We did not get very far with it. Since it is a question which takes one into the realm of the psyche itself there was – it seemed – no answer that can easily be given. You could state, Marjorie observed, that the amnesia arises from the way in which, in forming the complete human individual, the psyche naturally associates with the physical body.

The association is looked at in Appendices III and IIIA which go into the nature of the psyche and of its disposition towards the physical body. The ideas run to some technicality; but, granted that amnesia rests with such disposition, there are clearly the elements of a mechanism in explanation of the past-life hypnotic phenomenon: the hypnotic suggestion, in circumstances of the co-operation of the patient, changes the psyche disposition in such a way as to re-establish selectively those channels by which memory-storage tracts of the psyche were in past lives accessible to the patient's consciousness.

But, all such matters of understanding apart, did I find out anything from my various follow-up conversations to throw light on the puzzling contradiction of communicator evidence which I came upon with Miss Dunn? Yes, I did. Lang's comments concerning other communicators from his world who deny the fact of reincarnation made a most interesting exposé. When I came to the point, he told me he had no wish to impugn the integrity of such communicators – he made this quite plain. "What you must know," he said, "is that they are people you would class very specially within the term *ecclesiastical* – besides which it is possible in our world to live in very isolated communities. These people are part of communities of this kind with few exchanges beyond their own boundaries. They have very special beliefs about the course life takes. They consider that people live their life on earth, and then go on after that to live in heaven as the final state. People holding such beliefs do not return again to earth."

Lang's last statement was consistent with his early assertion that a reincarnation is always voluntary, and a matter of aspiration. But Lang had more to say. It was in fact not strictly true that no one ever returns to earth from such communities. "There is a leak," he continued, "and it cannot be prevented. Reincarnation is the natural course, and in the end these special ecclesiastical dogmas are powerless to stop the leak. Eventually a true understanding comes to people, and they follow that."

"You may be sure that reincarnation is the general rule," he asserted most positively, "and it is so with all ordinary people, and with all classes and callings of life." I gathered that people holding and professing religious belief are almost always to be included amongst what he called *ordinary people*. With the specially formed communities he had spoken of, one was concerned with views that are overwhelming strong.

He said, if I had any doubts, that I would inevitably discover the truth of reincarnation for myself. He knew so far as he was concerned that reincarnation is a fact – *because he could remember his previous lives.*

Chapter Sixteen

SCIENCE AND A NEW APPROACH

Introductory Comments

The chapter begins with important developments that enable the psychical phenomenon of materializations to be understood rationally. But the outlook of the chapter runs at the same rational level far beyond the ambit of this phenomenon.

The phenomenon today is often regarded as a curiosity of small significance. What follows will show that not to be true. The phenomenon when it is understood – and as will be clear – is like a springboard to a new view upon the world. With this it will be seen why Marjorie had impressed upon me so strongly (Chapter 6) that she attached strategic significance to knowledge; in particular knowledge on the lines of the new physics.

It will also be seen, purely as an incidental, why such great scientific investigators of materialization as Sir William Crookes, Sir Oliver Lodge, Sir J. J. Thomson, Lord Rayleigh (all prominent physicists) and Charles Richet (physiologist and Nobel Prize winner in the field of Physiology or Medicine in 1913) failed notably to gain insight into the phenomenon – though assured of its fact. The then physics – the only science to which they could turn – was inadequately advanced. In the past half century science has changed radically; and it is able to offer now sufficient basis for good insight into the phenomenon.

Beyond the materialization phenomenon the selfsame basis holds out also an entirely wider understanding of the nature of the world.

Materialization Phenomena

I return to the nudge – as I called it at the start of Chapter 14 – that Marjorie gave me with the conclusion of our second meeting *via* Mrs. Young. And I return to when – shortly after – I realized Marjorie wanted to go into detail concerning her materialization in my bedroom.

Then I had witnessed, so it seemed to be, the same flux of matter of some kind from my body which is often evident in photographs taken of materialization events – the flux I also noticed in photographs Miss Dunn showed me at Stanstead.

In Marjorie's materialization I had observed this emergent flux take on form –

the form of her face – in much the same way that can be gathered from the photographic evidence of similar events.

What is the nature of the emergent matter? How is it possible that it can be dislodged – as presumably it must be – from the human body from which it is thus taken? How can this be done without harm to the human body? How, moreover, having become detached in the first place is it forced out of the body? By what means then is it caused to assume the features of some other-world person (as I had seen with Marjorie)? How is it eventually returned, and the original situation restored? These were questions that I saw now to be posed. I did not know the answer to any of them.

To assist their study I asked Mrs. Young if she could give me another meeting. She was willing to do this; but I realized that the difficulties attending it were great. The mind of Mrs. Young must be almost devoid of the concepts of science – and it was in such terms that I knew we must progress if we could. Marjorie was acutely aware of the problem; and she was clear that if she tried to *talk* to me – even in the simplest scientific language – the mediumistic mechanism would falter: she would be able to convey little or nothing to me. Despite this we had the meeting; and it was certainly not unsuccessful.

Mrs. Young could receive images; and, even if she could not understand them, she could describe them for me to interpret their scientific significance. This was the tactic to which Marjorie primarily resorted. While it was slow, it was also effective.

When I left the meeting I knew that the emergence of the formative matter from the human body is due to two separate beams or fluxes of radiation – radiation akin to light. One beam has the role of detaching small fragments of body matter. The other is devised so as to expel them. This expulsion is by virtue of the pressure that radiation can exert upon matter lying in its path. It is the same kind of pressure by which the stars are inflated; and which is exhibited by the light and other radiations from the sun as such radiation forces the tenuous matter of the tail of a comet to lie in a direction always outwards from the sun. It is light-like radiation pressure, Marjorie was telling me, which is active to drive fragments of body matter out from the tissues of the body when once they were freed.

But how are the expelled particles initially detached? Marjorie invited me to contemplate the disruptive force that light can exert upon matter.

In broad terms it is not difficult to follow what she was expressing; but the more detailed aspects call for some preliminary explanation.

Firstly it is useful to go back to the Greek idea of the atom of a substance (Chapter 8): the minimum particle of the substance which cannot be further reduced in size by splitting short of the loss of the characteristic properties of the substance. Today we refer in general to such least particles as *molecules* – reserving a rather particular meaning for the term *atom*. This is primarily because it has been found that there exists in nature a range of fundamental substances which are fundamental in the sense that all other substances can be formed from them; but also because, this being so, it is convenient to call only the least particles of the fundamental substances by the name *atoms*. On this convention we can say that all molecules are built up as groups of these atoms. The atoms can be thought of as the building bricks of the structures of

149

molecules. The fundamental substances are known as elementary substances or elements.

Clearly the atoms which in combination constitute a molecule must hold to one another more or less tightly. Chemists refer to the grip by which one atom binds to another in a molecule as the bond between them; and as a matter of physics it is known that any such bond corresponds to a certain energy. If this energy – which is spoken of as the binding energy – is supplied appropriately the bond will fail and the atoms fall apart.

Marjorie – it was clear – was reminding me that the electromagnetic energy of radiations like light can be disruptively transferred to atoms to destroy the bonding between them. Here quite obviously was the essence of a mechanism by which molecular structures of human body tissue could become broken up into part structures – fragments of the originals. Moreover, with such a mechanism, it was not hard to see how fragments detached in this way could be formed of a size sufficiently small to allow them to be forced under radiation pressure through the interstices of the body tissue: so that they could be expelled from the body. Without for the moment tracing it further that was the theory, as I gathered it from Marjorie, of the formative matter of materializations. This matter, she was instructing me, is the matter which Richet, encountering it in practical studies, called *ectoplasm.*

By this time we had fully taken up the session period which Mrs. Young could give; and I was enlightened – *and left puzzled also*. What sort of light was it that Marjorie was speaking of? Any light-like radiations of which I knew could not harmlessly penetrate the body to an appreciable depth – or if they did then I felt they could not possess the level of energy necessary for the bond-breaking processes.

Going over the ground I came strongly to the opinion that Marjorie was not thinking of any light-like radiations of the kind that we know in our world. The radiations she had in mind were electromagnetic radiations belonging to her world. This I felt sure of as a mental impression from her – an impression that was later confirmed.

It helps the understanding of the ideas Marjorie had been conveying through Mrs. Young to consider what it means to say that light is electromagnetic. The study of electric and magnetic forces was greatly advanced by Michael Faraday in the latter part of the first half of the 19th century. One of his achievements was to show, experimentally, that these two forces of nature are interrelated: knowing about the one you can know also about the other. In 1855 James Clerk Maxwell, basing his ideas on those of Faraday, showed mathematically how electric and magnetic forces could be brought together into one unifying and symmetrical theory. The mathematical equations recognize explicitly the symmetry between the two forces. It is a theory which is outstanding. That is true to an altogether remarkable degree: long before relativity was formulated, and for unrelated factual reasons, the theory satisfied the requirements of mathematical form which relativity was going to lay down as general prerequisites of validity. But then again in a remarkable way the theory predicted of the electric and magnetic forces a very special result: the two forces acting together, in a perfect example of the symmetry shared between them, must be able to propagate in a *wave motion* with a speed which is just the speed of light. Light for long had been regarded as a wave motion of some kind. Now the actual nature of the motion was revealed: it was electromagnetic. In 1886 Hertz carried out experiments which verified these ideas.

Couple with such ideas the principle later established (on experimental grounds) by Lord Rutherford, that the structure of the atom is electrical, and it becomes apparent how a wave train of light in falling upon atoms can exert an influence upon them – an influence which could even be sufficient to disrupt any bonding between them. These were ideas implicit in Marjorie's image-dominated instruction.

Her exposition was given in the February of 1978. I had already participated in a meeting with Dr. Lang, Marjorie being also present, when the subject of materialization was to the forefront. That was in the January of 1978. It was not a meeting taken up especially with the explanation of the subject. For that reason, and not only from the general standpoint of the present section of this chapter but also from the standpoint of the meeting with Lang, it seemed a benefit to set down first of all, as I have, Marjorie's illuminating explanation of the underlying mechanisms.

At the meeting with Lang there was not the time to go into the functioning of materialization – this he was leaving to Marjorie. What he did was to carry out a most impressive experiment.

His aim here was to illustrate the phenomenon itself; and in doing this he used me as the subject and physical medium of the demonstration. He wanted particularly and practically to exhibit the character of ectoplasm.

Early in the meeting he had indeed explained that ectoplasm consists in material fragments derived from the body tissue of a medium, and that these are of a wide variety. The fragments can – as such – be used to build up the tissue structures of another human body. What Lang now proposed to do was to detach such fragments from my own body and to collect them – in a small quantity – so that I could see for myself what ectoplasm looked like.

He asked me to recline on his operating couch; and he said I was to relax. He next took a wad of folded paper tissue and laid it across my forehead. It largely, but incompletely, covered my forehead; and it was entirely dry as he laid it in place. There was little more than a second's pause – and then I heard, it seemed in my ears, a rasping hiss which was brief in duration, of the order of a second. A moment later he was saying: "Take off the paper, and look at it." I removed the paper; and rose from the couch. The paper was still dry – except that a patch about the size of a 2p piece lying on the side placed next to my forehead was coated with a clear pink liquid which reflected light well. Apart from the pinkish colouration, the liquid had the appearance of glycerine. There looked to me something like 100 milligrams of the fluid; and it was starting slowly to soak into the tissue. "That," stated Lang, "is ectoplasm from your body." I noticed how there was an area on my forehead – corresponding in location to the patch on the paper – which was tingling. The tingling area was quite dry. It continued very slightly smarting for the rest of the afternoon, and during the evening; but next morning the sensation had cleared up.

Talking with Marjorie in a mediumistic conversation to which I shall very shortly come, she told me that the fragment size was never much more than a few millionths of a centimetre. She also then informed me – hard to credit as I found it – that I myself had been the source of the radiations detaching and forcing out the fragments from my body. Lang had been able to induce in me such an emission of radiant energy; and that was exactly what she had accomplished when she had materialized near to me just after I had settled into bed (Chapter 1).

But Lang himself, with the demonstration, wanted me to know more of the subject and especially about the materialized form. The ectoplasm, as it built up the form, did not normally take on the full density of body tissue. Although it built up true body tissue, there was this difference. You could say that the texture is spongy. Nevertheless, so he stated, it is firm to the touch. It is also a little warmer than normal body temperature – by something like one or two degrees centigrade. As often happened, Lang's medical interests caused him to divert from the subject – but to say something of distinct interest. It would be clear to me now, he told me, that he could take body matter from his medium and transfer it to a patient, so as to reconstruct a damaged organ. On a particular day he might, in total, use up to seven pounds of George Chapman's body weight.

Lang turned to procedural matters affecting the study I was making. There were unfortunately various difficulties which must be hampering to the study – and to the whole developing programme that Marjorie had in mind. To pursue these things with Lang himself – in more than a cursory fashion – must encroach impossibly upon George Chapman's time. Mrs. Young indeed had rendered most useful help; and Lang rated her sensitivies at a high level; but with her mediumship I would find that progress – of the special kind Marjorie now wanted to make – must be painfully slow. It seemed that assistance of a rather different nature was needed. Tentatively Lang spoke of Mr. William Elton – whom I have already mentioned in Chapter 13. Elton, he said, could work in a deep, if not a full, trance state; and Marjorie would be able to use him. Of his present address Lang was uncertain; but if I could find Mr. Elton, and he was willing to help, then advance should be greatly speeded. This in fact was vitally important because there was much more ground than just that of materializations to be entered upon. George Chapman was able to tell me how I could make the necessary contact. Fortunately Mr. Elton agreed; and before long communication became very usefully extended.

The first meeting *via* Mr. Elton – with its strong element of the unexpected – stays in my mind as a highly eventful occasion. It was on the 13th April, 1978. Mr. Elton I found to be a man well into his sixties. His greeting was cordial; but he enlightened me when I had come to know him better that it disguised considerable uneasiness concerning the fact I was a scientist. I did not understand this when he told me. The advances of science have rested simply with careful and patient enquiry. There is however I am now aware an apparent history of psychical enquiry allegedly scientific but more akin to the Spanish Inquisition than to science. That I merely note – it was exactly what Elton had had in mind.

Mr. Elton is possessed, I found, of no training or interest in science; and – from the standpoint of evidence and in regard to the scientific information I was to gain through him – this has to be rated an advantage.

There was the disadvantage of his lack of scientific vocabulary; but this lack was not total; and there was never the need to resort to the picture language which, as Dr. Lang informed me at my next meeting with him, he and Marjorie had decided would be necessary at the February meeting *via* Millicent Young.

The session lasted about an hour and a half. It took Elton something like fifteen seconds to adjust to a condition of light trance. He functioned at first – if briefly – in a manner entirely identical with that of David Young: although he became aware of other-world visitors present, he remained fully aware of me, and could hear and speak with me. Holding this awareness condition he shortly however went on to speak under the control of one and another of the next-world visitors. In subsequent sessions he allowed his control state to go deeper. He then became entirely unaware of me; but very directly responsive to the other-world person speaking through him. If for instance it was Marjorie and she smiled then her smile lit up his features. If she laughed then he laughed. If I tripped up in my thoughts as I spoke, a half-puzzled half-teasing expression might appear on his face. The state, though deeper than on the first occasion, never became the full trance practised by George Chapman. The voice I felt – though carrying modulations characteristic of Marjorie if it was she who was speaking – always remained essentially the voice of William Elton. Sometimes it could be deeper, or crisper, or faster distinctly than that naturally of William Elton; and I assumed – having no real basis of comparison except in Marjorie's case – that these differences reflected the personalities speaking through him; but there seemed to be present in every instance a background of quality that was Elton's. With Marjorie the tone was a softer one than with Elton himself.

Going to the meeting I had taken with me a sheaf of listed questions; and I had anticipated that I should be able to start on these as soon as Mr. Elton had adjusted his mental state appropriately. I found myself, on the contrary, being addressed at some length by a person who talked with authority, and at the same time with the natural affection that exists within a family. It was Marjorie's paternal grandfather.

He had been making a wide study of present-day thinking in our world, he stated; and he related it to the course of human evolution which must take place as the future develops. Compared with the present state of the world, mankind would finally attain tranquillity. That would lie with the increase of man's mental powers and of his knowledge. He placed stress upon knowledge, and contrasted it with the unrealistic notions spread across the world at this moment. As man gained in knowledge, and correspondingly in wisdom, so his mind would arrive at an inward peace and an outward and far more profound sensibility of the great beauty of the Universe.

At the start of the monologue I had felt disconcerted that precious question time was being lost; but as this unanticipated oration proceeded I recognized I was listening with an increasing interest. The speech lasted about twenty-five minutes, and its conclusion made clear its prime aim: it was to encourage me in the writing of this book.

Marjorie had also brought my mother's mother. She, too, encouraged me to press on with my researches and my efforts. There were others present – one to my surprise, Ludwig Boltzmann, whose ideas (significantly) lie at the root of modern physics. In the end Marjorie spoke – at first on purely personal things. With her characteristic vivacity she became teasing – and I enjoyed her light-heartedness. After that she was serious – her accident, tragic without question for both of us, was the means by which she could expand my horizons as she never could have done had she lived. Then I received the go-ahead: "Fire away with your questions."

There were many; and I was unsure if time would avail for us to get very far with them. About forty-five minutes had already gone. But Elton was able to continue his trance state for another three quarters of an hour, and this was sufficient.

He had told me before we started that he could not promise a session time of more than an hour. Thinking very much of this I hurried therefore with some points on the book that I wanted settled. This brought me quickly to the subject of materialization.

I was keen before anything else to obtain verification of what I felt I had learned from Marjorie through Mrs. Young. I found that I had understood Marjorie then without mistake; but she immediately took the subject much further – first making the statement (to which I have referred earlier in this section) that when she had used me as a medium it was I who had been the source of the respective electromagnetic radiations which were operative: those detaching the ectoplasmic fragments from my body tissue and those forcing the fragments free.

In demonstrations of materialization mediumship the situation, she then said, was often similar – but not always. There was an alternative course of procedure in which the operative radiations are produced by special apparatus. By this, of course, she meant apparatus constructed in her world by scientific experts of her world. I could think of this equipment – to get a rough idea – as a rather complicated laser. It was necessarily complicated because the number of different vibration frequencies of the radiations needed was great; and the frequencies required moreover to be exactly chosen. I will explain the broad significance of these particular statements shortly; but for the moment I will continue with Marjorie's statements.

What she next said was as interesting as Dr. Lang's comment on the texture of the materialized form. She in contrast was talking about the medium's body tissue which supplies the formative ectoplasm. The effect of the fragment-detaching radiations upon the body tissue is to leave it *in a porous state which might be described as finely honey combed.* The tissue becomes depleted in many small regions (within each body cell); and these depletion regions are more or less uniformly distributed throughout that part of the body from which the fragments are taken. On this fashion, while a considerable amount of matter may be withdrawn, the general body structure remains intact and there is no disastrous depletion. The effect follows naturally since the radiations interact at random with the tissue.

In regard to the materialized form itself, this form becomes apparent because the detached fragments released in order to construct the form settle upon the (psychical) body structure of the materializing next-world person. They use this body structure much in the sense of an aligning template (vis-à-vis its likeness to the physical body and its similar body-cell size). Depositing themselves in appropriate dispositions under the influence of this guiding structure they then link with their neighbours. As they link they yield up the binding energies of the linkages, and the whole mass of reconstructed tissue becomes raised in temperature in consequence – by the small amount which Dr. Lang had mentioned when speaking on the subject of the texture of the materialized form. The structure tends to be incomplete, Marjorie added, because deposition is contrived to occur throughout so large a volume that the number of fragments available is far from sufficient for full tissue formation.

Normally, therefore, though true tissue is made, the materialized form is highly sponglike (though not visibly so). Thus – as Dr. Lang had stated – it is distinctly less dense than body tissue naturally.

Why did Marjorie speak of the use of a large number of radiation frequencies? – and why was it necessary for these to be exactly chosen?

The answers are highly informative. For one matter – and of a distinct and general interest – they suggest a next-world physics running on lines closely parallel with those of the modern physics known to us. For another – and but one amongst others bearing more immediately on the materialization phenomenon – they show why it is that the fragment-detaching radiations free fragments of body tissue from the person providing the ectoplasmic material but do not free particles of the clothing worn by that person.

To throw light upon the situation I have to turn to principles which constitute the start of the modern theory of matter. This theory in recognition of an outstanding characteristic is named *quantum theory*. Fortunately, although quantum theory at large is not simple, its starting ideas contain no special difficulty.

At the outset of Chapter 12 I alluded to the divide lying between the scientific thinking of the 19th century and that of the 20th. The impact of quantum principles takes us to the moment of cleavage itself; and in fact to the year 1900. In that year the great German physicist Max Planck formulated with mathematical precision the point of view which came radically to change the scientific outlook on the world. It concerns all interactions between electromagnetic radiation and matter.

These interactions include just that kind of interaction by which, when you sunbathe, you experience the thermal radiations from the sun warming your body. You feel the warmth because the interaction between such radiations and your body transforms the electromagnetic energy of the radiations into thermal energy in the matter of which your body is formed. Then again the interactions Plank had in mind include interactions that work in the reverse sense. An example lies in your experience of cold should you walk into the freezing atmosphere of a cold room, a room devised specifically for refrigeration. Your body matter emits electromagnetic radiations at the expense of the thermal energy content of your body – and in the room you feel the loss in a sensation of chill. We do not have to think merely of radiations of the character of thermal radiations. The electromagnetic radiations of rather higher frequency which we call visible light can similarly be emitted and absorbed by matter – likewise those electromagnetic radiations of very much lower frequency known as radio waves. Generally speaking matter is emitting and absorbing electromagnetic radiations all the time – and over a wide range of character.

It is necessary in outlining Planck's theory to turn to two concepts which it will be seen are of prime significance. We have considered the energy of electromagnetic waves. Wave energy is one prime concept. Wave frequency is the second. What specifies a particular character of electromagnetic radiation is the wave frequency of its motion. This frequency is the recurrence rate of the oscillation or vibration, at any given point, of the wave motion. The two concepts and the way in which they are together involved are vitally important in the new outlook in physics. Max Planck was the first to demonstrate the momentous nature of this new outlook.

Planck was facing the impasse the physics of the 19th century had reached when trying to account for the known characteristics of the interaction of electromagnetic radiation and matter. There had been done much experimental work. This was in regard to steady-state conditions of interaction – in which the absorption of electromagnetic radiation by matter is just balanced by the emission of electromagnetic radiation by the matter. Such conditions can hold in a totally enclosed cavity – of which an oven is an example.

The experimental study had revealed clearly the way in which in such equilibrium conditions the density of electromagnetic energy that is related to a given frequency varies from one frequency to another. There was always a frequency at which the energy density peaked. For higher frequencies it steadily fell away. Existing theory – classical physics – could give some account of the rising energy density below the peak. It entirely failed to account for the peak and the steady fall beyond it. Greatly astray, it even predicted that the total steady-state electromagnetic energy within a cavity like an oven must be infinite! The last result known as the *ultra-violet catastrophe* is one of the reasons why classical physics had to be abandoned.

Planck was able to construct a new form of theory that accounted exactly for the experimentally determined energy distribution in equilibrium conditions. He was able moreover to show how the peak of the energy distribution shifted with the operative temperature – entirely as was found experimentally.

To arrive at the new theory Planck turned to certain very fundamental ideas of Ludwig Boltzmann – which earlier he had intensely opposed. They were that physics should recognize in energy a similar *discreteness* to that which we see in matter in the form of atoms. Planck therefore considered that the absorption and emission of electromagnetic energy by matter must be in unit amounts – no other quantity of energy ever being involved. The unit amount he called a *quantum*. Absorption and emission had always to be in whole numbers of *quanta*. To complete the theory, the magnitude of the energy quantum had to be a universal constant multiplied by the wave frequency of the interacting wave. The universal constant is a very small number, which is now termed Planck's constant.

Max Planck's striking success in quantum terms with the problem of interaction at the interface between matter and radiation was followed by Einstein's equally striking and successful application of quantum ideas in 1905 to end the impasse in physics over the emission of electrons from matter under the action of incident light. Einstein showed that with electromagnetic radiation the energy quantum is not something to be found just at the interface with matter: it was characteristic of the form of the electromagnetic field itself. The electromagnetic field is naturally to be thought of as a hail of quanta – photons as they are now called.

The quantum picture in mind, consider the laser-like apparatus of which Marjorie had spoken. It was apparatus of her world emitting, it is only natural to imagine, radiations of her world. In questions to Marjorie, aimed at checking and double checking that my understanding of the materialization mechanisms was parallel with hers, I started at this point. She assured me that the radiation from the apparatus is both of her world order and is electromagnetic. What I then inevitably inferred from the fact of the apparatus emitting radiation of specific frequencies only, if very many, was that there exist corresponding quantum energies present in the radiation which are equally specific. I also anticipated that these energies must be chosen to match the many differing binding energies of the bonds which needed to be broken in order to detach specific fragments of the tissue structure. If there was an absence of any frequencies corresponding to the binding energies of bonds of the atomic structures of clothing, it followed that clothing would be left intact. Again, with the general low level of interaction between the physical orders of this and the other world, both the fragment-detaching and fragment-expelling radiations must be highly penetrating: a thing which was essential. As to the radiation pressure exerted by the fragment-expelling radiations and forcing the detached fragments out through the body tissue, it was clear that by correctly choosing radiation frequencies to match the quantum absorption energies of the detached fragments the radiation pressure would conveniently affect the detached fragments only and have no influence otherwise. I was able to check all such issues satisfactorily with Marjorie.

In the process of checking, I gathered a fact concerning the formative materialization mechanism which I had suspected. The detached tissue fragments which are deposited upon the (psychical) body structure of the materializing person are held to this jig-like body structure by forces of the nature of van der Waals forces – the selfsame kind of forces which normally hold the psychical body to the physical (Chapter 12).

There were also certain ideas finally to round off the subject. When the transposed matter must necessarily be returned, the whole process is operated in reverse. The materialized form dematerializes under the influence of radiations like those which detached and expelled the ectoplasmic particles in the first place. Now formed again by this process of dematerialization the particles redeposit themselves to complement the tissue they had left depleted in the course of their original formation. In the course of this redeposition they settle into correct position under the aligning influence of the psychical body of the person from whom they had been taken.

A further point, relative both to the initial materialization and to the subsequent dematerialization, was that if detached tissue fragments in their transposition processes are to continue to experience the selective (quantum) driving forces which drive them to deposition, then the fragments must retain their identities. They could become broken down into other particles by the activity of (relatively high energy) white light, and the driving control would not then operate for them. This was a reason for the normal use of (low energy) red ambient lighting in demonstrations of materialization.

With her explanations of the materialization phenomenon in the quantum fashion of the new physics, Marjorie had made good a first and significant part of her scientific objective.

Mystery?

In May, 1978, a month after my Elton meeting, I was talking once more to Dr.

Lang at Aylesbury. It was partly to discuss material for the book, partly to go over some of my newly acquired ideas on materializations. I also wanted to put to Lang a speculation based on this understanding that might resolve an enigma now close upon two thousand years old.

According to the records, with the death of Christ by Roman crucifixion his body was placed in a rock tomb. It was done in haste because of the imminence of the Sabbath and because of Jewish restrictions upon what could be done on this day. The tomb itself was new and belonged to the wealthy Joseph of Arimathaea. He was a member of the town council of Jerusalem, but had not voted in support of the demand for the death of Jesus. In recent times a rock tomb site has been discovered nearby the Damascus gate; and the site has been shown on archaeological studies to fit well with the New Testament account. The location lies close to the present-day bus station on the Damascus road. This station is at the foot of what is now known as Skull Hill, but called in the account Golgotha: "the place of the skull." The bluff of the hill presents a strong semblance of a skull. I am aware of these local facts since my sister has visited the location. It is not the traditionally held site – which does not fit with the records and seems to have been fixed on arbitrarily by Helena the mother of the Roman emperor Constantine the Great (who initiated the evolution of the Empire into a Christian state). The unresolved enigma attaches to the tomb and starts with the night following the Sabbath.

It was necessary to complete burial preparations; and some of the followers of Jesus went very early in the morning to the tomb. The tomb they now found contained no body; and the large closure stone had been rolled aside. What creates the mystery is that the Jewish council had asked for and obtained from the Roman governor, Pontius Pilate, soldiers to be placed on armed guard over the tomb. The intention behind this step was to prevent followers of Jesus stealing the body and then fraudulently declaring the resurrection of Jesus as propaganda. But neither the bewildered disciples, nor the Roman sentries terrified by events they had seen, or the Jewish council knew what had happened. The body on the evidence was never moved – but never found.

If that was the situation it is one which minds brought up only in classical science tend to find incredible. Yet it seemed the quantum explanation of materialization processes could put things in a different light. A scientific rationale of events, which did no violence to the record, looked very possible. Next-world persons arrived as a mission at the scene in the early morning hours. The body was then irradiated to bring about its dematerialization; and the products of dematerialization were used to materialize some members of the mission. It was these materialized persons who brightly illuminated (as I had seen Marjorie in her materialization) terrified the sentries, rolled away the closure stone, and included the 'angels' who later addressed some of the disciples. It was these persons also who folded up the grave clothes and placed them as the disciples found them.

When I had spoken with Lang to review certain ideas concerning materialization, I turned to this speculation on the mystery of the unoccupied tomb. He assured me at once it was more than speculation, even very likely speculation: *it was known to be fact*. Marjorie was present at the meeting; and she had been well aware that I wished to discuss the subject. She had even gone to the trouble of ascertaining the actual time taken to dematerialize the body – and she broke in: it was nearly two hours. Lang did not disagree with this statement. There however for shortness of time we had to leave the matter.

But I came back to one aspect of it in a fascinating talk with Marjorie (*via* William Elton) in October, 1988 – just after the long-anticipated carbon dating of the Shroud of Turin had finally been made and announced in the news media. This shroud, it had been widely believed, was one of the linens found lying in the tomb by the disciples of Jesus when they discovered the tomb was otherwise empty. Since the announced carbon dating placed the origin of the material of the Turin Shroud as falling between 1260 and 1390 A.D. (corrected in the official statement of early 1989 to 1270 – 1380) it seemed with the announcement that the shroud could not by any stretch of imagination be such a relic. My talk with Marjorie made it clear that to hasten to this conclusion was to be over ready to see things in black and white only: there were halftones and overtones present of great interest.

The immediate reason not to be over hasty is that with detailed knowledge of the Turin Shroud it is a strain upon credibility that, fashioned totally in a medieval context, it should have been fashioned in the actual form which it takes. It possesses on it a pale sepia double image of the full figure of a man – as though, had it been the original grave wrapping, the body had lain full length on it leaving an imprint; and then, the cloth having been folded over to cover the full length of the body, it had equally acquired an imprint from the body. What is striking is that the two imprints are totally unnatural – they assume however a natural expression on photographing and inverting the scale of light values. Why, one cannot escape asking, should a medieval artist – contrary to the great realist striving in art of the period – ever conceive of a portrayal in so strange and unreal a mode? That question would be satisfactorily answered if the fact was that the artist had in front of him at the time the original cloth with the same strange kind of image on it. If so, it would also be natural for him to show as he does the crucifixion nails having been driven through the wrists – this in contrast to the fact it was not known in medieval times how that was the manner of Roman crucifixion. Artists without exception had shown the nails through the palms of the hands.

There is an early history of a cloth image of Christ: the image "not made by hands". The words represent the fact that the image was not in pigment. The earliest reference is by St. Jerome quoting from the lost "Gospel of the Hebrews": Jesus apparently gave an instruction. It was on one of his appearances to the disciples after his death. He wanted to ensure the safekeeping of his shroud. But this was, for purely Jewish reasons, an intense embarrassment – the shroud was "unclean" and "defiling" to touch. Moreover it carried something totally banned from Jewish practice: namely an image. For such reasons it was utterly unsafe in Jerusalem, or anywhere in Palestine. In the end it was taken by Thaddaeus, who was one of the outer circle of "the seventy", to Edessa (now the town of Urfa in south eastern Turkey) and presented there to King Abgar V. For the purpose of presentation it was folded in four after doubling so as to show only the head of Christ as a portrait. Folded thus it was overlaid by a trelliswork of gold bands.

Secure in Edessa only in the very short term the shroud slipped out of history in 57 A.D. – and when the tide suddenly turned against the Christians in Edessa.

Ian Wilson, an Oxford historian, has maintained in his work *The Turin Shroud* (Victor Gollancz, 1978) that it is nevertheless possible to trace the shroud, with some fair certainty at least, to the start of the 13th century. It apparently was found in Edessa in the 6th century during extensive rebuilding of Edessa at the direction of Justinian, then emperor-to-be. The building works were necessary subsequent to very heavy flooding. From Edessa it was taken to Byzantium in 944. There it was frequently displayed in the Church of St. Mary of Blachernae. But it became lost again when in 1204 Byzantium was looted by the Crusaders during the Fourth Crusade. Certain facts point to its becoming the possession of knights of the order of the Templars, who brought it back with them on their return to France. Remarkably in 1314 two principal Templars of which one was Geoffrey de Charnay, principal of the order in Normandy, were burned at the stake on the order of the French King, Philip the Fair, for idolatrous veneration of the image of a head.

Notably also in 1356, on the 28th May, there was completed a collegiate church built by Geoffrey de Charny at Lirey in central France. There is ground for thinking this Geoffrey was great-nephew to Geoffrey the Templar – difference of spelling is of little significance in those times. Geoffrey de Charny was one of France's greatest generals. Four months after the inauguration of the collegiate church he was killed fighting at Poitiers against the English led by Edward the Black Prince. Very shortly after this the shroud which is the Turin Shroud was on exposition at the church Geoffrey had built at Lirey.

What Marjorie stated in her conversation with me was that, from her own researches, the tracing of the circumstances of the original shroud by Ian Wilson is essentially correct; but the experiences of the de Charny family had impressed on them that any exposition of the shroud, the original shroud, which had come into their possession might hold dangers for its continued existence which they could not risk. By an extremely ingenious technique a copy was made for exposition. First a figure was sculptured which would give a reasonable resemblance of the strange image when the sculpture was heated so that it would scorch lightly a sheet of linen laid over it. The scorching thus copied what was in fact a scorch image in the original. It needed several attempts to succeed; but a highly accurate image was finally obtained. The image of the Turin Shroud is thus *virtually* a true relic, although the linen material dates back only to the Middle Ages. (The original, on Marjorie's evidence, was hidden for safety not far from Poitiers; but, fragile as it already was, it became subject to rapid deterioration and has long since totally fragmented.)

These statements on the Turin Shroud would be of small account if they did not create the setting for a supremely important question: how was the image caused in the very first place? The statements do clearly create the setting; and the question is a riddle which, like the enigma of the empty tomb, the studies of this book are as Marjorie pointed out particularly well able to resolve. The answer rests with the death process and the activity connected with the electrical body in these conditions. The answer also rests, as Marjorie specifically maintained, with special intent.

Appendix III shows how with death there commences the controlled annihilation of the very great number of electron-positron pairs forming the electrical body. The annihilation energy of each pair is itself great: 1.05 mega-electron-volts. If the total annihilation energy is disposed of steadily over several hours, as it is normally controlled to do, it provides no special effect. Could some sudden flux of the annihilation energy – releasing much greater densities of photon energy – be sufficient to cause scorching of the linen? Very certainly it could – it would require the intent to produce the sudden flux. Moreover, the mechanism would naturally give the strange inversion of the light values which is so untrue to life.

Physics

The Encyclopaedia Britannica describes physics as the "scientific discipline that is concerned with energy and matter and their interactions with one another". The language even for the non-scientific reader cannot fail, at the stage we have now reached, to be familiar. Very much earlier – as in Chapter 8 – I had wanted to find out if the same kind of language applies in the next-world existence: whether there was a real physical aspect of that world in which one could gain enlightenment on lines resembling the physics of our own experience. Marjorie had said categorically there was – it could be called a parauniverse (Chapter 10); and now with materialization processes and the radiations of next-world order used to control them she was clearly thinking of such radiations just like one would in modern physics. Keen for comment I mentioned this specifically to Lang at my meeting with him of May, 1978.

"Yes well, you see," he remarked, "*we live in a quantum world exactly as you do.*" His response triggered off in me a vision of atoms constructed and behaving almost the same as our own atoms. Perhaps he read my mind. His next statement was: "We have atoms here that correspond very much to your own. We have an atom of hydrogen with a central proton and an electron orbiting round it, just as you have an atom of hydrogen in your world – only our electron is a different electron, and our proton is a different proton. They are very much smaller than yours." To have developed this conversation in detail would have made demands on time that was not available; but I could see there existed a strategic question which, if settled, might enable me to embark upon some important homework: a study that could make the physics situation much more clear.

The question related to the radiations from an atom. Such radiations have much to say concerning the character of the atom that emits them. I felt I knew, by transfer of thought from Marjorie, what roughly is the vibration frequency of the light by which they see in her world – that frequency if right must be of great significance.

Since I want to go on to talk of frequencies that are exceedingly high I will digress, for the sake of those not mathematicians, to introduce a shorthand which saves the writing of long sequences of zeros. If we write down the number *one million* as we normally do, namely as 1,000,000, there are six noughts. In the shorthand of index notation of which I am speaking, a million is written 10^6 – and it is a way of stating that a million is the product of six 10's. The number 6 is called the index. In a very simple extension of the shorthand one writes the fraction which is one millionth as 1^{-6}. I mention this extension because I shall also want to speak of numbers which are exceedingly small. As another example of the shorthand, one hundred million must, following out the principle, be set down as 10^8.

Turning back to the subject, the order of the frequency of visible light as we know it is 10^{15} vibrations per second: a very large number – and rather unmanageable expressed normally. Referring correspondingly to light of his world I told Lang it was my impression that its frequency was immensely greater than that of our own – in fact you would have to multiply the frequency of our light by a factor of more than 10^6 so as to equal it. I added that the correct multiplying factor was nearer to 10^8. Lang nodded agreement – certainly, he said, the right multiplying factor was more nearly 10^8 than 10^6. The light frequency we are speaking of is thus of the nature of 10^{22} vibrations per second (a number represented by 1 followed by 22 zeros – ten thousand million million million). My anticipations were that with this figure, *the rough value of the frequency of the visible light emitted by next-world atoms*, I could move forward to discover near enough such fundamental things about these atoms as their size and their massiveness.

But that was not all: I felt it might be possible to find out something on certain major questions. I had accumulated a number of special problems. Why was it that material forms and constructions of the next-world were naturally so permanent (as I noted in Chapter 8)? How (in Chapter 13) was it that, handling a vehicle so fast as her flying machine, Marjorie's brain and reflexes were able to meet the inevitable demands for fantastically rapid action? How, too, was it possible for her body to withstand the enormous accelerations and decelerations of such travel? Our bodies here would disintegrate into pulp under forces the merest fractions of those which her body – normally and naturally – must be able to withstand. The study, because fundamental, could conceivably answer these questions also. In fact, it answered them all from amongst its various conclusions. And thrown in freely it became apparent (as I explain in detail in Appendix III, *The four-dimensional psyche presence*) why the (psychical) body of the next life does not require the intermediary device of the electrical body in order that the psyche should be able to control it (Chapter 4).

To carry me across the gap between the physics of this world order and the physics of the next I required, as I saw when I came to look at things more closely, several stepping stones. My foot was already on the first – I knew the frequencies of visible light in the other world. The next stepping stone lay there in front of me in the form of the elementary quantum theory of the atom due to Neils Bohr. From the way Lang had spoken I felt confident that this theory held good for a hydrogen atom of his world as much as it did for a hydrogen atom of our own. The reason specifically why I looked upon the theory as my next foothold was that it directly relates the frequency of radiations from an atom to the nature of the atom itself.

This theory as it happens is not so much a theory of why in fundamental terms an atom is like it is as a deductive answer to the question of how the atom must be organized if it is to emit the radiations which, from the experimental studies, it is known that it does. With the work on the atom by Lord Rutherford in 1911 it had become clear that the structure of an atom like the hydrogen atom is on the pattern of a very simple solar system. A massive positively-charged particle, a proton, holds in orbit around it a relatively light negatively-charged particle, an electron. The electron is compelled to circulate about the proton by virtue of the electrical force of attraction which – corresponding to gravity in the solar-system pattern – exists between electrical charges of opposite kind. This picture became the picture of the Bohr theory of the atom when in 1913 Bohr introduced into it the principle of quantizing. It was at the time he was studying under Rutherford. What Bohr proposed was that the motion of the circulating electron must be seen restricted to certain special orbits. This limitation was a bold step contrary to accepted physics. It quantized the orbital motion of the atom – in precise technical language it quantized the angular momentum of the circulating electron. This momentum could assume any one only of an equally spaced series of values, starting with a least value set by Planck's constant (actually equal to Planck's constant divided by 2π). The spacing was equal to this least value, and therefore all values of the series were whole-number multiples of the first. With each value there was a specific orbit, and the larger the momentum value the larger the orbit. The quantizing of the angular momentum automatically quantized the energy of the atom. Consequently the larger the momentum value the greater also the quantized energy of the atom.

It was here that the theory linked up perfectly with Planck's theory of radiation emission and absorption by matter. An atom could move up or down in Bohr's quantum scale of orbital momentum and energy by absorbing or emitting respectively a quantum of radiation energy according exactly to the quantum rules of Planck. On this footing the vibration frequencies present in the radiation from emitting atoms mirror precisely the internal transitions – from one quantum state to another – producing the radiation.

If an atom is in its lowest state it cannot of course radiate – it can only absorb. In its lowest state, which is also its most common, the orbital radius is least, and the orbital size then may conveniently be said to specify the size of the atom.

The Bohr theory was vindicated and explained in fundamental fashion – and with a far more developed view of the atom – by the major advances in quantum theory beginning in 1925. But the Bohr picture provided me with an entirely adequate basis for my present purposes.

I needed other stepping stones. For one, I felt sure that the law of force between electrical charges must be of the same essential nature whichever world order I was concerned with. More explicitly I was thinking of the way the advances in quantum theory since 1925 had enabled the mechanism of the electric force between electric charges to be understood: a continuing and inevitably arising exchange of photons produced the force. The mechanism must surely be the same for both worlds; and I took that as firm ground. Its validity was later confirmed to me by Marjorie. I assumed also that in the two world orders protons and electrons stood to one another in the same ratio of masses. I felt this could be made a further stepping stone. The assumption I learned is certainly not exactly true – though closely so. However I found that despite these stepping stones I still could not proceed unless I knew the relative density, in similar circumstances, of the two world orders of matter. I needed that as a still further stepping stone.

On this front I can only say that I experienced an intense pressure to take the density of our world order as greater in the ratio of about 100:1. Marjorie explained to me in due course that the pressure came from her. At one point I felt there might be some ground to contemplate a ratio of 1000:1. But then I found myself being pushed away from this figure, and compelled to write the 100:1 ratio into the calculation.

What I knew could not be assumed was that Planck's constant possessed the same value in both worlds. On the contrary – and this in truth was what the whole calculation was about – I could see that using the starting data of my stepping stones I should be able to arrive at some fair estimate of what Planck's constant must be in Marjorie's world.

From the quantum account I have given thus far it will be clear that the value of the constant imprints an altogether primal stamp upon the physical character of the world order in which it operates. It fixes the grain size, so to speak, of radiation; and in regard to atoms it decides the gradations of their internal states – so that it determines atomic dimensions. The whole texture of a physical order hangs upon it.

All of these ideas set the stage for a second meeting with Marjorie through William Elton. This meeting took place on the 5th July, 1978.

On the occasion Mr. Elton assumed immediately the deeper control state which I have described in the section on materialization phenomena. Marjorie's grandfather was again present; and once more he spoke first. It was on the broad philosophy of life. He confirmed some of the things Dr. Lang had told me – in particular he affirmed that a sequence of several or many incarnations into the life of this world is a natural part of the developmental process of the human ego. However knowing the work load which Marjorie and I had on hand he quickly passed the conversation over to her. I was soon giving Marjorie a summary of the assumptions I had used in my attempt to explore the main physical characteristics of her world. I also told her of the results that, on calculation, flowed from these assumptions. She accepted the assumptions were correct or closely correct.

In regard to the conclusions I came as directly as I could to the acutely interesting question of the relative atomic scales of the two worlds. Lang had presented his world on a much finer pattern than ours: his atoms were much smaller than ours. I considered that now and fairly closely I had come to know by how much they were smaller. But I had to make my approach from the standpoint of Planck's constant – the arbiter of scale as I have explained.

I told Marjorie I had found that this constant in her world was diminutive to a fantastic degree in comparison with what it is in ours. 10^{-30} was the result I had derived for the approximate ratio of the next-world value to our own – meaning that our value is the greater in the ratio of 10^{30} to unity. (If you write that ratio in full you will need to write down a number containing 30 zeros.) Marjorie's comment on my stated figure was that I was nearly right. It would be more nearly correct to say that the ratio is 10^{-29}. That figure was accurate to within about 10 per cent.

Going to my assumptions she said I ought to allow for the fact that the frequency of their visible light is not higher than ours just by a factor of 10^7 – which I had told her I had taken in my calculations as sufficiently accurate – but by a factor which is two to three times higher still. I ought also to take into account the fact that her type of proton was, relatively to its corresponding electron, lighter than ours in the ratio very nearly of two to three. If I took her more precise figures into my calculations I should find her corrective statement on Planck's constant was true.

Here, I remark that Marjorie gave values in fractional form rather than decimal, because – in an important mediumistic respect to which I shall come – she realized that Elton's mind was familiar with fractional relationships, but was not well versed in decimal.

When, a few days afterwards, I worked through my calculations again, introducing the allowances Marjorie had told me to make, I arrived at a ratio equal to 10^{-29} multiplied by a factor of 0.87. It will be noticed that the factor 0.87 brings about a difference from the value 10^{-29} by a little more than 10 per cent: just about what Marjorie had stated I should find.

One might reflect that the agreement between my corrected result and Marjorie's prediction was scarcely astonishing. If she and I were thinking along identical lines, and neither had made a mistake of calculation, then my new result – inevitably – was only the kind of result I should have found. For myself it would have surprised me had things turned out otherwise. As critique however the situation was intended to bear more than its own immediate significance. Marjorie had seized on the approximate nature of my calculations to make her prediction and so extend the logic of events of Chapter 14 even more strongly. The anti-realist view of psychical phenomena was in no small difficulty with the logic of the two episodes of that chapter. As I showed at the end of the chapter, when considering the logic of this present prediction, such a logic detracts even more disastrously from the plausibility of the anti-realist position. Strictly for the purposes of this argument it is sufficient to say that its factual background has here been set out. Yet having seen a little of the setting in physics which called for the quantum view, it is possible to add highly material comment. The anti-realist outlook arose historically from the belief that the inability of classical physics to accommodate psychical phenomena must be a profound objection to their reality – and that this must mount a main requirement they should be explained away. We have seen in the quantum connection – and once more it comes as disaster for anti-realism – that classical physics is not even able to accommodate major physical phenomena. This is a fact still scarcely realized.

In the immediate scientific context, and continuing with the conversation of the meeting, I was able to take up now the subject of atomic dimensions. I said to Marjorie that, corresponding to the minutely small value I had arrived at for Planck's constant in her world, it seemed her kind of hydrogen atom was so small you could arrange 10^7 (ten million) of them side by side across a single diameter of one of our own hydrogen atoms. These latter atoms, it gives a more concrete idea to say, are themselves so diminutive that a side-by-side row of 10^8 (one hundred million) of them could scarcely exceed a length of one centimetre. Marjorie's reaction to the figure of 10^7 came reassuringly. That again was nearly right, she answered. If I amended my assumed figures in the way she had been telling me, I should find it to be an underestimate – though it did not materially change things.

I said to her that there seemed to be one highly important consequence flowing from the exceedingly small scale of such atoms. It was physiological, and when one came to contemplate the speed with which electrical changes could be propagated in the nervous system of the human body. This speed depended largely on chemical change – which relates intimately to the influence one atom exerts upon its neighbour in handing over to it an orbiting electron. The smaller atom could enter more quickly into chemical change since the orbital circulation time was less – orbital velocity was I had found virtually the same.

Nervous impulses in bodies like our own here are, it is true, transmitted in electrical fashion along any one nerve fibre; but they are transmitted by a process which is chemical from one fibre to the next. The chemical process is relatively slow and therefore it is dominating in determining the overall time it takes to pass on a nervous impulse. Thus the speed of nervous transmission depends essentially upon that of chemical change – and so almost entirely I thought upon the time of electron exchange between adjacent atoms. A next-world atom, I remarked, by virtue of its extremely small dimensions must be able to exchange an orbital electron with its neighbour in a minute fraction of the time it takes for one of our own atoms to effect the exchange. Assuming the next-world nervous system similar to our own I would expect the activities of nervous tissue to proceed at a *very* much faster rate in next-world bodies than with us. I argued, in fact, that commensurate with the diminutive scale of next-world atoms the nervous control processes of the next-world human organism must be able – potentially – to operate millions of times faster than those of the human body here. That would resolve the nervous response and reaction problems of her space flight.

Marjorie responded that broadly speaking all this was so. The electron orbital speed is the same with her atoms as with ours. Since human bodies of her world operate in generally similar ways to ours, I was thus justified in concluding that for them the speed of nervous activity – and thus the speed with which the brain could function and muscles could be operated – is almost unbelievably faster than with us.

Mentioning this striking disparity between the activity rates of the physical and psychical bodies to Lang at my next meeting with him at Aylesbury, he commented that the slowing down he inevitably experienced in taking over the use of his medium's brain was something with which he had to bear. I had not spoken of chemical processes but – significantly – he called the slowing down "the *chemical* slowing down".

In referring this physiological subject to the exchange of orbital electrons between neighbouring atoms I did not stop to look at this particular aspect of the activity of atoms with any closeness. It was unnecessary in the circumstances; but I want now to give it further attention because it a key factor in the strength, and durability, of structures – the next subject which I took up with Marjorie.

Earlier in the chapter, in the section on materialization phenomena, I considered the bonds which hold atoms to one another in the formation of substances. The forces which constitute such bonds are the forces that determine the mechanical strength of solid substances. They are commonly called the forces of cohesion; and for a long time the exact way in which they arise eluded physical understanding. Eventually in 1927, and with developments in the quantum view of matter bedwarfing any such initial phases as have been entered upon in this chapter, it became evident that cohesive forces are (precisely) calculable. When two closely adjacent atoms exchange orbital electrons, then – so the mathematical theory showed – it is possible for a binding force to exist between the atoms. Thus the forces of cohesion are electrical; and they must depend upon the electrical charge carried by the electron. Comparing Marjorie's world of matter with the kind of matter known to us, I could see that by applying these ideas an understanding of the relative strength of structural forms in her world must be possible. Besides strength, I might understand the natural permanence I noted in Chapter 8.

Fundamentally I could see that in the ability of a structure to withstand acceleration forces, and to resist impact forces causing erosion, the vital factor is the ratio of the binding force which can be exerted to the inertial mass which is immediately effective. In the accelerative situation this mass is the mass of the accelerated structure. In erosive impact it is that of an impacting body or particle. But I had found in my studies comparing world with world that the charge-to-mass ratio of an electron must be 10^8 (one hundred million) times greater in Marjorie's world than with us. This was a deeply significant figure. It showed that the electrical forces of binding counted for *very* much more in her world than in ours. I did not know by exactly how much – the calculations are anything other than simple – but it stood out that the difference must be enormous.

Marjorie supported all these ideas. She accepted as near enough my figure of 10^8 giving the relatively greater ratio of charge to mass of her world electron. A more accurate statement would place the ratio at three quarters of my value; but that was not material to the argument. The argument was certainly the key to understanding the immutability they naturally experience with structures of her world. And it certainly showed why in her flying machine her body could safely withstand its tremendous accelerations. When I asked her by how much they exceeded the safe limits for our bodies here, she quoted a factor of 10^5 (an excess by one hundred thousand times). On simple calculation the acceleration time, at these levels of performance, to one fifth the speed of light (Chapter 13) can be seen to be of the order of a mere ten seconds! (Marjorie has said the best time she has made is seven seconds – that feels physically very tense.)

This is a point suitable to say more about William Elton's mediumship. It would have been greatly simplifying had there been a medium available whom Marjorie could have used in just the same way that Lang made use of George Chapman. It was totally clear that Lang could express any thought he wished through Chapman. Marjorie put the circumstances precisely to me when – at another meeting through Elton – we found time to talk of the degree of expression which he was able to make available to her: she had to work through the intermediary of his mind – whereas George Chapman was able to permit Lang to bypass his medium's mind. If she could not find a counterpart to her thought in William Elton's mind she could not express that thought through him. I remember an illustration of this when Marjorie's grandfather failed entirely with one sentence in his opening remarks. The sentence was a nonsense. I interrupted to say I could not follow him. He apologized and tried another way of presenting his meaning – which succeeded. Marjorie was wary of this kind of difficulty. That was why – as I have already noted – she had used simple fractions rather than decimals when we had come to arithmetic values. She was able to circumvent difficulty with the index notation, so useful for very large numbers, because with the way things went I used the notation first. Taking up the question of Planck's constant I stated my derived figure for the ratio in the natural way with the words *ten to the minus thirty*. She had then only to say that I should be almost exactly right if I changed the figure *thirty* to *twenty-nine*. I noticed that after I had used the index notation a few times Marjorie was able to venture it successfully through Elton – as if, so to put it, his mind had by then become programmed to the notation (though in separate and normal conversation with Elton it was not something I found that he understood). This matter of index notation is only one example of the way that Marjorie had to choose her thought carefully in handling scientific topics in order to transmit her ideas without hitch. It was Elton's own mind all the time that was directly controlling his speech apparatus – in contrast with Lang Chapman where it was Lang's mind which was in the direct control of Chapman's articulation.

Having explained the need for understanding the mediumistic mechanism in the case of William Elton, and for exercising an appropriate technique in its use, I particularly want to state that William Elton was always most ready to give his mediumistic help; and that such help has proved invaluable to the writing of the latter part of this book.

As well as the matter of mediumship there is one which is more general that I must also comment on. It is something that affects all conversation, but tends to bear especially upon mediumistic conversations because of their relative brevity. Language is more open to misunderstanding than is often credited. Therefore I endeavoured to bring in a factor of redundancy into my mediumistic discussions – not altogether remote from the fashion of cross-examination in a court of law. Marjorie understood my intentions well enough; but at the second session *via* William Elton she made my practice of them the excuse for one of her dry sallies: "I suppose you do imagine we know what we are talking about!" Her use of the plural *we* was to include one or two august next-world persons who as at the first Elton meeting were in fact present to lend the support of their authority and knowledge. Possibly the incongruous element of my interrogatory of such company sparked off Marjorie's sense of humour. I had been pursuing this cross-questioning for nearly half an hour – solely to be sure I was forming the right ideas. That I am certain was understood and accepted patiently by all present; but a good thing can be overdone, and to halt me Marjorie (I am inclined to think) felt this ploy (strongly in her own vein) measured up well.

Dr. Lang appreciated the need for cross-interrogation. He and George Chapman went so far as to grant me a special three-hour session so I could make sure that in my writing I should be expressing no misapprehensions. This special session, accepted with great forebearance by Lang throughout, picked up two points – minor only but showing the need for the session and how misconceptions can interpose themselves unsuspectedly in the communication of ideas.

A New World-View

What I had been learning thus far in the present chapter could scarcely be experienced except as a powerful intellectual upsurge. And it was an upsurge in which the ideas of modern scientific theory are the implements of the knowledge Marjorie had earlier been looking to.

The upsurge had originated with the explanation of the materialization phenomenon; and then it had advanced to a wider rationale where certain major problems long held over came also, fascinatingly, to be resolved.

In steering my developing thought along this route as I have described, Marjorie undoubtedly made the materialization phenomenon the starting point because that was a simple logical way of going about her task. But two important things stand out concerning the materialization phenomenon. For a matter of fact – and despite the poor repute in which the phenomenon is held in the minds of many researchers today – it constitutes a prominent feature in the history of psychical investigation. For a matter even more important, it epitomizes the historical character of the approach to the psychical field *via* science. The approach exemplifies typically the impasse – noted by historians of science – which becomes reached with the inadequate paradigm: that block to further advance invariably encountered by a pattern of thinking too restricted in basic deductive power.

Great forward strides in the practical study of materializations were made by Sir William Crookes. He was both eminent physicist and chemist; and he was recognized as one of the great scientific investigators of psychical phenomena of the late 19th and early 20th centuries. Dominated by the restricted paradigm of classical physics his scientific colleagues intensely disapproved of his investigative work. And Crookes himself could put forward no rational accounting for the remarkable materializations he had studied. He died in 1919; before ever the quantum outlook had come to fruition; or ever had truly found appreciation. As Marjorie demonstrated to me, the paradigm of the quantum view of the world was the key to the problem. It was the key not to hand for Crookes.

The way Marjorie was handing this key to me it assumed significance altogether beyond the answer to the materialization problem. With the solution to the problems I had been holding over it seemed to present a wide and fresh outlook on the world. It was a view that was pluriversal: the view in which two radically different values of Planck's constant dictate the characteristics of two distinct physical universes. This twofold conception held in one quantum rationale the understanding of our own physical Universe and of the Universe forming the background to Marjorie's existence – the physical universe she had earlier described (Chapter 10) as a parauniverse in relation to ours.

There was immediate opportunity to try out the explanatory powers of this new world-view. The problem solving of the last section does not include two problems – most distinctly major – of which I have also taken some note. One is the interpenetration of the two physical Universes of the twofold total world. The interpenetration of two material worlds that are essentially non-interactive but co-extensive is an idea mysterious in the extreme to ordinary ways of thinking. I gave it some attention in Chapter 13. Then separately, in mysterious contrast to the unamenable nature of matter as we know it when it comes to the influence of mind, there is the remarkable responsiveness of next-world matter to precisely this influence. Marjorie brought into being both a cottage and a garden on the basis alone of mental activity (Chapter 7). What has the new rationale to say on these two questions? They must pose their own significant test.

Coming to consider them, the first took me to the strong realization I now had that the two Universes share in the same pattern of formation – so that they derive in fact from the same raw stuff. The derivation depends on quantization of this stuff. We have already had an example in the quantization of the electromagnetic field to produce photons – the minute quantum packages of radiation that travel through space like a fusillade of machine-gun bullets.

With the great development of the quantum theory commencing in 1925 it became clear at large that the stable – and all-importantly, therefore, the enduring – states of the raw stuff of the physical world lie with its quantization. These states can be worked out, and an early theoretical triumph was to calculate the photon states from the raw stuff of the electromagnetic field. From the vantage point of this broad theory of particle states any root distinction between matter and radiation, superficially greatly dissimilar, is seen to disappear. The atom, or any particle whatever (for instance a photon or an electron), is the result of quantization of the raw stuff of a field – not a field in general as simple as the electromagnetic field, but a field of a class that includes the electromagnetic field as a special case. (I note that Dirac, the recognized early exponent of the new quantum mechanics, paid little attention to the physical reality of these fields – preferring to dwell on "the beauty of the mathematics" describing them. Some physicists have inclined to treat the fields as mathematical only. But founders of the new mechanics like de Broglie and Schrodinger saw this unjustified: they held the fields to be real. Gauge transformation of the field relating to an isolated electron provides a way of deriving from this field the electromagnetic field between the electron and another electron, when the latter is introduced into the situation. The reality of the electromagnetic field is not questioned – the conclusion on the reality of the original field before gauge transformation is obvious: the field must be real. However, the reality of the fields is not vital to the argument that follows.)

A point to bear closely in mind about all such fields is that they are wave fields, and that as such it is a natural property for them to pass through one another (in the technical language they superpose). An illustration of this wave ability is given in the analogy of waves on the surface of water – these waves show no difficulty in running through one another. One has only to think of such waves incident on, and their reflections from, a breakwater. Matter for such reasons is not fundamentally impenetrable to other matter, but fundamentally interpenetrable. This is at the heart of modern physics.

But how does it happen, then, that we naturally and commonly experience matter in an impenetrable guise?

Modern physics is able to explain very exactly how this guise arises (instances of which – ironically – in ordinary experience are so exclusively dominating that with everyday frame of mind we find it hard to imagine why anything different should ever occur). Modern physical theory demonstrates that particles of matter tend inevitably and constantly to be creative of other particles. This creative activity can result, on an exchange basis, in interaction with other matter. Impenetrability is something that is bound up with interaction and its forces. Quantum theory is able to show just how such forces come about.

These ideas take us to the crux of the problem of the interpenetrability of the two different quantum Universes. The interactive forces of the one tend – with the vast quantum gap – not to be felt at all by the other. The character of the vast quantum mismatch will become the more clear later in this section. With the mismatch neither Universe has any difficulty in occupying one and the same space as the other. This is not to argue that interaction between the two Universes never occurs. Where it does it is not to a degree having any bearing on the question of universal interpenetrability. Materialization phenomena form an example, and one in which the interaction is specially contrived.

With quantum principles there lies, again, the key to the difficult idea (difficult by common or garden standards) that mind in some *direct* way can shape and manipulate next-world matter to its will – and with ease. The idea is not one that the old physics can cope with, any more than it could with the materializations investigated by Crookes.

What mind is bears inevitably. Given a proper regard to the nature of mind an approach taking up the conceptions of the new physics can bring understanding to this next-world compliance on the part of matter. It must be a reasonable hope that the explanation should throw light on the fact that no ready similar compliance exists with our own kind of matter. I want to show that a quantum rationale meets with these points. But first there is the question – it has to be the very pressing question – of how mind can affect matter at all.

A philosophical answer to the question is apparent from the analysis of Appendix V. Without such analysis on the other hand, quantum theory itself suggests an answer; and it proves distinctly helpful. Quantum theory offers a strong pointer in the direction of energy. Following this pointer is how I will start to take up the argument.

We have seen in the Bohr picture of the atom the way in which the quantum state of an atom can only be changed, say to the next higher quantum state, if the atom is given a package of energy of amount equal to the difference between the higher-state energy and that of the existing state. The change can happen if the atom absorbs the energy of a photon of radiation. This illustrates the fact in quantum mechanics that it is energy which fixes the state. To change the state, energy must be added or removed. It follows logically that if mind is going to modify an atom, and change the state in which it exists, then mind must be able to add or remove energy – and to the extent at least of the minimum difference between the energy levels of the various states.

In further talk with Marjorie *via* Elton I understood from her that in her circles quantum mechanics is looked on as most certainly expressing the truth in such regards. The statement makes comparison with the conclusions of Appendix V the more interesting.

A main conclusion of this appendix is that mind for one thing and energy as we encounter it in modern physics for another fall together in a broad common category: in the sense of being able to say that mind is energy-like. More precisely it can be said that in a logical sense the nature of mind is overlapping with the nature of physical energy. Mind therefore is equipped for energy interaction with matter. The question left over is the question why mind is particularly competent to manipulate matter of next-word kind, but singularly incompetent to influence our own.

Here from the ground occupied by modern physics the clue to the situation comes easily to hand. The quantum of energy needed to change the state of a next-world atom, in comparison to the energy quantum entailed in the same change in an atom that is an opposite number in our world, is vastly smaller than the latter quantum. To put a figure on it, and in the light of data appearing earlier in the chapter, the ratio is in the order of 10^{-21} to one (something like one thousandth of a million-million-millionth compared with unity). In any one effort

– and Marjorie assured me this was so – mind is more than easily capable of supplying the microscopic quantum. It needs on the other hand a mind far beyond the normal, and of very great power, to support the effort of supplying a quantum of 10^{21} times greater – one that will effect a corresponding change in a corresponding atom in this world. With the ability to take matter through one change of quantum state there is clearly the ability to carry out a whole sequence of like changes. But in this world order here, mind normally is not able to make the very first move.

I take the opportunity of the much clearer idea of next-world quanta now arrived at to go back and look again at the quantum mechanisms of the materialization phenomenon. It is a step which better understanding calls for. In the explanation that has earlier been given, the materialization processes use specially devised photon beams, and the photons are photons of next-world order for the sake of their penetrating character. At the stage we have reached, the vast energy gap between the naturally occurring quanta of the two world systems has just been made specifically clear; and normal energy quanta of the next-world system are clearly seen to be altogether too insignificant to have any effect upon our world. How then do the next-world type beam photons exert any influence? How are they able to release tissue fragments, freeing them from the ties of the stable quantum-state relations with neighbouring atoms? The problem at first sight might appear daunting; but it is not one to which the quantum physicist will attach any real difficulty. Marjorie actually threw out a clue at the time by comparing the photon-beam source with a laser. In principle photons are not restricted to the energies they are normally found with. They may have quantum energies that are exceedingly large integer-related multiples of the common quantum values. A laser is a device capable of generating such unusual photons. Especially if photons like these are of very high frequency the problem of bridging the energy gap disappears. The whole matter is one of express contrivance towards the required end. Tightly bunched groups of a very great number each of photons of normally occurring type, and particularly if they are of very high frequency, offer an alternative technique. The bond-breaking interactions are then of multi-photon class.

The explorations we have been looking at in this chapter and made with the help of the ideas of modern physics bear, as I see it, a greatly significant aspect: they tend to remove any demarcation like that between 'natural' and 'supernatural'. I mean this in the sense that they immensely extend the reasoned outlook it is possible to take on the world.

Transfiguration Phenomena

In this section it will become apparent how the reasoned view upon the world can be extended much further.

Transfiguration was the subject along with materialization that Lang had been keen I should study (Chapter 14). But it takes one far more deeply into the processes of physics and into the nature of the psyche. If only for this reason, the phenomenon could not usefully have been considered at any earlier point in this chapter. There is also the very good reason that I had not thus far any practical acquaintance of the happening.

Mrs. Young ventured that she had given a demonstration which she knew deeply impressed the person watching it; and she volunteered to attempt a like demonstration for me. We arranged a special meeting; however I saw no changes that I felt could qualify as transfiguration. Despite this I happened upon success. With no plans laid beforehand, I encountered the phenomenon on a second meeting with Miss Jeanette Dunn. That I want to turn to now; and I remark on my endeavours afterwards to discover the principles by which the phenomenon could be understood. It took me several sessions of discussion with Marjorie, talking to her through William Elton, before these principles became fully clear to me. I aim here to sketch them in simple outline. The more thorough-going aspects of the study will be found in Appendices III and IIIA.

The first move came from Miss Dunn. Early in October, 1978, I received her telephone call to say she expected once again to be staying at Stanstead for a while – it would be in the fairly near future. If, she suggested, I liked to spend a day at Stanstead while she was there – as I had a year ago – it might assist me in my studies: just as on my first visit.

What was settled was that I should go – and on the 27th of the month. Since Miss Dunn wished to leave for her home in South Shields later in the day it was agreed that I should try to arrive around nine in the morning.

On meeting again with her, the news I first gathered seemed to imply that the present occasion would not be so valuable as the previous. The only psychic demonstrations and facilities to hand which had been arranged at the college for the day were restricted to healing. They scarcely met with my immediate interests; and it looked as though it had been a mistake to come to Stanstead without making some fairly definite plans beforehand. But it was not a mistake.

Miss Dunn reminded me, with a little hesitation, that she was herself possessed of some psychic faculties – possibly she would be able to help instead. Concerning her own abilities, so it proved, Miss Dunn underrated herself. While she was proposing that we draw upon these abilities, I recollected her telling me on my first visit that besides clairvoyance she held some sensitivity for transfiguration. She had hinted she might attempt it on another occasion. The recollection raised the hope that she would now make such an attempt: perhaps later that morning – after we had relaxed for a while in conversation.

First of all, because she was interested in my researches, and because she felt the early scientific pioneering of the psychic field had not been since pursued as it ought, I tried to convey in outline what, over the gap between our meetings, I had come to see was the bearing of modern scientific knowledge upon the psychic. More than an hour passed rapidly in this talk. Eventually, thinking that the circumstances might be appropriate, I recalled to her what a year ago she had said about transfiguration; and I proposed that now was a favourable opportunity to demonstrate the phenomenon. Miss Dunn thought it would be worth trying.

By way of background I must state that I had, as our meeting was beginning, remarked on Marjorie's attendance with the same general aim of exploring presented opportunities as the time before; and I must add that, when I made this remark, having recollected the transfiguration possibility with Miss Dunn, I was keenly wanting Marjorie to seize upon the opportunity to express herself in this special way. I must also comment that, by the time I actually proposed the

173

attempt, Miss Dunn was already well aware of Marjorie's presence. She could both see her and hear her.

I asked Miss Dunn if she felt the light level – which was poor – might nevertheless be too high; and whether I should draw the curtains. She replied that the light was not disturbing her – whereas the act of pulling the curtains might well upset her present poise. She told me she would let this state, a state of trance, go deeper. Since however she wanted to avoid a full state of sleep, she asked me to talk to her; and keep talking.

I waited a moment before starting to speak – and as I waited I noticed Miss Dunn's lips becoming more full and more curved in a most reminiscent manner. I started to talk describing the changes. Then – while it may be difficult to believe – I saw the mauve lipstick on her lips change to the vermilion colour that Marjorie normally chose to suit the complexion of her face and her general appearance. At the same time the cheeks became the more rounded cheeks of Marjorie's face – and, with the rounding, slight creases formed at the corners of the lips: in a way I recall so well.

Besides, deserting Miss Dunn's comparative paleness, the cheeks assumed Marjorie's more lively hue. Suddenly Jeanette Dunn's body jerked. She had been almost flopping in her seat. The jerk caused her posture to change to upright; and then, the posture completed by a slight backward tilt of the head, I was witnessing once again a more than familiar carriage. The total effect – conveying a remarkable experience – was highly emotive. But next all these changes – having been realized and held for a few seconds – started rapidly to fade. It was Jeanette Dunn again, relaxed into her own sitting posture, with her own mauve lipstick, and her own features in her own complexion.

Understanding of what I had seen was something on which I tried to gain Marjorie's mind in my evening and, these days, often early morning sessions with her. I have explained the difficulties I experienced at first when trying to gather impressions of a scientific nature – but despite my initial failure of the flying machine (Chapter 6) I did in fact move on gradually to more success. Subject to check by an independent channel it became a *modus vivendi*. Picking up direct scientific impressions from Marjorie in preparation for my Elton meetings made it far easier and quicker to cover the ground of my talks with her at these meetings. It was largely by just this process of direct reception from Marjorie and then of confirmation, amplification, or correction by her at the Elton meetings that I was able to learn the ideas, fundamental to the understanding of transfiguration, which I have set out in Appendices III and IIIA.

Appendix III is particularly concerned with the physics of the electrical body. Appendix IIIA centres on the way in which as a matter of physics the psyche focuses its presence upon the individual.

The physics of those circumstances is important in any situation in which a mind acts on the nervous system of the physical body. It is important in the normal situation where the mind concerned is the owner of the physical body, and where it interacts with that body. It is important in the unusual situation in which it is some other mind that interacts with the selfsame body. The unusual situation is present in transfiguration; and therefore, to be specific, what happened in the transfiguration which took place as I looked on at Stanstead occurred because Marjorie's mind was able to achieve access to Jeanette

Dunn's system of nervous control.

How did it come about that Marjorie could take control? Why, too, if this access became possible on the occasion, is it not normally possible?

I can give a short answer to these questions that is apt to convey a false impression of simplicity where no real simplicity exists. Yet this answer does express the essence of the matter: essentially there exists a sense in which the psyche of the individual is all-enveloping of the purely physical aspects of the individual. The statement implies that the psyche throws up in some way a physical region of influence or presence. Such a concept of the psyche presence is made more precise in Appendix III, *Conductivity form, neural coupling and psyche presence*. By virtue of such an all-enveloping psyche presence, you – as the rightful owner of your body – alone react with your body (Appendix IIIA). Your own psyche screens your body from control by another psyche – regardless of how the other psyche may approach. To this, one must add however, that there are circumstances in which the protection may cease to be complete. The psyche of an individual may retreat, voluntarily or involuntarily, from its fully-enveloping role. Another psyche presence may then be able to influence the previously inaccessible physical body. This, I was assured by Marjorie when talking with her *via* Elton, is the principle by which she was able to modify Miss Dunn's features: Miss Dunn voluntarily redeployed her own psyche presence to permit the access that Marjorie needed.

These very broad ideas, Marjorie went on to say, operate in other connections. For instance in hypnotic regression, as described in Chapter 15, the fundamental redisposition of the psyche of the hypnotic subject not only makes available in its realistic way the memories of past events but it can bring about a less than fully-enveloping state of protection. The possible intruding psyche of Chapter 15 then has opportunity for its own expression through the hypnotized subject.

This may look a rather different account of what happens compared with that given in Chapter 15. There the door was seen as possibly opened to the intruder by a partial retreat of the psychical body from the physical. The two accounts are not really differing – they represent different aspects of one situation. The needed redisposition of the psyche for the regression to be effective tends in the first place to a relaxing of the association of the psyche away from the physical nervous control system of the patient. This is a first and basic consideration. A second consideration ranking with it is that the bonding between psyche and psychical body is a specially fundamental thing. It has to be so or the psyche would not transfer automatically to the departing psychical body at death. Withdrawal, even if partial, of the psyche from the physical body therefore entails some withdrawal of the psychical body. The regressive situation under hypnosis thus tends to partial retreat of the psychical body; but any relaxing away of the psyche – as in the regressive situation – is liable to leave the protective action of the psyche against intrusion short of complete. (In Chapter 15, where Lang removed completely the patient's psychical body in order to convey verbal instructions through his patient, the patient's electrical body would inevitably have been removed along with the psychical body – as made evident in Appendix III, *The four-dimensional psyche presence*. On the face of it that would have left Lang's psyche presence without an electrical body, normally located, by which to control the patient's vocal system. But Lang would have had no difficulty in withdrawing electron-position pairs from the patient's removed electrical body to serve as a temporary electrical body in proper juxtaposition to the vocal system.)

A similar and again unintentional mode of vulnerability to intrusion holds with the heavily-drunk person. This case was cited by Dr. Lang, in Chapter 15, as a parallel example. I discussed it with Marjorie in the sense of withdrawal from an irritant drug.

Marjorie moved on to our own mutual interactions. She took up the very broad ideas of the subject in relation to our personal 'messages' – both originally and since her death. If the intended communication – for the sake of argument – should be from her to me, then with her intention and the volition of it there occurs the projection of her psyche presence to juxtaposition with mine. I instinctively recognize her mental state (of volition) by virtue of my sensitivity to her; and by pure psyche-to-psyche transfer. Characteristically I experience a physical sensation of minor order, because I automatically reduce in small degree my psyche-presence protection. If circumstances permit me to give my mind to these events, I may follow up by allowing her projected psyche influence a more full direct access to my physical system through a more full redeployment on the part of my own psyche presence. The level of sensation of the message at the same time becomes very much stronger. Since her death and even with communication reversely, from myself to Marjorie, exactly the same conceptions apply because (Appendix IIIA) the next-world individual is in similar principle subject to an enveloping psyche presence.

There were operative the same broad principles, Marjorie continued, in her control of William Elton – and as, for instance, at that very time she was expressing herself to me through his trance state. In the readjustment of his psyche, when he falls into his trance condition, he hands to her psyche – upon its projection to impinge on him – a degree of direct access to his nervous control system. That was why he smiled when she smiled, or gestured his hands when she gestured hers. His psyche adjustment however did not give to her like access to his speech apparatus; and for access there she was compelled to go through the intermediary element of his mind, relying on the responsiveness of his psyche to pick up her thoughts.

Reflecting here more fully on the nature of such mediumship it seems appropriate – as an incidental matter – to recognize that its telepathic character confers a most valuable freedom of communication in regard to language. Lang affirmed (Chapter 5) that a thought has existence apart from the language that may express it. Therefore with mediumship like that of William Elton, a Chinese communicator may be expressing himself in his native Canton, but the communication through the medium will be in the medium's, say, natural English – and despite the medium's entire ignorance of Chinese dialect. This compares with trance mediumship in the style of George Chapman where direct control of the medium's speech by the communicator enables the speech to be very exactly that of the communicator; but by the selfsame fact any translation facility with language is totally ruled out.

But such incidentals aside, the enveloping of the individual's physical nature by the manifesting presence of the individual's psyche is clearly an important principle. As I have pointed out, the principle in fact is not as simple as it might sound. The more precise situation is made clear in Appendix III, and in greater detail in Appendix IIIA. In this situation the electrical body has necessarily to be considered; and in relation to the psyche presence. The physics of the electrical body brings in quantum ideas of modern physics which far transcend the simple ideas of classical mechanics. The relation moreover of the psyche presence to the electrical body is something that entails more dimensions of space than the customary three of visual perception. Here – quite separately but having some bearing – one may note that, with the mechanics of general relativity, physicists have recognized the customary ideas of space are inadequate to describe reality.

This is a chapter that turns upon explanation. What can be said of the extraordinary change from mauve to vermilion in the colour of Jeanette Dunn's lipstick? That must be a question almost clamouring for a rational answer. It is hard to see how the nervous-control ideas here envisaged at the heart of the transfiguration phenomenon could possibly account for the change. Putting the point to Marjorie her response was that the lipstick events were purely a materialization effect. Just as in her appearance to me I had acted as a materialization medium so Janette Dunn had also co-operated with her in that particular way. The red 'lipstick' was a film of matter overlaying the mauve lipstick and was briefly formed by materialization processes. Miss Dunn's transfiguration was not an example of transfiguration pure and simple – in the nervous-control sense. It combined in this sense, the two separate phenomena of transfiguration and materialization.

In a corresponding way, Marjorie added, her materialization to me was not just a matter of materialization processes. Had that been so, I would not have seen her. The room was quite dark. She had to make the materialization luminous. Her psyche created photons to raise the energy states of the atoms entailed so that these atoms radiated light on returning to their normal states – in a way similar to that in which light is caused to be emitted by the screen of a television picture tube. The physical phenoma of the psychic field, she stated, were often combinations of phenomena basically different from one another.

And when they were not combinations they could even then range widely in degree.

As example she said that in certain circumstances the materialized form can be made to speak. Had she, materializing in my bedroom, been able to replicate her physical form much more completely, and so as to include the speech apparatus and lungs, she could have spoken to me in the normal way. Firstly she reminded me that in her world there is an atmosphere – moreover that the human body follows closely our pattern here. Therefore people speak to one another over short distances in the same vocal way that we do – even if they use thought transfer for longer distances. Then she pointed out that a materialization adhering (by van der Waals forces) at every point to the psychical body upon which it is superposed must be animated in strict accord with the motions of this psychical body. Given a sufficiently full materialization it follows that she would only have had to speak as she commonly does in her world and her materialization would have spoken very characteristically in her own voice – the more so if the materialization allowed her the monitoring action of hearing herself speak.

But the cardinal principle of this section is the basic transfiguration mechanism: the instrusive control by an alien psyche of the individual's nervous system. It is this intrusive principle made operative through the relaxation of the

177

screening protection natural to the individual's own psyche presence. Reverting to it in some mediumistic review talks, Marjorie emphasized the importance of exactly this principle for the understanding of wide aspects of the psychic field. It collates, fascinatingly and rationally, aspects that otherwise seem to stand unconnected.

There was the subject of the clicks attaching to Dr. Lang's mode of treatment of his patients. I noted in Chapter 3 the loud clicks I had experienced when laying on the couch in his consulting room. They were linked specifically with particular operations he performed. I also noted in Chapter 9 how Iris reported hearing loud clicks with Lang's first night visit to her – in order to deal with her stomach-ulcer condition. Marjorie explained that in such operative conditions Lang needed to act intrusively He needed to relax the patient's natural screening against alien-psyche intrusion. This relaxation, she told me, is certainly not difficult when the patient is basically co-operative. But the patient's psyche must be strongly influenced to bring about the relaxation. It helps if the medicals present in the operative team exercise a concerted influence. This was why I had noticed Lang snap his fingers lightly when giving me helpful treatment on some of my Aylesbury visits. That was to time the collective effort to relax his patient's screening. I had heard clicks, so it seemed in my ears, far louder than any such finger snapping. It was because the screening is essentially electrical, and because it is electromagnetically coupled with the nervous system (Appendix III). The relaxation of the screening is rapid; and this induces an inevitable strong transient electrical disturbance in the auditory nerves. On the experience of it, and in regard to certain night visits to me by Dr. Lang, I comment that having told him how the clicks woke me up I did not after that hear the clicks on his visits. This was, Marjorie confirmed, because Lang then used a much slower rate of relaxation. The electrical disturbance was still caused, but it entailed only sound frequencies that were inaudibly low.

Psychic healing may, superficially, seem quite unrelated to clairaudience. Yet Mrs. Young (Chapter 11) stated that she always heard a click in her left ear before she became clairaudient. What precisely are these clicks she hears? Could they conceivably be the same in nature as the clicks I experienced when Lang was treating me? The answer – given by Marjorie – is definitely yes. Mrs. Young relaxes her psyche-presence screening to allow intrusion by the communicator. This is so that the psyche presence of the communicator can influence – electromagnetically – Mrs. Young's aural system. That is the mechanism of clairaudience. With this understanding of it from Marjorie, I asked William Elton if he heard any clicks when entering upon the clairaudient condition. He did not appear at all surprised by the question. He said that he heard a click on some occasions; but on others not. The inference from his statement is that at times he enters into the clairaudient relaxation of his psyche screening in a much more gradual manner than at others.

Marjorie made some other remarks which set the deep-trance mediumship of George Chapman in a most interesting light. If in her transfiguration of Jeanette Dunn it had been possible for Miss Dunn to redeploy her psyche even more radically, and to the extent of handing over the direct control of her speech apparatus, then Marjorie could have spoken through the transfiguration in her natural manner. With the use in addition of Miss Dunn's auditory channel, to allow the normal monitoring of speech production, Marjorie would have been able to talk in a very exact replica of her natural voice. The mediumship of George Chapman, when he is controlled by Dr. Lang, can be seen in these terms: it is an extreme form of transfiguration. Dr. Lang takes over very fully from George Chapman; and in a marked contrast to what might be called the *overshadowing* condition in trance mediumship such as William Elton's.

Looking back on the transfiguration study it had proved far more absorbing than I imagined possible. The so greatly interesting point was the degree of general understanding that it brought. When the mechanism of the transfiguration phenomenon is realized then it can be seen as rationale of psychical phenomena of various differing kinds. There were particularly the special slants thrown upon contrasting mediumships of the trance state like William Elton's and George Chapman's. And surprisingly, the same mechanism shows how in normal life an individual is able to support his individuality and remain as a unit free of direct external interference from other minds.

A most significant matter embedded in this last respect is that here the unusual phenomena of the psychical field are to be seen merging – in identical root fashion – with the every day. The world palpably is integrated in a far wider rational degree than we tend to credit.

Remarks

A natural desire for simplicity in the approach from science has – almost fervently – dominated much investigation of the psychical field this last half century. Oversimplifying, the motivation has enmeshed thinking in a web of false limitation. Appendix I is a logical exercise of disentanglement on that account.

To present the position more explicitly, there is the statement made numerously this century that the great difficulty with psychical phenomena lies with the inability to accommodate them within a rational scheme of thought. The statement expresses exactly the unreal web of thinking spun by an oversimplification of scientific approach. The very coarse trawl must inevitably fail to catch the finer examples of marine life – but it is a delusion to conclude from such an actual trawling that these examples do not exist. The kind of science invoked in the over simple view can be summed up in the one word *Newtonian*. Certainly Newton inspired scientific thought powerfully – and up to the time of Einstein, and of quantum mechanics with de Broglie. But the physical knowledge of this century shows Newtonian thinking massively inadequate, and incompatible both internally and externally. Such thinking is now the thinking of a discarded physics (Appendix IV) – a fact mostly as yet unappreciated. The daunting deficiencies have been made good in the new physics; furthermore with fantastic advances. We have seen in the present chapter that, applying the new knowledge, this kind of knowledge is able in its radically different and open-ended fashion (Appendix I) to handle psychical phenomena in the rational way.

Chapter Seventeen

CLAIRVOYANT PORTRAIT

My second meeting with Jeanette Dunn at Stanstead realized 'spin-off' which I appreciated deeply and personally.

The events concerned took place in the period just before the transfiguration in which Miss Dunn assumed physically so many of Marjorie's attributes. In that period, as I noted, Jeanette Dunn was clairvoyantly seeing Marjorie. Knowing that as a professional artist Miss Dunn could quickly make sketches of people I seized on the opportunity. I asked her if she would make such a drawing of Marjorie.

Miss Dunn agreed to do this. She produced her sketching pad; and she stated that she would only draw what she could see – she would fill nothing in by artistic license. She said that she did not want me to see what she was drawing while she was still sketching. This, she remarked, was to make it the more difficult simply to regard the sketch as the result of thought transfer of an image from my mind. I can add that I had never shown Miss Dunn a photograph or likeness of Marjorie; and – importantly – that while I did in fact visualize Marjorie both before and during the period in which Miss Dunn was sketching it was never except in full face. Seated as we were with Miss Dunn's position on one side of a table while mine was on the other it was possible for Miss Dunn to hold her pad below the table level out of my sight.

Before starting to sketch, she allowed herself to relax for two minutes or so with eyes closed. Marjorie, I sensed, was near to and behind my left shoulder. Having gathered this impression it hardly surprised me, though it was interesting, that Miss Dunn's gaze when looking up periodically from her pad was always in the direction of my own location of Marjorie.

After about five minutes, Jeanette Dunn handed me the sketching block. Her drawing is shown in the reproduction. The aspect inclines strongly to profile: a view which I had not anticipated – and a view hardly to be aided by my visualizations.

Miss Dunn commented that Marjorie looked much younger than when she died. That was true. Miss Dunn's suggestion to explain this was that Marjorie probably wanted to give me an impression of herself when she was, say, twenty-three. Bearing in mind what Dr. Lang had told me concerning appearance (Chapter 10), I reflected that Miss Dunn had seen Marjorie as more youthful because, following the common trend in the next life, that was how – with the passage of time – she had become. It was more youthful than when scarcely a

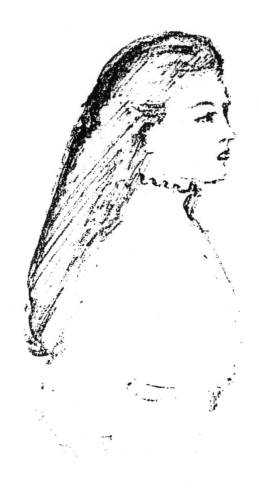

by Jeanette Dunn
Oct. '78.

year after her death she had materialized so close to me.

In due course I studied the likeness in detail. I took account of the features, the form of the figure, the shape of the head, the height of the forehead, and the general character and poise. It was all certainly very true to Marjorie, even if a younger Marjorie. But there was a question of her nose. At an early age an accident had resulted in a permanent change. This I was told was greatly a matter of maternal grief. For myself I felt that the changed form – the only form that I knew – was not unlikeable. Critically, I did not regard the different nose of the sketch as a detail that was untrue – because I knew the accident would have left the *present* (psychical) form unaffected. Showing the drawing to Marjorie's mother there was no dispute that it was authentic to the undamaged profile.

With opportunity I also showed the drawing to George Chapman. After his deep-trance sessions, and while resting, he invariably finds himself in a clairvoyant state (Chapter 18). Looking at Miss Dunn's sketch, Chapman remarked that having in this way seen Marjorie on several of her visits to Aylesbury the sketch might suggest a face slightly narrower than in reality. William Elton also has variously seen her, and he independently made the same comment. I have since been able to see Marjorie clairvoyantly many times myself, and to the support of these views. But it must be said that an aspect which is almost a side view will in the nature of things not give a good guide to the width of a face.

Speaking in a purely personal way it is clear to me in various respects that Marjorie had aimed to achieve a picture of herself which she knew would give me pleasure.

Chapter Eighteen

GEORGE CHAPMAN

George Chapman's contribution to this book is large. Was it a *sine qua non?*

To venture upon what might have been the historical sequence had circumstances been different always leaves room for question; but I am inclined to think that without George Chapman I should never have written these pages. My fear that the medium could or would somehow mislead – not well sustained as I have shown – must, I believe, have prevented me from going on to cover the kind of ground which I have. Of course, George Chapman is a medium; yet he is of the rare kind which one might say is highly self-effacing. The term *full trance* which denotes his mediumship rather suggests the general abeyance of the medium's own personality. We saw in Chapter 16, *Transfiguration Phenomena* how, in rational terms, such mediumship is to be regarded; and it supports the idea of abeyance. This non-presence of the medium was assuring. It was a quality which as I experienced it in my continuing and most natural talks directly with Dr. Lang sidestepped my doubts, and created the conditions for making headway.

George Chapman himself however has, just on this account, been forced deeply into the background. In the present chapter I want to achieve some remedy for this; and I want also to trace the way in which George Chapman became the remarkable medium which he is. At this stage – with the ground which has been covered and the insight which has been gained – that is possible not just as a narration of the mysterious but as something which can be intelligibly followed and understood.

My correspondence with George Chapman gave him a rudimentary idea of my aims and my conversations with Dr. Lang; but limitations of time did not allow me to keep him well informed, and I should like to place on record my appreciation that despite poor lines of communication he so generously continued to give time at the end of patient schedules for these long talks with Lang. Our correspondence was marked by my explaining to George on more than one occasion my feeling – with the very special part he was playing – of the importance to the account I hoped to give that we should find time for a talk about his mediumship.

I was therefore glad in May, 1977, to receive his suggestion that we have a chat over tea on a customary visit to Aylesbury – it would be when he had sufficiently recovered from his period of trance. This led to a talk with him in October, 1977.

At that time George was regularly handing over the trance use of his body to Lang for periods lasting six hours without a break – periods of a duration which are, I believe, quite exceptional in psychic experience. Dr. Lang was then commencing treatment of his patients at 11.30 a.m. Allowing time for George to readjust, our talk was in fact not until late in the evening.

George told me of the way that, confusedly at first from trance, he regains his normal senses; and then how he becomes aware of an intense thirst. He counters this by drinking great quantities of strong tea. The facts might sound curious; but they clearly relate to what Lang said on the repair of patient tissue in his operating practice. When examining a patient and diagnosing a damaged organ he may – as I have quoted him in Chapter 16, *Materialization Phenomena* – repair the damage by the use of matter taken from his medium's body. The transfer of the matter to the patient, so Lang then made clear, is by materialization processes; and George obviously has to make good this loss. The loss, on Lang's statement, may well be considerable. But here the quantities of tea constitute a needed first step – and they help, as George said, to waken him and restore his vitality. On that, he added, a shower is a further aid; but, temporarily, he is in need of complete physical rest.

Out of interest I took up this point with Lang when next I could speak with him. He informed me that – with the great physical demands he was placing upon George and despite this rest – George would not in fact recover of his own accord to a sufficient degree for him to meet the same demands day after day. Lang and his medical team therefore stay on after George comes out of trance; and, while George rests, they put right the physical depletion he has suffered.

The conversation had not gone far when – taking me again into known territory – George broke in as I was speaking. It was to say that he could see Marjorie standing near the chair in which I was sitting. He was able, he remarked, to do this because – as I mentioned in Chapter 17 in relation to Jeanette Dunn's sketch of Marjorie – he remains in a state of heightened psychical sensitivity for some time after his full-trance state. Marjorie, he said, was close to me and on my left. He described her. When he did this, instead of calling her Marjorie, he switched to using the name *Margaret*. This did not come as anything new because it only took me back to David Young's use of the name for her (Chapter 8); and to Dr. Lang's explanation later on. But it was interesting. With George, I had never referred at any time to Marjorie as Margaret; or told him there had been such a change; and, keen to know the reason, I asked him why he used the name.

He replied that after trance he often saw members of the assisting team which Dr. Lang had brought with him. Marjorie was sometimes with the team, so that in this way he had come to know her; but *Margaret* was the name by which she was addressed. She was smiling at us, he informed me, as he was saying this. I remarked that I knew Margaret was the name she had now adopted; but that it had impressed me when quite unexpectedly he had referred to her like that. He went on to add that the sensitivity by which he was now seeing her often stayed with him for hours after trance – exactly as was so now. On many occasions he would see people he did not know; but, in the end, the sensitivity would fade and his perceptions would revert to normal.

Listening to George, as he continued and told me more about himself, the impression started to form in my mind of a man impelled expressly, constantly and irresistibly by destiny. Even when a boy, events shaping for him as they did, he was to experience an urge, a powerful urge, onwards to some long-unclear ultimate future.

He was born in Merseyside in 1921, and brought up by his mother until she died when she was twenty-nine. He was five years old at that time.

His mother had been a gifted materialization medium. On his saying also that she was a practising Buddhist, I asked if that had any special ethnic significance. His answer was no. But she felt the great importance of practising the Buddhist teachings – at the same time she held firmly to the Church of England; and she had endeavoured to bring him up in it.

His deep and steadfast intent to regain contact with his mother, if that was possible, formed with her death a drive which helped him attain his ultimate goal.

On the outbreak of the Second World War George entered the Irish Guards, in which he had an uncle; and before long he transferred to the Royal Air Force, and finally to the R.A.F. Regiment. At the end of the war, and since he wished to obtain early release from the Air Force, he applied to join the Aylesbury Fire Brigade. Demobilised in May, 1946, he thereupon became a member of this brigade. Two years earlier, at the age of twenty-three, he had married; and in 1945 his daughter Vivian was born. Her early death was a second tragedy in his life – and it reinforced his deep motivation to bridge across to the 'other world'.

Respecting his initial endeavours and searchings, as he looked back upon them, I felt myself in much sympathy with the George Chapman who was then trying to find his way. On these matters one has to think of him very much as the practical man – setting store by what put him in touch with reality.

Concerning the subject of mediumship, at that stage, he had many doubts – and he derived no help from it; or from the Spiritualist meetings which on a few occasions he attended. His development seemed to be left entirely in his own hands – *and* to 'chance'.

He told me – and what he had to say seemed to fit clearly with his final goal – that he was always fond of animals. When a boy in Liverpool he ran a local animal clinic. He was happy to take in any sick animal of the neighbourhood; and he noted that in his care these animals invariably regained their health, and rapidly. On this account, he felt sure he possessed some intrinsic healing ability. When he joined the Aylesbury Fire Brigade he met, as one of its members, a Mr. Leslie Miles. Miles previously had practised as a solicitor. At the time, he was suffering from a back injury. Chapman made an offer to Miles to heal him of the injury – by applying his hands to the affected region. The offer was accepted; and, as Chapman anticipated, Miles was cured.

The interest that Miles had in "psychics" now entered importantly for George. With three others they would form a ring, using a tumbler and each placing one finger on the glass.

George commented that in doing this he felt they might be taking risks; and he said he did not advocate the indiscriminate use of the technique. But on more than one occasion he had felt he must accept risk in order to gain advance. I am inclined to think that on these occasions George Chapman was in fact running no risk. Marjorie has explained to me that so much depends upon one's frame of mind. If one indulges in psychic practises "just for kicks", then one may run into problems. You tend to attract other-world persons that are of the same attitude as yourself. If by your attitude you attract bad types you cannot expect to escape trouble. It is exactly like forming associations in this world. In George's case, I envisage that what he gained was the interest and the help of those devoted to the good of humanity.

The tumbler experiments apparently had not been tried for long when a message was received which greatly impressed him. It gave him an assurance that he was concerned with real things and was on the right road. The message stated that a relative of a named member of the ring had died. This was news to the member; and it was confirmed immediately upon making a telephone call. The message seriously encouraged him to press forward and marked a main juncture in his development.

Ambitiously – and still in 1946 – he gave his mind to the projection of the psychical body. Each day relaxed in a chair he would spend lengthy periods – usually of three hours duration – on his own and with this form of projection as his aim. It was not long before he achieved it; and then, he said, he was able "to look at his physical body sitting in the chair". This was altogether the turning point for George.

Thinking about it after our talk, I felt it could be instructive to put some questions to George about the experience. We were able to have another chat in May, 1978, and I will turn now to this occasion and to our conversation then. Reminding George of his statement, I asked him exactly what he saw. To the ordinary person the statement, I explained to him, must conjure up a vision of the room with its furniture, part of which was the chair in which George's vacated body would be reclining. Was that what he meant to convey? George's account in reply was rather different. There was no room, no furniture: *just darkness – and the reclining body which he recognized as his own*. In this projective description, I noted the same basic characteristics of my own projective experience (Chapter 5): the lack of the familiar details, and their replacement by a general darkness.

The two experiences tallied – and I note that, if the reason for this darkness is not obvious, the darkness is simply that due to a natural lack of illumination in the outer space of the next-world. There remained nevertheless one very good question: if in the projected state it is not possible to perceive physical things like chairs and tables, how did George Chapman succeed in seeing his physical body? The unsolicited completion of Gorge's account goes a long way to yielding the answer. In the fashion, he stated, in which his physical body appeared to him it was illuminated by a glow primarily located around the outline of his body.

This further highly interesting statement I discussed subsequently with Dr. Lang. On Lang's explanation the lighting proceeded in part from George's electrical body – and in part from a psyche residuum which remained with George's physical body (Appendix III, *Normality, disease, mediumship, death and birth*).

To trace through the situation in outline, the transfer by George of his psyche presence – in a principal way – to his projected psychical body enabled him to make this latter body his new agent of visual awareness. Then, as the light of the glow from his residual psyche presence and from his electrical body (retained by this presence) scattered off George's physical features, so he became aware of them through this fresh – next-world – channel of consciousness. I comment that had George more carefully looked, he could have perceived some of the chair that was supporting his physical body. It, like his physical body, would – if not so noticeably – also have scattered the light to which the eyes of his psychical body were receptive.

George's statements and Lang's discussion were deeply interesting. In his discussion Lang went on to make some further illuminating observations; and – since I want to give them – I briefly turn aside so that their significance will be more clear. In the first place George had presented a good description of the kind of visual experience that goes along with psychical-body projection. But Marjorie had learned a highly different projective technique (Chapter 11) for gathering visual, and other, data of sense kind. It worked – so I came to be instructed by her – for sense data of either world and, most remarkably, it rested with no sense channel whatever in the normal way. It was an activity simply of the psyche alone.

Lang took the opportunity of the discussion to contrast George's visual experience with that of Marjorie's acquired technique. He commented that the kind of projective account given by George is not characteristic of the sort of projective experience of which Marjorie had told me. "That sort," he corroborated, "makes no use of the psychical body, and the projection can be be termed *pure-psychic* projection. With this kind of projection," he made the special point, "the ordinary picture is restored: things look as they normally do." It is the kind of projection which Crookall studied (Chapter 5), mistakenly regarding it as psychical-body projection.

Having used projection of the psychical body for so long as he now has, it is a very simple matter for George. He can accomplish it regardless of circumstances; and, to my personal knowledge by demonstration (Dr. Lang then taking control), in a matter of a second or so. It is nevertheless a help if he is able to relax comfortably in a chair.

To return to the talk of October, 1977, I thought it could be instructive to put to George a caveat by Marjorie: that the return of the psychical body is liable to induce a state of shock – for which reason she was not keen for me to practise such projection. George remarked that the return needs to be controlled with care – too rapid a return will result in sensations of nausea. He had had to learn such things on his own; and it was one of those instances where he felt he needed to accept the element of risk.

Very soon after mastering psychical-body projection he found he could also achieve projection in terms purely of the psyche. This enabled him to visit his mother and his daughter. From these visits he would return, he said, with memories of his meeting with them.

Sometimes with psychical-body projection in those early days he found on regaining normal consciousness that his vacated physical body had been utilized for automatic writing; or that, beyond normal accountability, things had been moved in the room in his absence. It was not long then before Dr. Lang appeared on the scene.

George told me that he did not remember dates particularly well – it was events themselves that mattered most to him. So as to when exactly Dr. Lang began to participate he could not state for certain. He recalled that Mrs. Chapman encountered some abdominal trouble; and that he decided he would try to heal her. Here I note that with this decision George (in order that he should be able to exercise a direct healing control) would inevitably have been setting up in relation to his wife a psyche-presence redistribution – a redistribution of the kind which I describe in Chapter 16, *Transfiguration Phenomena*, and which Marjorie and I automatically establish every time we are in communication through our 'messages'. Both Lang and Marjorie independently have confirmed this point. George's psychical body was at this moment relaxing away from his physical body; and he had become open to the kind of control which Dr. Lang was to practise through him. In his account George said he leaned forward, his hands reaching out to heal his wife's abdomen. Just at that point Dr. Lang in fact took over and announced his presence to Mrs. Chapman. Dr. Lang informed her he would treat her and cure her of her complaint. Mrs. Chapman was cured: that, George believed, was the start of Dr. Lang's return to medicine – in a long practice which developed extensively here and on the Continent.

Checking this account and relating these details to Lang, they were corrected in part by him. "Ah, yes," he said, "George does not keep records, and it was a long time ago. Mrs. Chapman did have a nagging tummy complaint, and I put things right for her then as George told you; but I treated patients through George several times before that. Some things stand out in people's mind more than others."

I understand that George possesses a considerable sensitivity to Dr. Lang's mind; but in regard to the healing he is instrumental in giving, and apart from the broader aspects, he has little acquaintance with Dr. Lang's methods. In depth they are not intelligible to him; and they have no special attraction for him. He was interested however, he told me, that when – using him as medium in the customary way – Lang was operating in a hospital in Paris one of the French doctors paid some attention to the mediumistic trance condition. The doctor found the pulse rate attaching to this state was remarkably low. I asked George what the rate was; but he replied that the doctor had not informed him and he had not asked. I put the same question to Lang. "Oh," said Lang, "feel for yourself"; and he held out George's wrist for me to count the pulse. It was barely over 30! "We keep all of George's physical processes at the lowest possible level," Lang remarked. "It is best in every respect – and least disturbing for me".

Dr. Lang and George Chapman from the intellectual standpoint are poles apart; but when it comes to the men themselves, and their essential motivations, they are greatly at one. From my talks with each of them, I know that they are dedicated in their separate ways to the task of healing people. They performed the task jointly and intensively without break for well over thirty years. Although some years ago George felt he must retire, going to live in Wales, he neverless continued his joint practice with Dr. Lang on a reduced scale – both in Wales and in Europe. There have been also visits widely cast, such as in India.

POSTSCRIPT

Scientific knowledge owes its status to the impressive fact that *it applies*: its principles are known at large to be borne out in practice. In our present age, when physical science is put extensively to use in engineering enterprise, the truth of the statement is abundantly illustrated. Such knowledge, characteristically, has long been harnessed in the confident expectation of engineers that *it will work* – and success in the multitudinous activities which constitute modern engineering overwhelmingly re-enforces the prestige that science enjoys.

When major advances are made in science and there comes about an extension of knowledge, then initially and literally this precise situation no longer holds good. Inevitably the opportunity for test by prolonged application takes time to present itself.

Nevertheless, there exists a vital respect in which – and due to which – the situation in a sense remains firm. It is this: that those who engage in the scientific exploration of reality do so with a degree of care which is especially distinctive of their work. It is such that the congnizance of it inspires in its practitioners a confidence which is of a very high order. A measure of the level of this confidence is the fact that the authors of papers, or reports, setting out their work most certainly anticipate that other workers will arrive at similar conclusions if they carry through work which is similar in kind. To this extent every such paper, or report, is implicitly an invitation to all those competent and equipped to demonstrate also the truth of what has been found.

When, in the past, experimentation was altogether simpler than often it is today the direct checking of conclusions was more, even greatly more, frequent – and its extent was seen as a main plank in the platform of science.

Now much scientific advance is possible only through large national or international funding. A notable instance is the recent identification of the carrier bosons of the weak force – decades after theoretical considerations pointed in their direction. The specific bosons were recognized practically by a group of physicists in 1983 in a twelve-nation effort at the Geneva laboratory of the European Organization for Nuclear Research. Repetition of work tends now, on grounds of the sheer scale of expense, frequently not to be the norm; but the scientific principle of distinctive care, and embedded in it an intrinsic and scrupulous good faith, is present always in support of the reliability of scientific work. Without the guarantee this offers there would lie to hand no assurance that the time and effort which can be enormously costly was other than a waste.

Psychical research may often be hampered on the score of financial means; but apart from that its nature inherently is apt to result in a sparsity of accomplishment. Some idea of the special reasons for this sparsity will no doubt be gained from the narrative of this book: the combination of circumstances appropriate to significant advance do not commonly occur. So advance runs, perhaps, more like those advances in modern science illustrated by the weak-force experimentation of 1983 – experimentation expecting little likelihood of immediate and independent check.

Exploration in the psychical field, sparse as it may be, can and must engage the same attitudes, and bring to bear the same qualities, that support such scientific experimentation. These attitudes and qualities include open-mindedness and boldness: factors of enormous importance in the momentous advances of present-day physical science. I am sure that, studying the nature of reality through its own disciplines, psychical exploration will increasingly exhibit reality in a much wider spectrum than is often at present allowed in popular thought – and exactly as modern physics itself looks to a far wider perspective (Appendix I).

Such conclusions as I have pointed to in this book concerning the spectrum of reality I am convinced can be reached by *any* serious and appropriate research effort, given the opportunity: this – just as in normal scientific research – regardless of differences of specific circumstances in the making of the approach.

APPENDIX

Appendix I

THE OUTLOOK FROM SCIENCE

In the Introduction I took note of – and rather as a misconception – the conflict thought to exist between accepted science and those unusual events which are psychical phenomena. Chapter 16 has shown that the ideas of accepted science – if by that we mean modern science – are an invaluable aid to understanding psychophysical phenomena. One has only to think of those of materialization processes. The relationship seen in Chapter 16 is totally distinct from conflict. Yet it is widely thought that psychical phenomena are inconsistent with scientific understanding; and thus must somehow be discounted.

I want here to trace how this kind of belief has come about – and show how the antithesis it conceives between psychical happenings and rational ideas is formally to be resolved. In the latter respect the present century has accomplished advances in logic that enable the resolution to be made at a fundamental level. They reveal in a powerful light the nature of the rational procedures of science.

We have to look at these procedures. But it is important to the tracing which I intend to give of the rise of the conflict, and likewise to its resolution, to understand such procedures in the form both of the traditional and their present day guise. To such ends I turn, in order to make a start, to scientific knowledge of the kind in which its potential for explanation is not only greatest but most firmly grounded. I look therefore to the field of physics, where such a potential has always been seen – though seen most of all in the physics of today. The physics of the present century, modern physics, furnishes – in an initial achievement – all the understanding of the facts of chemistry; but – among many other major accomplishments – it has spectacularly come to be regarded as the instrument of enlightenment in biology, and yet again in cosmology. Such wide-spreading abilities inevitably place physics at the heart of science.

That central position was discerned long before physics took on its modern guise and brought about the eruption of understanding of the present century. There has long existed a deep impression that in our experience of the real world all that could be explained was either already understood by physics, or else would become so – expectedly before long – in the course of progress.

What has been much in mind in speaking of explanation and understanding is the part played by scientific knowledge in the long-traditional guise of physical laws. Against this background the conceived paradox between science and psychical events may be put like this: that knowing the laws of physics they seem to be directed to regularities of pattern in the sequence of events that do not naturally accommodate the psychical type of phenomenon. Therefore if the deep-seated and long-standing impression of the universal powers of explanation on the part of physics holds good there must be no room for psychical phenomena in rational thought.

With this approach it is obviously necessary to look closely at the nature of scientific knowledge. I shall show in doing so just how the approach is fundamentally flawed. It makes assumptions – uncritically – concerning the scope of physical laws, whereas the assumptions are not justified by the logic of such laws. The paradox has been precipitated by these false assumptions. So I look specifically to the formal structure of the knowledge of physics.

It places an important emphasis upon its fundamental and traditional character to contemplate firstly what such scientific knowledge is not. Aggregate knowledge – if that signifies just a collection of facts – is not what is meant by it. A long list of specific truths does not – in the relevant sense – make this science. In its essential nature, it is propositional – and the propositions are few but comprehensive. This is precisely what is implied when it is said that the basis of physical science is *scientific law*. Thus any branch of physical science is at root and traditionally a set of postulated general statements, its laws. Each of these ranges over a vast multitude of particular facts; and, by analogy, one can think of it as a portmanteau – with the contents of the portmanteau representing the multitude of facts embraced within the general statement of the law. On this fashion the knowledge of physics is a *systematized* form of knowledge: a body of knowledge rounded up and organized under the general propositions which are the laws of the system.

Saying that this is the essential form of physical science, I stress that it is so with physics as, in the course of its traditions, it has developed classically – and I stress it is so, in consequence, with the view of science entailed in the conceived paradox. In a qualified manner it can also be said true of the revolutionary new physics which has taken over this century. I shall come to this new physics in detail. But I specifically note that in this physics there is a formal development of direct and highly significant relevance to the paradox. For the moment I continue with the traditional form.

By its strategic packaging, not only is knowledge greatly simplified but there is conferred great power. It might be said that this power is akin to the power of the generalizing symbolism of mathematics – which allows broad considerations of logic to be effected most conveniently. Thus the power of physics is operative in the logical consequences of its laws. And specific consequences follow in prescribed conditions. In this way the phenomena of the real world become predictable in a vast range of circumstances. The achievements of science, operating thus, are often remarkable; but it is simply a matter of logical deduction from the premises that are its laws. Science is powerful because of its logical technique.

Euclid's treatise on geometrical knowledge presents an excellent example – and indeed the archetype – of the technique. What is characteristic of Euclidean geometry – apart from a needed vocabulary for expressing certain primary concepts – is a set of basic postulates: propositions, termed axioms, which are accepted as to their truth. Starting out from such a fundamental scheme – which is called today in logic *a formal system* – geometry consists in the erection of an edifice of geometrical truth derived from the starting system purely by the processes of logic. One can think of science based on law by way of analogy with geometry; and the analogy is important. It is so because geometry, and such science, can be seen as differing illustrations of the same thing: the systemized knowledge of a formal system.

Knowledge of this kind has come under the closest scrutiny since the turn of the century. Study first arose with the interest then springing up as to the true nature of mathematics – and of arithmetic. In the years 1894 to 1908 there was published a first answer to this question by the Italian mathematician Peano. A little later (1910-1913) there was the outstanding treatise, *Principia Mathematica*, by Russel and Whitehead, seeking to show that the whole of mathematical truth reduces to the basic principles of logic. The burden of the treatise has not come to be accepted; but it is of no small significance that at the time of its writing, and for long before that, there had been a broad climate of opinion – indeed an unquestioned belief – that, if only the right collection of starting principles could be discovered, then *all* truth could be derived from such principles. This was an implicit, even fond, hope. If realized, such a goal would supremely vindicate the 18th century Enlightenment views concerning science and its ability to explain the entire world.

It was of course recognized that, beginning with any known starting system, then so much could be proved from it, and no more. The rules of algebra for instance were – strikingly enough – known not to admit of the proof of the so-called *central theorem of algebra*. As shown by Gauss, in his famous doctorate thesis, a starting system of greater deductive power than algebra is needed to prove the theorem. Whilst recognizing such limitation, the hope nevertheless was and continued to be cherished that eventually the fully-deductive system would be found: in terms of which no true proposition could escape proof.

The hope was shattered by Kurt Gödel in 1931, with the publication of his paper headed: "On Formally Undecidable Propositions of Principia Mathematica and Related Systems". The paper might be said to be the most momentous of the century.

Its rating apart, it has written an entirely fresh chapter in the subject of logic. What it sets out to demonstrate – and what has in mathematics become accepted by mathematical logicians – is that as a conclusion of pure logic, and no matter what mathematical set of starting principles (assumed true and therefore consistent) is gathered together to construct a formal system, there will always exist true propositions statable within the vocabulary of the system whose truth remains undecidable by the system. Certain of these propositions – perhaps all – may be provable in a system of greater deductive power; but in regard to this latter system there will then exist, of necessity, true propositions that likewise are not provable *within it*. So formal deductive systems may be arranged in a hierarchy in an open-ended fashion, some proving what others cannot prove, but *not one* (nor the totality of all such conceivable systems) capable of deductively establishing all truth.

Because the formal-systems proposition demonstrated by Gödel is that *the capability of a formal system inevitably falls short of proving all true propositions expressible within the system,* this systems proposition has come to be known as the *incompleteness theorem*. Its proof is set out in treatises on the foundations of mathematics. It is not a proof given for *any* formal set of propositions whatsoever. The formal set considered is inherently mathematical. But the mathematical element does not exclude the knowledge of physical science from the scope of the theorem. All the fundamental statements of physics which constitute its laws are mathematical. The incompleteness theorem applies to science in a basic way.

What follows is that the hope of the existence of an all-proving system of scientific knowledge – and with it the paradoxical contrasting of the facts of psychophysical phenomena – was only possible prior to Gödel thinking through in logical detail exactly what is entailed in issues of axiomatic-type deduction. With this analysis and perceiving that the formal systems of science divide the true into the provable and the unprovable, it is evident that unprovability itself can never discriminate between valid and invalid. It can never be decided just on the ground that a fact of experience will not fit (in a logically derivative way) into scientifically demonstrable knowledge that that fact is inconsistent with this body of knowledge. This is the resolution of the paradox.

In an inversion of his incompleteness theorem Gödel pointed out that a test of the validity of a deductive system is the finding of a fact (statable of course within the terms of the system) which lies outside the set of all propositions provable within it. The all-proving system must necessarily be invalid (through internal inconsistency).

The axiomatic method of handling knowledge in bulk is the highly convenient and greatly powerful alternative to the intractable, if very basic, simple collective method of cataloguing and classifying all true statements. The present century above all others has seen the triumph of the axiomatic method. It has also discovered very clearly its logical nature and limitations (still not widely realized).

But physics today has found it vitally necessary to abandon the climate of thinking in which it had grown until the present century. Inner contradictions, and contradictions with nature, discovered over a period now nearly a hundred years ago have been removed by the radically different formulations of modern quantum mechanics. A question of greatest interest ensues: how, looked at closely, does this mechanics compare with the Gödel logic?

It must come as a shock to many people to be told that the fundamental principles of quantum mechanics are of such a kind that they have nothing at all directly to say upon the occurrence of physical events. The older physics set down its laws as specific statements on typical happenings. The new principles as they stand fall entirely short of this – despite their overwhelmingly greater inherent power of explanation. The fact is self-evident to the expert few. Steven Weinberg, Nobel Prize winner for Physics in 1979, expressed the fact in his Dirac Memorial Lecture at Cambridge in 1986. He compared the fundamental principles of quantum mechanics to an empty stage. It is a good analogy. And you have to add the actors – from real life – before the play can be written. Quantum mechanics will then say what can happen in the play. Vitally and characteristically quantum physics for such reasons is *open* to the real world, picturing the real world progressively as the real world dictates. But more precisely just how does this come about?

Turning to the wave mechanics which is the basis of modern quantum theory the wave equation – due to Schrödinger – for the wave function of a physical system occupies a strategic position in the theory. Given the wave function, all the quantum states of the system are inevitably given also. All such states, and thus the physical nature of the system and its activity, therefore rest in the solution of the wave equation. To be able to solve the wave equation it is necessary to know what is the so-called Hamiltonian operator which is a main feature of the equation. This operator takes its form from the energy considerations holding good in the system. The description that quantum mechanics gives of the system and of its behaviour depends accordingly upon what we know in the first place, and in the light of experience, in regard to the energy conditions.

If for example we look on the energy conditions in a particular rudimentary way, then it is possible to derive from the Schrödinger equation the Newtonian laws of motion for a particle in a field of force (or a slightly more accurate version of these laws). If in a different and rather less rudimentary way we consider a free particle like a free electron, thinking of the particle from a relativistic viewpoint, then quantum mechanics is able to attach to any such free-particle system a quantum package of intrinsic angular momentum which is just the (spin) magnitude ascertainable by experimental procedures. Taking things differently again, and if we consider a system of the kind in which one electron exists in the presence of another, the Hamiltonian operator has to comply with the fact that each electron reacts to the electromagnetic field of the other. Quantum mechanics in these circumstances points to a remarkable state of affairs. In the space surrounding each electron there are continually created and annihilated photons which convey momentum between the two electrons. With this transfer of momentum it is seen how the known electric force between charged particles (an unresolved mystery in earlier physics) comes about; and, beyond this, there is given exactly what form it takes – namely the form that relates the force to the inverse square of the distance separating the particles.

It is possible to extend the foregoing progressive situation, taking other Hamiltonian operators appropriate to other types of energy conditions more developed than those just contemplated. In this way quantum mechanics opens up from itself – given the knowledge of specific energy conditions – a fascinating array of vistas upon reality, each with its system laws, and after the fashion of the open-ended hierarchy implicit in the incompleteness theorem of Gödel.

The mode in which the principles of quantum mechanics align with the incompleteness logic is that of a second degree of generalization. All formal systems, and thus the laws of any specific branch of physics, are sets (as we saw earlier) of general rather than particular propositions. With any one general proposition there is a direct correspondence in detail between the general proposition and any fact which is a specific statement of the general proposition. This is characteristic of axiomatic systems and the laws of classical physics. In classical physics the laws thus epitomize the real world – or aspects of it. That is how the principle of generalization operates. In quantum mechanics a further degree of generalization is brought in through the use of operators. Schrödinger's equation generalizes the Hamiltonian operator. This introduces the Gödel style of open-endedness and hierarchy. The hierarchy is implicitly present in the single symbol of the Hamiltonian operator. But at the same time, with the symbol, the ability directly to epitomize is lost. When through the knowledge of experience of the real world the operator recognizes the specific considerations that apply with an actual set of physical conditions, then the Schrödinger equation is able to provide the general form of expression of traditional physical law that is capable of direct interpretation in particular-propositional fashion. Stating the specific form of the Hamiltonian operator transforms the Schrödinger equation from a non-epitomizing statement to an epitomizing one – that is to say when the Schrödinger equation is then appropriately solved. The central principles of quantum mechanics are therefore not constructed on the formal-systems lines of classical physics. But with any actual specification of energy conditions they can be transformed to a corresponding formal-systems pattern.

The important logical significance of the new physics of quantum mechanics is that this physics is manifestly open-ended. Classical physics, it is true, is in fact open-ended; but it is only implicitly so – in the sense, but scarcely realized, that all formal systems must be open-ended. Without this critique it is an easy step to see classical physics – in principle at least – in conformity with the (even now strong) Enlightenment view of science: as knowledge able to explain all fact; and, in closed fashion, rejecting as false all statements (however factual) which are not deducible logically from its system.

From all of this there flow far-reaching considerations. Classical physics if taken uncritically can lead one to think that mind as an entity external to physics does not exist – rather that mind can be recognized only as some interplay of purely physical realities. The point is illustrated if for example – and ignoring the critique of formal systems – the motion of an electron is regarded without exception, no matter what the circumstances, as described by the laws of classical physics. Then – keeping thus to classical physics – some special motion of an electron in the brain must perhaps be looked on as a thought. Given this is right, it will be clear that the thought can reflect *only* the total *physical* circumstances present. Classical physics has no means of entertaining conceptions beyond this. On such grounds there has arisen the idea that all psychical issues must be finally traceable to the living brain. This is a position which finds itself in great difficulty (see for instance Chapter 14). Quantum mechanically there is no such difficulty. Quantum theory takes a form which enables it to relate to mind where classical physics cannot. And it lays down but one requirement in regard to the interaction of a physical nervous system with a mind external to the physical order: it is that such a mind enters at the level of energy into the activity of the total psychophysical situation. If mind can enter like this then a Hamiltonian operator must in principle exist by which the Schrödinger equation will determine the physical aspects of the activity.

Quantum mechanics is open-ended therefore, in this Hamiltonian manner, to mind-body interactivity in the idealist sense; that is to say provided mind in this sense is able to express itself after the fashion of energy in modern physics.

The proviso is a remarkable one contrasted with the entirely independent but similar formal demand of the Plato sense-perception logic considered in Appendix V. Mind it seems, although existing independently of the physical world, must be able to assume the guise of physical energy.

Having come this far, and having surveyed the logical terrain in its various scientific aspects, it is possible – with the ground thus prepared – to make, simply, one further statement: a statement of very great significance. Laws of science like the laws of classical physics are not absolute.

The implicit assumption that they are absolute was an important element in creating the paradox with which this appendix is concerned: they were seen as fully unyielding. The assumption is not true: all such laws, we know in the new physics, are conditional upon the circumstances which give rise to them. The actual fact of the circumstances is more fundamental than the laws. That is written on the face of quantum mechanics – and with a change of circumstances the laws may change too.

This can be illustrated in the context of the well-known laws of conservation of energy and momentum with a free particle. The laws were derived in the first place from the Newtonian laws of motion. Until quantum ideas came upon the scene it was never imagined there could be any departing from these central laws: they must inevitably be complied with, precisely and always. In the new physics it is certainly possible to find circumstances in which the laws are exactly true: they are the circumstances in which the particle location is entirely indeterminate! To introduce location into the situation the laws have to be broken – at least to some extent. One cannot advance far in the new physics without encountering that fact.

In the climate of the new physics it is never a surprise if in new circumstances a law is no longer found to be true.

Appendix II

PSYCHIC HEALING AND ETHICS

I am concerned in this appendix with the kind of healing described in Chapter 9; and I want to consider the objection levelled against such healing that I remarked on at the end of the chapter. It was an objection I had encountered in the form of a moral issue.

Again the situation is apparently one of paradox: the healing is good, but the privilege entailed in it – and especially in our egalitarian age – is not. If a resolution should fail to be forthcoming, it would be arguable that this healing is not supportable.

The matter lies really with clarity of thinking: on reflection it quickly becomes plain that much less ground exists for seeing in the paradox a true conflict than with the scientific issue of Appendix I. There the primary misconceptions could only be straightened out in the light of fundamental advance in mathematical logic – or of a philosophic appreciation of the difference between modem physics and a view which was taken of classical physics. In the present instance the misconceptions are far more superficial.

They undoubtedly arise because moral judgements are, commonly, not made with the same care and precision that is found in mathematical and scientific argument. Moral principles in day-to-day usage are laid down without any check on the bounds of their validity, or any statement of the conditions in which they apply.

In illustration consider for example the famed principle, due to John Stuart Mill, of *the greatest good for the greatest number*. It is without doubt a notable and important guide; but in that entirely unqualified form it is not difficult to discover the kind of situation where to apply the principle leads at once to manifestly and horribly wrong consequences.

Imagine a hospital in which there are two terminal cases: one suffering from a heart condition, the other with liver trouble. Both could be saved if they could have respective organ transplants as a matter of urgency. But suppose contingencies are such that the needed transplant organs are simply not to hand. Then imagine there is a visitor to the hospital with a sound heart and a sound liver – moreover it so happens, by some quirk of circumstance, that it is known these particular organs meet specifically with the transplant requirements of the two terminal cases. Imagine next – to develop the argument – that these organs are removed arbitrarily from the visitor and used in successful transplant operations on the two otherwise terminally-ill patients. The visitor will now most certainly be a terminal case. On the other hand with these operations the overall initial situation, of two terminal cases and one healthy visitor, has been radically transformed. There is in consequence only one terminal case, the visitor, and the two patients who were dying are well on their way to recovery and health. The transformed situation is a perfect expression of the Mill dictum: the greatest good spread over the greatest number. But the morality of the transformation is entirely a different matter. Obviously, devoid of provisions to preclude false situations, Mill's principle cannot always be applied. Stated baldly and without safeguarding qualification, as it invariably is, it has to be described as *too strong* or *too decisive* a principle.

The social-justice principle, at the heart of the paradox with which we are concerned, runs on the lines *not possible for all therefore not right for one*. It similarly is over-strongly decisive. This is immediately demonstrable if we turn, yet again, to a dramatic medical situation.

Consider there has been a train disaster – and consider it to have occurred in remote terrain far from organized aid. Imagine that were is nevertheless some sort of road or track nearby along which a doctor on holiday, and as it chances at that time, is motoring. He has easy access to the wreckage, and to the many dying and suffering. In the nature of things he can help some, but very far from all. Giving all effort to the task confronting him he would not for one moment dream of reasoning to himself: "I know the social justice principle which says *not possible for all therefore not right for the one (and so not right for the few)* – I must do nothing and drive on." He would give all the aid he could as his clear moral duty. To save the social justice-principle from such *reductio ad absurdum* the principle must be made less decisive by appropriate qualification.

The needed revision is accomplished without difficulty on perceiving that the principle, in its essence and in valid form, must derive from a particularly simple logical consideration. The logic, altogether clear, is that if something in particular holds good in relation to one person then inevitably that same thing must hold good in relation to some other person, given that precisely the same circumstances exist with the latter. The qualification of the same circumstances is the ground for what holds true in relation to *both* persons; and it is the means of comparing between them. The revised form, however it states the logic, must contain this necessary qualification – and in some such words *as other things being equal*. With the qualification it is evident that had it been equally possible to attend upon all the suffering then it would have been wrong for the doctor to select some of the injured for treatment and not to treat the others.

That, with the train accident, is the only conclusion to be drawn from the principle when it is validly stated. Failing the equal possibility of attending all the injured then such constituting the circumstances, and exactly for this reason, *there is no conclusion at all to be drawn – because the situation lies right outside the scope of the validly-stated principle.*

The situation with the healing of Chapter 9 runs parallel with that of the train disaster.

Appendix III

THE ELECTRICAL BODY – AND THE PSYCHE

Initial Remarks

There were aspects of the electrical-body system too technical to find a place in the main text. They are angles from physics, and from the philosophical standpoint. Considering them now they lead to a more extensive view of the subject – so that the neurological activity of the system is better seen; and in relation to normality, to disease, to mediumship, and to death and birth.

Like the two preceding appendices the stimulus to enquiry was paradox: here, the paradox which became evident early in Chapter 12. The resolving of this paradox shows in terms of modern physics how the electrical body depends on the psyche for its existence.

The whole appendix sees the electrical body in this vital context of the psyche.

The antimatter paradox

When Lang introduced me to the notion of the electrical body (Chapter 4) it was in fact the philosophical content of the subject which primarily attracted me. The concept seemed to have something important to say on puzzling and long contemplated questions: how is the mind able to affect the body? And how through the body can it sense the physical world? When, on the other hand, he said that the electrical body is an ensemble of electrons and positrons (Chapter 12), my attention became diverted to – what seemed to me – the far more pressing question of the stability of such a system. Lang had made it evident that the electrical body always outlasts (if only marginally) the physical body – yet at first sight, and from what is known of the character of positrons, there was no reason apparent why its lifetime should be more than a minute fraction of a second. That looked a very great problem.

I will give briefly the facts concerning the positron. Its existence was predicted on theoretical grounds by P.A.M. Dirac at Cambridge in 1930; and in 1932 it was observed (without knowledge of Dirac's work) by Carl Anderson of the California Institute of Technology. This was in some practical studies on cosmic-ray particles.

Dirac's theory is deeply instructive. It arose from his investigations of 1928, at the time when the spread of the new understanding in physics was permeating –

even bursting upon – the world of science. All events, but especially those on the scale of the atom, these hitherto profoundly a source of mystery, were – in their mathematical description – to be seen represented by a wave equation; and this wave-mechanical procedure, so it proved, accounted for the many physical phenomena which had baffled explanation.

Rather earlier, Einstein had propounded, and gained wide acceptance for, his theory of relativity. This theory stood in essence as a critique of the theories of physical science in regard to their mathematical form. A theory – and such was the critique – could not be looked on as truly correct unless this form met fundamental requirements. These, technically, were certain demands of invariance.

Dirac's special concern was the search for solutions to a wave equation that satisfied the relativistic critique. Up to that time wave-mechanical theory had made do with an equation that disregarded the invariance demands and so was non-relativistic. Dirac's results were astonishing – and in part then incredible to many physicists.

A first conclusion was that to every fundamental particle known to physics there must exist an *antimatter* obverse: an antiparticle. If, for example, there were electrons in prescribed conditions, then in these conditions a specifiable expectation existed of encountering antielectrons – positrons as they came to be called. A positron is a particle of the identical mass of an electron, yet possessing the precisely opposite electrical charge.

Coupled with these conceptions there was the extraordinary idea that particles could become 'unobservable' by assuming states of negative energy – in which states they became of negative mass. Difficult as this was for the mind to grasp, Dirac accepted the apparent implications of his mathematics and (guided by well established principles of statistical mechanics) went on to suppose that all such possible states (infinite in number though they were) must be filled by particles except perhaps at the topmost levels. The possibility of these exceptions Dirac regarded as holding out the explanation of antiparticles. The absence of an electron, for instance, with respect to a negative-energy state constituted a positron. If, therefore, an ordinary electron (that is to say one of positive energy) should give up just that energy which would enable it to drop into such an unfilled negative-energy state then, falling into this state, it would not merely become unobservable: it would destroy the real and observable positron represented by the unfilled state. So – and there was found full experimental support – any encounter of an electron with its antiparticle, the positron, could be expected to bring about the mutual and immediate annihilation of both particles. The energy to be given up is easily released – in the manner for instance of two photons emitted in opposite directions, and with a total energy not less than 1.05 mega-electron-volts. These ideas forced the problem – and the paradox – present to my mind when Lang calmly affirmed that the (stable) ensemble of electrical particles forming the electrical body was constituted by electrons and positrons.

In view of the intrinsic difficulty of the subject, I did not then (as I explain in Chapter 12) try for a discussion of the problem – the talks with Lang allowed of so little available time. In the circumstances it is not surprising that coming finally to express the difficulty to him he did not go into detail. He was content to point out that the electron-positron ensemble did not exist on its own; but – and this averted the catastrophe I envisaged – in the direct presence of the psyche. When he made the statement it was with an air of certitude which conveyed to me beyond doubt that he understood both what was the difficulty in my mind and what conceptions enabled its resolution. The reassurance sharpened my expectations of a full solution to the problem.

In discussion meantime with Marjorie, through the mediumship of William Elton, she had told me that physicists in her circles most certainly supported the Dirac mathematics and in particular Dirac's theory of the positron as an unfilled negative-energy electron state. I did not at that time express to her my difficulty with the stability of the electrical body; but it was the more clear that the problem bore exactly the character in which it had first formed in my mind.

Reflecting and taking account of Lang's clue, I looked for problems in physics already resolved which possessed some likeness of nature. It seemed useful to pay particular attention to the phenomenon of electrical superconductivity – long a mystery since its discovery in 1911.

The question with this effect was how an electrical current once it had been started in conditions of sufficiently low temperature could then continue virtually forever, so empirically it appeared, given only such conditions. In the normal course of events the free electrons in a metal – which by their coherent flow constitute an electrical current – rapidly lose their energy of coherent motion if the impelling force causing it is removed. This energy is lost since it is converted into random (thermal) energy of vibration of the so-called ion-lattice structure of the metal; and the conversion occurs because the electrons collide with and are scattered by the lattice. In superconductivity the important fact which came to be perceived in a quantum-mechanical study was that specific pairs of free electrons experience a special mutual interaction by virtue of the conduction circumstances. The interaction is of the nature of a bonding and it is strong enough – in the prevailing conditions – to prevent the occurrence of energy-dissipating interactions with the lattice by electrons of the pairs: the electrons do not have the energy to satisfy the scattering conditions. The pairs are referred to as Cooper pairs after Cooper who, with Bardeen and Schrieffer in 1957, first presented this explanation of the superconductivity phenomenon (to gain them the Nobel Prize in Physics). Since the pairs are inhibited by their bonding from interacting with the lattice, they keep their energy of coherent motion and so create the permanent state of superconductivity.

The bonding is due to what is termed a phonon exchange; and this exchange takes place between the electrons of a Cooper pair through the intermediary of the lattice. A phonon is a quantum package of energy of mechanical vibration – in the present circumstances the vibration is that of the ions which form the lattice.

The phonon exchange produces a force of interaction between the Cooper-pair electrons in the same (broad) kind of way that photon exchange between charged particles (as explained in Appendix I) produces the known electric force between these particles. It seemed to me that the solution of the instability problem with the electrical body, and in the light of Lang's clue, might rest in a photon exchange of bonding nature between the members of electron-positron pairs: an exchange taking place through, and being made possible by the presence of, the psyche.

Granted such a mutual interaction, it could if sufficiently great inhibit the annihilation interaction. In fact it would do so if the thus-produced binding energy of a pair exceeded the 1.05 mega-electron-volts mutual annihilation energy of the pair. To give an idea of this energy, it is about fifty times the energy needed to accelerate an electron of the scanning beam of the picture tube of a television receiver.

Arranging a special talk with Marjorie through William Elton, she confirmed these ideas. The binding energy induced by the psyche in electron-positron pairs was, she said, of the order of 2.0 – 2.5 mega-electron-volts. The photon exchange, she also told me, was to be understood in terms of the quantum physics of her order of existence (Chapter 16, *Physics*).

With the aim of presenting the picture a little more fully, Marjorie asserted that the psyche acts to enhance very greatly the emission of photons by the pair particles in relation to their normal exchange-force emission of photons. The stimulation of emission – as indicated by her figures – is so intense that the particles of a pair give up twice or more than twice their normal mass-energy to the photon field created by the process. Environs carry this energy instead of the particles; and the particles fall to negative energy states. Ordinarily in such highly-negative states they would not be expected to emit photons – that is a very necessary reason for the psyche stimulation of emission. The psyche-stimulated photon exchange producing the negative states is, as Marjorie also asserted, an exchange purely between the individual particles forming the pairs and the psyche.

The essential basis of the electrical body thus clarified, it seemed important to gather more if possible of salient details. I had noted that if the electron-positron pair density should be of the order of 10^{10} pairs per cubic centimetre, then current densities akin to one ampere per square centimetre could quite feasibly be set up in the ensemble. In this there might conceivably lie an accounting for the magnetic effects which some individuals (including children) have allegedly been observed to produce at will – causing for instance the deflection of magnetic compass needles (Chapter 10). In my talk with Marjorie, I was corrected by her on the figure I have quoted for the pair density – normally the pair density is something like 10^{13} pairs per cubic centimetre. Marjorie pointed out that the normal level of current flow is of the order of microcamperes per square centimetre. That level was quite sufficient to induce the neural currents which control the physical body.

The electrical-body current flow bears a one-to-one relation with the neural currents similar in broad respect to the one-to-one relation that holds between the input and output currents of an electrical transformer. The electrical-body current flow moreover contains various components of the general form of the neural impulses travelling along a nerve fibre.

The four-dimensional psyche presence

Why is the psyche unable to induce the neural currents directly, without the intermediary of the gas formed by the electron-positron pairs? That appeared a fundamental question; and seeing no answer I put the question to Marjorie in the talk part of which I have just recounted.

The character of the answer was entirely unexpected. Marjorie's response was firstly this: *the psyche presence does not interpenetrate matter – it only approaches as closely as it can.* Then better to make me understand what she was wanting to convey she turned to the very strong binding-energy interaction we had been speaking of; and to stress its extreme tightness she went on to say that the electrical body was held to the psyche presence – and the psyche presence to it – as though the two were *glued together.* As she spoke I envisaged a proximity of a very close kind indeed. "Then it seems," I remarked, "that the psyche presence must act on the electron-positron gas from a range of only 10^{-13} centimetre, or thereabouts" – a range no more than the approximate particle size of electrons and positrons. I did not have any clear idea in my mind when I said this of what it entailed; but I think very certainly that the remark was consequent upon my direct sensitivity to Marjorie's thought. Marjorie supported my comment, telling me I was thinking the right way. Immediately I saw the fundamental explanation I had been seeking. On Marjorie's initial statement, and if the psyche presence was to control directly the charge carriers of the nervous tissue of the physical body, it must (bearing in mind the molecular aspect of such tissue) do so at a range greater than 10^{-13} centimetre by a factor of 10^6, or close to that (the factor expressing roughly the relative size of particles like molecules compared with those like electrons). Therefore the psyche must be better able to control the electrical body than ever it could the physical neural system in the direct sense – and with, so it seemed, a fantastic order of advantage. Because of the inverse square law of range with the electric force, I suggested that this advantage would be in the ratio of 10^{12}. Marjorie told me that I had the right idea. It seemed a very major clue: one that perhaps explained why normally, and while the psyche – which must be looked on as a distinctly weak influence – can successfully control the electrical body, any direct influence by the psyche upon the physical body (and upon this-world matter in general) is out of the question.

And then an assumption implicit to what had just been said became apparent. I remarked that I thought there was something of much and indeed prime import which had been left unstated. The argument without saying so was assuming in the first place that *the psyche presence impinges upon the three-dimensional world of matter from the direction of a fourth dimension of space.* This was entirely the fact, Marjorie replied – and she added that the psyche presence is itself four-dimensional (she had not plunged straight into such ideas for reasons of the limitations of mediumistic mechanism).

I comment that when Marjorie said I had the right idea on the advantage of the electrical body I felt she wanted to tell me I was also exaggerating. I did in fact sense her mind correctly, so she explained to me long after; but to say just why I exaggerated would at the time have been too difficult. Fields, in particular the electromagnetic field, do not necessarily propagate in the same way outside the ordinary three dimensions of space of our world as they do within it. The multi-dimensional physics which arises inevitably on the introduction of the fourth dimension of space – along the direction of which, in the picture one has to understand, the electrical body and the physical neural system are slightly separated – calls for a superposed (exponential) attenuation factor for fields that propagate along this direction. The superposed attenuation may be looked on as due to a special distortion of the metric of space as it is encountered in this particular direction. It is a distortion without which the ordinary three-dimensional world would not be defined. It follows that my ventured 10^{12} :1 advantage for the electrical body must be reduced to allow for the fourth-dimensional attenuation. The electrical body does not in fact couple tightly with the physical neural system as I first supposed; but very weakly only. The electrical-body advantage is represented actually by the ratio 10^5 :1, not by my 10^{12}:1 figure. As a separate correction to what I had ventured, the fourth-dimensional spacing of electrical body and physical neural system is slightly greater than 10^{-8} centimetres – instead of the 10^{-7} centimetre spacing I initially assumed, thinking then of molecular size. With however an actual advantage in effectiveness of 100,000 times, the merit of the electrical body is still very great.

But, gathering my first understandings, I possessed a new illumination. It lit up at once a part of Lang's instruction on the electrical form of body. In answer to a question, he had stated that on the death of the individual the electrical body becomes discarded (Chapter 4). With an understanding of the necessity for the electrical body in our present existence, it was now clear why this kind of body is unnecessary in the next; as he also told me. Since the atoms from which the psychical body is formed are smaller even than the electrons and positrons of the electrical body (Chapter 16, *Physics*), the control of the psyche over the psychical body must be even more complete in the absence of any control intermediary than it is over the physical body here with the aid of the intermediary. The next-life body is influenced directly by the psyche at even shorter range than is the electrical body indispensable to us in this life.

The significance of another part of Lang's instruction on the electrical body also became clear at the same time. I should have appreciated it when I first realized the tight coupling to the psyche presence of the electron-positron pairs. In the terms in which Lang put it, the electrical body "appears to cling" to the psychical body as the latter moves away from the physical body at death. The reason was now obvious. With death, and having no further use for the physical body, the psyche transfers its prime activity to the use of the psychical body. The transfer notwithstanding, the electrical body naturally and for the time being remains tightly bound to the psyche presence. The psychical body thus has the semblance of acquiring the electrical body. (The apparent acquisition does not last for long. The psyche allows the electron-positron binding energy to decrease to the point at which the pairs mutually destruct in a sequence of annihilations. In the course of these the electrical body slowly fades out of existence.)

Statistical physics of the electron-positron-pair gas

There was another fundamental question where I also hoped for clarification in my talk with Marjorie of the previous section. How do the electron-positron pairs behave as a whole – even if only in the widest possible terms? What – in the more ordinary language of physics – are the statistical characteristics of the gas which they constitute? I had become interested in the question and thought I had insight into it – it seemed to present a next natural step on the road to understanding. Talking with Marjorie I obtained agreement on an answer.

The physical conceptions necessary to the answer again go back to the important theoretical work of P.A.M. Dirac in 1928. One of the distinctive features of this work was that it showed how a particle may possess an intrinsic degree of momentum – that is to say without having any translational or straight-line velocity of motion. On the macroscale a spinning top gives an idea of such momentum. Without moving anywhere, the top nevertheless possesses internal motion and therefore momentum – angular momentum – by virtue of its spin. Studying particles like the electron Dirac found an analogy to this spin momentum on the part of such a particle. And the analogous quantity had to be present strictly in quantum fashion. The quantum unit was precisely the unit of angular momentum any integral multiple of which Niels Bohr had seen was to be attributed to the orbital motion of an electron in an atom: a momentum which if attributed then the radiation spectra of the atom could be accounted for. Now, however, Dirac discovered – and it was entirely from his unification of relativity theory and quantum mechanics – that particles such as the electron were concerned intrinsically with just half the Bohr unit. It was what a few years earlier had been conjectured from experimental work on radiation spectra. Contributing to the theoretical picture, and in 1934, it was shown by Pauli and Weiskopf that relativistic quantum mechanics is capable of accounting besides for particles not having any spin momentum at all. It was evident moreover, on very simple grounds, that particles must exist having intrinsically the full unit of angular momentum. Thus when an atom radiates a photon and its total orbital angular momentum is reduced thereby by one unit, that one unit must (for reasons of momentum conservation) be the intrinsic angular momentum of the emitted photon. Particles in fact, depending on their nature, may have an intrinsic angular momentum which is, in general, an odd or even integer multiple of half the full unit.

The actual number of full units to be attributed to a particle is said simply to be the spin of the particle. It is a number which is specially characteristic of the wave function that in quantum mechanics represents the particle. In the technical language it is said in the instance of the electron that the particle has spin-½; and in the instance of the photon, spin-1. A particle devoid of spin is said to be of spin-0. Spin may naturally occur with the opposite sense of rotation. One then speaks say of spin-(-½), or spin-(-1).

It is necessary to go into this degree of detail because widely different considerations can apply to half-spin particles as compared with those of unit and zero spin. They apply when one is interested in the behaviour of the particles in aggregate; that is to say in an ensemble. It is a fact entailed in the representation of a particle in quantum mechanics by a wave function that, with a system of half-spin particles of the same kind in which the particles are all in the same energy state, one cannot set up the wave equation for the system – because the wave function of the system vanishes. This result is understood to mean that systems of two or more such particles cannot exist. The statement is an example of a highly important principle in quantum mechanics known as the Pauli exclusion principle. On the other hand no like exclusion exists with systems formed of similar particles of unit or of zero spin.

When one seeks to apply these ideas so as to ascertain the behaviour of the electrical-particle gas forming the electrical body, two things in particular need to be recognized: firstly, like the Cooper pairs in electrical superconductivity, the effective particles of the electrical-body gas are the composite electron-positron pairs; and, secondly, the spin value of any composite particle is the algebraic sum of the spin values of its component particles. Since the electrons and positrons of the electrical body gas are both half-spin particles, and are each likely to possess negative spin just as much as positive, electron-positron pairs will exist with spin-(-1), with spin-0, and with spin-1. These are the only spin values of the pairs; and it follows that for any of these three classes of spin any number of pairs can exist in a single energy state. This is not a circumstance which would exist were the gas particles say of half-spin – like with a simple electron gas. There, any given energy level can take on no more than two electrons (and then only if the spin settings are different). The probability distribution for the occupation of the various energy levels in this case works out on the lines of the so-called Fermi-Dirac statistics. The gas statistics for the pairs constituting the electrical body is radically different. With the spin results worked out the statistics must be on the similarly well-known Bose-Einstein lines.

In this conclusion it is important to note a very special point: the particle pairs are of negative mass – because the environs energy of the pair bonding is so great at the expense of the mass-energy of the particles. The kinetic aspects of the gas are therefore in part singularly unusual. The mobility of the pairs is not enhanced by increasing the energy level of the gas – to increase the gas mobility the gas-kinetic energy level must be reduced! On the other hand, and in the usual way, the gas will have temperature above the absolute zero so long as it retains any mobility.

One possibility with the gas is that only the zero-energy gas-kinetic state is occupied. If this possibility were realized, the ensemble – which then would be at zero absolute temperature – would exhibit no mobility; and there would be no current flow.

That is not however a condition of no utility to the psyche in its relation to the neural system – far from it. Should the psyche be faced with the condition it is entirely free to set up any currents, and any current variations, it pleases in the gas. It has just to lift and switch charge pairs to energy levels of appropriate mobility. That is a matter of creating fluxes of photons, and thus of momenta, on the part of the individual particles of each pair concerned. It is a creation process which inevitably has to be psyche stimulated; and the accelerations, or decelerations, are not just equal in magnitude but mutually opposite in direction between the particles to take account of their opposition of charge sign. In the result, and incidentally, the gas is naturally raised to a temperature above the absolute zero.

The foregoing gives a summary of combined developments in which I made some analysis on my own and Marjorie, over an extended period, gave me impressions – all with a view to mediumistic discussion. Main issues were gone into in our talk of the previous section; but there were some subsequent and similar mediumistic conversations.

One point made in the latter conversations was that because of regularities in the psyche-driven currents of the electrical body the actual gas statistics only approximates to a fully-random statistics. Actual temperature in consequence is correspondingly an approximation to that simply with the Bose-Einstein statistics. We noted also that should the density of the charge pairs be materially less then it would be necessary for the psyche to drive the pairs into states of rather greater mobility in order to achieve the same currents. In these circumstances the operating gas temperature is raised somewhat further above the absolute zero.

Normality, disease, mediumship, death and birth

In the continuing talks with Marjorie, and at times with Dr. Lang, I heard more on the functions and functioning of the electrical body. This information was distinctly various; and it was by no means limited to the norm.

But, falling in the normal category, I was told that many considerations had to be entertained apart from those of the control at will of the movement of the physical body, or again of the activities present in sense perception. Marjorie stated that the psyche, acting through the intermediary of the electrical body, exercises many continuous controls on the physical body that must be classed in contrast with intentional activity: controls over the many actions of the physical body that naturally are automatic or involuntary. Such routine activities are enhanced by the stimulus from the psyche; and inversely they are less effective if the psyche is itself less able to exert its influence.

With such functions any weakening of the energies of the psyche is reflected in a weakened drive of the electrical body; and, in consequence of the reduction of the activity of the electrical body, the individual experiences a loss of physical tone.

On functioning, Marjorie discussed – as a basic question – what decides the operating temperature of the electrical body. We have seen (in the preceding section) that the driving of the electrical currents is one factor. It is a mobility-inducing factor. There was, she said, apart from slight thermal coupling but one other main influence: that from the neural system. This has to be viewed rather in the light of the effect which an electrical load circuit has upon a driving circuit: therefore the influence has to be thought of as constantly tending to reduce the mobility of the pair carriers. The temperature settles essentially in the balance between the influences of the psyche and the neural system. A typical value for the temperature on the absolute scale is fifty degrees.

To this Marjorie added that the constant tendency for the neural system to reduce carrier mobility is evident to most effect during waking hours. There is then a persisting tendency for the electrical-body temperature to fall – although recovery occurs during sleep. When Marjorie made this striking statement – striking because I could see no reason for the recovery – there was not the opportunity at the time to go further into the subject.

The first occasion this was possible was in a meeting with Lang. He informed me that it related to an effect of background radiations of his world upon the psyche, which in the state of sleep became susceptible to them. Once again I was left puzzled for lack of the opportunity to go yet further into the subject.

It was Marjorie who gave me the clue – a *very* remarkable one. The psyche, she explained, is always tending to create energy. That is a pronouncement incomprehensible to classical physics – but modern physics is open to the idea; and in this respect I shall return to the conception towards the end of this appendix. For the moment I shall simply continue with Marjorie's explanation.

During sleep, it was true the psyche becomes sensitive to the influence of the background radiations of which Dr. Lang spoke. It is then, as a result, made more active in energy creation: the creation rate may be increased five times. The reserves of energy of the psyche are then built up which had been run down during wakefulness.

On the same occasion Marjorie went into the overall pattern of energy flow from the psyche to the neural system – in the control of the latter by the psyche. Because of the negative mass of the charge carriers of the electrical body they are in the ordinary sense precluded from the radiation of photons. They must however radiate photons of our world order if they are to induce current flow in the neural system. The emission of such photons in fully adequate degree is in fact accomplished by the stimulation of the carriers by the psyche. It is the energy of stimulation on the part of the psyche that provides the energy flow from the electrical body to control the currents of the neural system.

Physical illness can drastically lower the mobility of the electrical body. In for example the disease, affecting the neural tissue, known as multiple sclerosis the neural tissue responds less efficiently than is normal to the control from the electrical body. For a specific level of physical activity, this places a much heavier drain upon the energy reserves of the psyche. The psyche finds itself in consequence less able to stimulate photon emission on the part of the charge carriers of the electrical body. This applies both in regard to mobility-control emission and to the radiation of photons that control the currents of the neural system. It is a twofold effect; and if the patient persists in endeavours to maintain physical activity it can bring about a rapid decline in physical control – the patient may collapse to the floor and be quite unable to get up. In Dr. Lang's treatment of such cases one measure taken is to build up directly the energy reserves of the patient's psyche. This restores the temperature of the electrical body to about fifty degrees absolute – and the patient feels much better with the elevation of the temperature to the normal figure. There is a tendency in all physical illness to reduce the energy of the psyche. (I quote an interesting comment in passing by Marjorie when discussing the foregoing with her. The fifty degree temperature is an optimum. At such a temperature a fully adequate mobility of the charge carriers is achieved; and a higher temperature would only increase the risk of spurious control from the random fluctuations that occur inevitably in all assemblies of particles.)

Realizing the relevance of the psyche to physical well-being, and thinking of the mediumistic state, I felt that it was not difficult to see why a medium like Mr. Chapman is so tired when he wakes up from trance session. To be more sure I took up the subject with Marjorie. George Chapman's own psyche has very largely to give way to that of Dr. Lang. Chapman leaves however a residual presence. This is to hold his electrical body available for Dr. Lang. The residual element does indeed influence the involuntary activities of the physical body after the normal fashion – but it is a reduced influence; and on waking George Chapman experiences the inevitable lack of tone. As Marjorie agreed, there is another and powerfully collaborating factor. So that he is himself less disturbed by his medium's automatic functions, Dr. Lang purposely slows down these functions (Chapter 18). This adds considerably to George Chapman's general feeling of fatigue.

In conversation with Lang I took up a point connected with the electrical activity of the brain. The electroencephalograph is a diagnostic and monitoring instrument of great value for the observation of such activity. It detects and displays the fluctuations, mostly strongly rhythmic, of electric fields found to be associated with the brain. I put it to Lang that the fluctuating fields so observed and normally supposed to originate solely from the brain – might have their even major source not in the brain but in the electrical body. Lang replied categorically that the electrical activity demonstrated by the electroencephalograph is to be attributed primarily to the electrical currents flowing in the electrical body. With the separation of the psychical body from the physical and the transfer of the psyche to the psychical body – taking the electrical body with it (as explained in the section *The four-dimensional psyche presence*) – the electroencephalograph trace will exhibit a collapse of activity. It is possible for such a state of affairs to be transient only – a temporary kind of death – because the psyche may in fact shortly return to normal association with the physical body. True death naturally entails no final return.

My conversations with Marjorie brought me information concerning the electrical body at the time of birth. With the delivery of the child, and following the norm of association after birth, the mother's psyche presence becomes extended to the infant. Inevitably, therefore, the mother gives to the child part of her own electrical body. She thus makes this, as well as the physical body of the infant, available to the psyche whose purpose it is to enter the present world by virtue of the birth. When the entrant psyche associates with the infant body, then the mother's interim psyche presence withdraws; and the child becomes a new human being. If as may happen – though rarely – defects exist in the infant body of so extreme a nature (Chapter 12) for it to attract no entrant psyche, the mother's projected psyche presence eventually leaves the child. The infant thus reduces totally to automatism.

Learning what I had of the events of childbirth, I observed to Marjorie that the loss must surely be made good to the mother of the electron-positron pairs given for the use of the entrant psyche. There was no real difficulty in this, Marjorie assured me. Electron-positron pairs participate naturally (as physicists know) in a continuing process, in which they are created at random, exist very briefly, and then – normally – cease to exist by self-annihilation. Pairs created, however, in very close proximity to a psyche presence can be captured by the psyche. Their otherwise automatic annihilation is, at the same time, prevented. On this fashion the deficiency necessarily suffered by the mother with the birth is made good in some fairly short period, such as an hour.

When, differing from the norm, the entrant psyche associates prior to delivery the mother's psyche sympathetically adjusts to allow the intrusion (Chapter 16, *Transfiguration phenomena,* also Appendix IIIA); but her contribution of electron-positron pairs has still to be compensated in the fashion just explained.

Psyche-matter interaction and philosophy

It will have been noticed how from an early point in this appendix the psyche is regarded as capable of purely physical activity. The bond-making photon exchange taking place, through the psyche presence, between the partners of electron-positron pairs of the electrical body is one important instance of the physical activity of the psyche. With context other than the photon activity of the psyche in binding the electrical body to itself, there had been conversations with Lang, and separately with Marjorie, in which it was put to me that the psyche is naturally a source of photons of next-world order. It was the explanation – in part at least – of the aural light perceived by George Chapman around his physical body (Chapter 18) when he first projected his psychical body. The explanation was partial because, as I was also told, electrons and positrons of the electrical body can emit photons of next-world kind.

Instances of the creation of photons by the psyche presence such as I have just noted – instances of psyche-matter interaction – must be of interest in the issue of mind-body interaction long contemplated in philosophical thought.

It was Plato who first gave the word *psyche* special philosophic significance. He used it to refer to a concept at which he had arrived by the analytical procedures first powerfully demonstrated by Socrates. The concept was by no means restricted to mind; but, as a principal example of the concept, mind was inevitably something that exists on its own terms – just as matter does. It is also true that Plato equally was constrained to see in mind the important contrast of the non-material. This contrast has remained ever since a major feature of philosophic thinking – and despite a great difficulty which has coloured the whole subject of mind and matter since the time of René Descartes. Descartes (1596-1650) who – apart from his fame amongst mathematicians – has been called the father of modern philosophy maintained the contrast in an extreme form. He placed *mind* and *body* in opposing camps, *absolutely*. It was an idea which tended to be greatly influential.

When, however, mind and matter are thought of as falling totally in mutually exclusive categories, one question is very hard to answer: how can these entities possibly interact with one another, as they so obviously must do in reality? The problem has proved insoluble – as clearly in the absence of any common ground it would seem that it had to. The fact – justifiably – supported materialist philosophers, like Gilbert Ryle, in their complete rejection of the Cartesian thesis: "the dogma of the Ghost in the Machine," Ryle derisively called it.

The evidence of this book concerning mind is however broadly *contra* Ryle and *pro* Plato; and it shows that the Cartesian dilemma is unnecessary – it should never have been created. *Mind which can emit photons* – and radically different in general nature as it clearly is from that of matter – *inevitably overlaps the category of matter*. Given common ground, as here one is, the problem stemming from Descartes vanishes.

Support for common ground between the categories of mind and matter, it must be noted, is forthcoming as I indicate in Appendix I: support deriving from the open-endedness which is characteristic of modern physics. Modern quantum physics can in principle deal with the mind-matter interaction if mind can, where necessary, operate like physical energy.

Appendix V takes the whole question further – by an analysis, going back to Plato, which is concerned with the logical and intrinsic nature of mind and energy.

214

Conductivity form, neural coupling and psyche presence

On many occasions Dr. Lang referred to the electrical body as the electrical-*pattern* body. Knowing Lang I did not doubt that this possessed very real significance. Whatever exactly he had in mind it seemed clear it must be found in the context he had laid down: that the electrical body is essentially something which *can flow*. At the same time there never had been the opportunity to hear in his own words what he meant when he included in his terminology the qualification of *pattern*. The present section arises out of my interest on the point; and from my feeling that the point would become clear with an understanding of the electrical body that, in regard to its coupling function, was more complete. On all of this I gathered some distinct enlightenment from Marjorie in further talks with Elton as medium.

They were in direct continuation of talks about the electrical body noted thus far in this appendix; and they went some considerable way towards a yet better conception of the nervous-response system of the human organism.

We started from the standpoint that the electrical body is essentially an electrical conductor – an electrical-flow system; and we turned to the basic question: what sort of electrical conductor? Thinking of the analogy with ordinary superconductivity, I remarked that in fundamental principle it must be looked on as a superconductor. Marjorie went along with this; but noted attendant circumstances to mask the superconductivity. The two basic couplings with the electrical body had to be taken into account: the coupling with the physical nervous system; and the coupling with the psyche. In circumstances in which the influence of these couplings could be considered vanishingly slight, the superconducting nature of the electrical body had the chance of prominence. Since, as made clear in the earlier section *The four-dimensional psyche presence,* the coupling with the physical neural system is of an extremely weak kind there is some justification for discounting any masking effect with this coupling – the more so the more quiescent the ambience. In regard to the psyche, Marjorie confirmed that the coupling is normally tight. But if the psyche should be highly quiescent then – lapsing interaction between the psyche and the electrical body needing very much to be thought of in the all-or-nothing logic of quantum situations – there must be occasions where the coupling is to be seen non-existent or virtually so. I mentioned a technical report I had noted in which the use of the extremely sensitive Josephson type of field detector had shown the presence of a sensibly unchanging magnetic field in the general vicinity of the solar plexus. Marjorie stated that this gave an instance of the quiescent conditions she had in mind – conditions that would allow of the long persistence of steady flow in the electrical body. The steady flow manifested itself to the detector as a steady magnetic field.

We considered next the question of the distribution of current flow: when an electrical current is induced in the electrical body what kind of path does it take? I proposed the principle of the conservation of electric charge as the foundation for the answer – one could then argue from the well-known form of the equation of continuity; and I commented on how in this equation local fluctuations of charge density – should they exist – were seen as affecting the spread of electrical current in their neighbourhood. Marjorie remarked that there were no grounds for supposing any such fluctuations to be significant. That being so the flow had to be in closed loops – loops precisely like the closed paths of the magnetic induction field.

I asked if we could give some thought to the way such current loops actually link with the physical nervous system. I did not then realize the complexities which any full answer to this question necessarily entailed. The special way – alluded to in the section *The four-dimensional psyche presence* – in which fields propagate in the fourth-dimensional direction was still something I had to meet with. I had no idea that the coupling of loops of current in the electrical body with say a particular nerve fibre must be subject to such propagation. But we talked; and Marjorie – anxious to keep to main principle and avoid massive digression on the complex details of multi-dimensional electrodynamics – simply stated that the effect of the coupling was to set up magnetic fields encircling strategic nerve fibres. The magnetic fields nested around the nerve fibres and, as she eventually expressed it, "fitting them almost like a glove." Changes in the magnetic flux encircling any given fibre control the current flow in the fibre. And the magnetic flux rests (as seen in the section *Normality, disease, mediumship, death and birth*) for its existence on psyche-stimulated emission of photons from the electron-position pairs of the electrical body. The whole system also is one which operates reversely as well: thus the physical nervous system is equally able to influence the psyche.

I said it was a natural assumption that the current flow of the electrical body should be strongly, if not totally, associated with the region of the brain. To this Marjorie replied that there exists also a minor complex of current flow in the vicinity of the solar plexus. This major and minor complex of current flow makes up the general pattern of current flow which Dr. Lang had had in mind when he spoke of the electrical body as the *electrical-pattern body*.

We came to the way the psyche is able to function in working relation with the current system of the electrical body. I told Marjorie that mentally I had received from her the impression of the total four-dimensional presence of the psyche interacting from a three-dimensional stratum or layer superficial or contingent to the electrical body. The impression was one I had properly received, she said. With that confirmation we went on to a discussion as to how it was possible for the superficial layer to enter into the interaction.

The discussion placed many ideas in perspective. Mind is a thing of various modes more radically various than ordinarily thought. In one mode it can perceive the force of reason. In another it can feel emotion. That is greatly different. Again, and again very different, it can express itself as will. Because of the influence of Descartes we have been conditioned to think that mind cannot express itself as physical energy. But it can – and this guise is no more radically differing than the others. These ideas are of deep significance for the present question. In modern physics it is plain that the only avenue offering a bridge between mind and the physical world – the only means for causing change in this world or being affected by its changes – is physical energy. In the contingent stratum mind, psyche, itself acts in the mode of physical energy.

The discussion then developed into a consideration of just how the energy field present to the stratum can in particular create and absorb photons. Such photon activity is necessary to the establishing of the binding energy of the electron-positron pairs of the electrical body. The answer is one which can be perceived by analogy. The kind of energy distribution present in a region in which photons are created and absorbed in purely physical situations is characterized by strong localizations of the energy and by its corresponding and inevitable fluctuations. *This* is the state of affairs which the psyche creates in the contingent stratum *and this active stratum is effectively the psyche presence.*

The conversation ran on from here in some rather interesting respects. First we considered the subject of the energy fluctuations of a complete system. The laws of Newton and classical physics say that no changes in the total energy of a complete system can happen. That is one of the fundamental symmetries of nature for classical science. It is now known in physics that the classical ideas were wrong on this. The nature of matter is such that energy fluctuations are necessarily and continuously occurring at random; and the classical law of conservation of energy is certainly violated in the short term. In the long-term average it is not violated. But Marjorie made the point that, even in the long term, the law is broken by psychophysical systems. The psyche – singular to state – possesses intrinsically an ability to create energy. The ability counterbalances the continuing energy expenditure of the psyche. It is active especially during sleep in order to maintain the mobility – and temperature – of the electrical body (activity referred to in this appendix in the section *Normality, disease, mediumship, death and birth).*

It is because of this creative ability, Marjorie stated, that a strongly creative psyche is better able to make good the mobility losses of the electrical body. The individual in such a case has less need of sleep than others.

Then there was a special point on photon creation by the psyche. It related to the electrical-body binding-energy considerations of the end of the section, in the present appendix, on the antimatter paradox. Running over their most basic aspects with Marjorie, she affirmed in restatement that photons created by the psyche are invariably photons complying with the diminutive value of Planck's constant relevant to next-world physics. The photons created in the region of the psyche presence to interact with the electrical-body charge carriers – carriers natural to this world – need therefore to be of a very high quantum order.

So Marjorie stated, the energy drain in this respect upon the psyche in setting up the photon field to bind the electrical body to the psyche presence is totally major. It far exceeds the ordinary energy demands upon the psyche in next-world existence. Next-world existence is one therefore of the experience of a very much greater available energy (in the ratio roughly of 100:1 compared with this existence).

Finally there was a comment by Marjorie on an inbuilt natural tendency of the psyche to limit quanta emission to very low quantum magnitudes. This acts to safeguard against catastrophic depletion of energy in creative activity by the psyche. The high-order quanta produced to retain the electrical-body charge carriers are produced in the specially-regulated conditions of the circumstance.

217

Appendix IIIA

THE ASSOCIATION OF THE PSYCHE

Appendix III has concentrated upon physical processes of the electrical body always seen in the context of the psyche presence. Doing this it has focused more on the part than the whole, on aspects more than the general picture. It is the whole picture I want here to make more plain – and by giving special attention to how exactly the psyche manifests itself.

Unfortunately the task is not rendered easy by the fact that the physical processes at large do not lend themselves to description against a background simply of the everyday space framework of three Cartesian dimensions. This, though, is not something new in physics. With the need to see the physical world operative in general and, following Einstein, in a curved space-time continuum it results that physical processes must often relate to ten Cartesian dimensions at least. Ten is the minimum to permit full and formally proper description; and if one dimension only ranks as time that means nine space dimensions have to be thought of. In so far as the overall view of the electrical body and psyche presence runs beyond the conceptual possibilities of the ordinary three Cartesian space dimensions the physical setting is not new in broad principle – the eventuality might even have been anticipated. As seen in Appendix III the eventuality is what Marjorie maintained to be the truth. It is important to consider it closely.

Dr. Lang had always talked of the electrical body as though it pervades the whole of the physical body. Then however following up his key remark on the stability of the charge-carrier ensemble which constitutes the electrical body, it appeared that this ensemble must exist in the form of a simple layer of thickness no more than the exceedingly small size of the electron. If the thickness dimension of this last statement should belong to the three Cartesian space dimensions in which the physical body exists then we have a nonsense: the electrical-body gas is restricted to a sheet of thickness greatly smaller than the size of an atom, yet at the same time this sheet is as extensively bulky as the entire human body. It was for this reason that in my conversation with Marjorie on the need for the electrical body (Appendix III, *The four-dimensional psyche presence*) I voiced my conclusion that all had not been made explicit: that it was more than the ordinary three Cartesian dimensions of space that was involved.

The ordinary dimensions were clearly entailed in one respect: that of the three-dimensional spreading of the ensemble – so that it could be said the electrical body was all-pervasive of the physical body (or something effectively that).

When however it came to stating that the thickness of the ensemble was of electron size, then this was in regard to another dimension of space altogether. The four-dimensional nature of the total space concerned had been implicit in the argument.

So, explicitly, the minute thickness of the sheet to which the electrical-body charge carriers are restricted has to be seen as lying along a space dimension other than any of the three in which the physical body extends: a thickness along a fourth dimension normal to all of these three. Since the restriction relates to this fourth direction of space only, no limitation is placed on the expansiveness of the electrical body in directions parallel with the ordinary axes of space. This expansiveness, to be precise, does not take place however in the three dimensions of what we ordinarily mean by space (in which matter including that of the physical body normally exists); rather it is in such a space after it has suffered a *small* displacement in the direction of the fourth dimension. I can thus paraphrase Marjorie (Appendix III, *The four-dimensional psyche presence)* to effect on the one hand that the electrical-body charge carriers move virtually "glued" to the psyche presence, and on the other that this motion lies *very close indeed* – close in the direction of the fourth dimension – to the physical body. One has to think therefore of the widely-spread three-dimensional extent of the electrical body as existing slightly to the side of the physical body in the direction of the fourth dimension.

The slight separation of electrical and physical bodies entails a weakening of the coupling between them. This weakening, as I have denoted in Appendix III, *The four-dimensional psyche presence,* is not of consequence for the effectiveness of the coupling – though the physics in detail is too technical a matter for this book. An important aspect of any such detailed consideration is the thickness of the physical body in the fourth-dimensional direction. It is a thickness of atomic dimensions. The separation in the fourth-dimensional direction of the electrical from the physical body is scarcely more.

But in discussion with Marjorie it became clear that simply to think of the electrical body as lying to one side of the physical body in this way is not to gain the full picture: the electrical body lies in fact on both sides of the physical body. Its charge carriers are to be found in exactly the same kind of way a small distance remote from the physical body in the other direction of the fourth dimension. The physical body can thus be said to be sandwiched between two electrical-body regions. Even then the picture is not entirely complete. There are not two separate electrical-body regions. The oppositely disposed regions are sub-regions only – if major sub-regions – of a single fully-closed sheet which, in the total and four-dimensional space we have to think of, is all-enclosing of the physical body.

The physical body by analogy is rather like a letter sealed within an envelope. The envelope represents the totally-closed fully-surrounding electrical body.

The psyche presence, virtually identical in localization with the electrical body, is similarly all-enclosing of the physical body – like a second and outer envelope. Its disposition enables it to act as a screen in preventing the electrical-body charge carriers from being affected by any field of influence, externally incident, of another psyche. The function is accomplished by absorption of the photon carriers of the incident field; and in accordance with the mechanism of photon creation and absorption by the psyche presence envisaged in Appendix III, *Conductivity form, neural coupling and psyche presence.*

All of this represents the picture in the context of our world here. What is to be said in the context of the next world? The logic of the situation would appear to demand a psyche presence active and located basically as described in Appendix III and in this appendix – subject though to the absence of the intermediary of any electrical body to aid coupling with the neural system. The demand would be consistent with Lang's statement on the way the electrical body temporarily clings to the psychical body at death – a circumstance occurring with the transfer then of the attention of the psyche solely to this body (and as I noted in the section on the psyche's four-dimensional form in Appendix III). There should be simply the active psyche presence disposed completely around the bodily aspects of the individual: just this and nothing more – but otherwise exactly on the lines set out in the present appendix.

Marjorie, when I suggested to her that these considerations represent the truth, agreed that they do.

She supplemented her confirmation by an enlightening observation on the binding together of the psyche presence and the psychical body. The binding is most certainly by forces of van der Waals nature; yet the forces are not strictly van der Waals forces – because, as normally understood, such forces are forces between atoms or molecules. Two hydrogen atoms for instance will attract mutually by inducing in each other a displacement of the centre of orbital charge. In contrast, the psyche presence although a physical manifestation is not an atomic manifestation. In such terms it is a matterless manifestation. But it is still, importantly, an energy manifestation; and localizations of energy follow closely the pattern of localization present with atoms. The localizations – although free of matter guise – enter into photon exchange (with the atoms of the psychical body) essentially as with the strict van der Waals situation: this to broadly similar effect.

The matterless manifestation of the psyche in a multi-dimensionally distributed pattern of physical energy that envelops the physical organism is, on the foregoing lines, the fashion in which the psyche associates with the organism.

Appendix IV

THE ANTI-REALIST VIEWPOINT

The aim of this appendix is an appraisal of the approach to psychical phenomena. Falling broadly in the class of miracles in earlier centuries, these phenomena had been accepted one way or another as an expression of activity from without the ordinary or natural order. What is – or should be – the view today?

As I noted in Appendix I there was by the end of the last century a great enthusiasm for an all-sufficient scientific explanation of the world of events. The power of rational thinking in physics had been widely perceived – it seemed that the human mind was close to holding the entire Universe in a firm grip. The new power widely fired the imagination and stimulated the intellect. In the field of psychical research this century it has been strongly felt that here were important guiding principles.

The effect, on a large scale, has been to turn the subject inside out. Facts had to be seen in a totally different way. That followed from the closed nature of this new type of thinking (Appendix I). When one reasons on the lines of such thinking – and even though the modus of it had not been worked out – the human spirit or mind must be a function entirely of the organization of the human body and its brain. So there could be no possibility of the human mind surviving death; and the effort had to be made to discern in events, hitherto thought clearly to express survival, only special activities or sensitivities of the living human organism and brain. With such sensitivities in particular, the full understanding of events had not to go beyond the ability to pick up for instance the thought processes of another living brain – or again, as it was hazarded, the stored memories attaching to such a brain; even perhaps in the extreme any sort of normal information whatever. Such considerations as these identify the anti-realist position towards which – with regard to the critique episodes – Chapter 14 is turned in practical test.

It is quite reasonable as an exercise to explore the possibilities attending a hypothesis. The exercise can be enlightening, and almost certainly instructive. Initial assumptions have to be judged however by the way they make things clear which before were obscure; or remove difficulties that may have seemed impenetrable. On these criteria anti-realist theorizing does not perform well. The special psychical events considered in Chapter 14 are as a whole *far* from illuminated by its ideas.

Had the blue rose been in my thoughts, the anti-realist task would have been comparatively easy: Mrs. Muir gathered the image of a blue rose because I transferred it to her – that would be reasonable explanation and would carry its clear measure of understanding. But against the tests reviewed anti-realist explanation becomes forced into unlikelihood and extremes of unlikelihood, even absurdity. The theory is totally embarrassed with the predictive events taken up at the end of the chapter – those which are described in full in Chapter 16, *Physics*.

There, I was told beforehand – by Marjorie – through the voice of William Elton the result of a quantum-mechanical calculation (a lengthy calculation) that I was to make in a few days time when I could turn to it. We are concerned here with a calculated number which had no existence at all in the ordinary and natural way prior to this announcement. The announcement presents a test of anti-realism which is altogether radical. As shown in Chapter 14 it defeats even the explanatory powers of the super-extrasensory hypothesis.

Virtually no room is left for anti-realist hypothesis to function in an effective way. It might be supposed that somehow and very quickly and unaware of it I worked out the calculation purely mentally; and that I did this just at the time Marjorie *seemed* to be proposing it through Elton – then that equally unawares I transferred the answer to Elton's mind, so that it could *seem* to come from Marjorie. But I insist that the calculation was utterly beyond any power of mental arithmetic that I possess. The calculation was, I repeat, lengthy. If alternatively it is to be supposed that Elton himself engineered it all, then difficulties are astronomically great ever again – Elton has no understanding whatever of quantum theory.

The test takes anti-realism to a *reductio ad absurdum*. One must suppose that the organization of the human brain is such (in a way not explained) that if two persons sit quietly in a room and one goes into a sleep state and talks in this state, the other responding, then – this being the total situation – abstruse and lengthy mathematical calculations can be achieved spontaneously (and entirely unawares) which neither person ordinarily has the mental power simply sitting there to carry through. This is the nadir of explanation!

Normally in the history of scientific development, arrival at such a state of impasse is taken as a call for a new avenue of thought.

On reflection the impasse is not a surprising turn of events. Assume it is a legitimate anticipation that psychical phenomena must find real understanding in terms of the scientific rationale of anti-realist ideas. Then the same true understanding should most certainly be expected with ordinary living events. It is an expectation that has met with disappointment. For example, it has been recognized that human memory is *not* explained by analogy with computer 'memory' – as in some such way it would need to be. Moreover, the question of knowing in sense perception presents great difficulty – it could be said the theory looks more like a theory of not knowing than of knowing. Further, in the psychology of blame the vital element of the freedom to decide is ruled out – in a closed fully-determined system it must be. Yet people do not feel they are to blame if they know they had no freedom in the circumstances. But they do feel they are to blame if they know they were free and their decisive action was crucial. The theory impugns the psychological facts. These instances are warning notices posted over the start of the anti-realist trail.

The rational core of the theory – classical physics – has this past half century been abandoned by physicists. Its inner contradictions spotlighted in the field of radiation by the *ultra-violet catastrophe* of Rayleigh and Jeans, its external

222

contradictions exhibited strikingly in photoelectric emission and by a total inability to account for the interior world of the atom all conspired to setting it on one side – and to the birth of the new physics. The rational core has its truth; but this truth is now seen within the scope of its limitations. So far from extending to the living world at large, the scope of classical physics is relegated to particular areas within physics. The quantum-mechanical ideas which have taken over from classical physics do not possess the closed form attributed easily and enthusiastically – but improperly – to science in the days of its early burgeoning (Appendix I).

Of highly significant contrast, the modern science of quantum physics is explicity open-ended. As a revolution, it is interesting that it was forced by purely scientific reasons (of the kind I have been noting) before ever Gödel's logic demanded a change in hitherto favoured conceptions of scientific formalism (Appendix I).

What has happened within physics over the last hundred years, and in particular with the upheaval of sixty or more years ago, is little known outside of physicist circles. There lie momentous events. They have occurred, and they have undermined entirely the thinking of the anti-realist position.

It has to be emphasized that now an altogether wider perspective is natural to science. Modern quantum mechanics is formally capable of dealing with the influence on a physical system of a mind existing equally in its own right and external to the system (Appendix I). In the light of the nature of quantum-mechanical theory the condition necessary to the interaction is that such a mind should be able to present itself to the physical system as a manifestation of physical energy. This important clue to the character of mind is considered from the standpoint of philosophical analysis in Appendix V, and supportively.

It may be noted that in a sense anti-realism was never so much a requirement of science as of a philosophic postulate (Appendix VI).

Appendix V

MIND AND ENERGY

There are two modes of rational thinking in search of truth: one speculative, the other analytical. In speculative thinking we say things, like: *if we may suppose that so-and-so (which we do not know well) is really like such-and-such (which we do know well) then that would explain why this-or-that-kind-of-occurrence happens as it does.* It is thinking which is of a pattern much followed in science. In analytical thinking we may say: *we know the nature of this specific entity, therefore it must be the case that this-thing-in-particular is true (because it is logically implied by the nature of the entity).* Philosophy is of both speculative and analytical kinds. Analytical philosophy makes understanding more clear. In a sense it does not add to knowledge; but its aim is to realize better, possibly much better, what we know already. It will be clear that its conclusions tend to a higher order of certainty than with science.

In this appendix I want to show that, distinct from science, certain analytical procedures are to hand which significantly illuminate the subjects both of mind and of energy.

It is much the fact that Marjorie has taken a major role and initiative in prompting my thinking on issues of this book. For some time it was clear she wanted me to become familiar with the reflections of Plato on the nature of existence. There were some difficulties entailed in this step.

A dissertation by Marjorie would have been ideal. But such a direct approach, and instruction by her through available mediumship, through the mind say of William Elton as medium, must have faced a big – if not new – hurdle: the appropriate concepts could be but scarcely present in the medium's mind. Using Elton as medium, I would have first myself to ascertain them, and of course their part in Plato's thinking, before we could begin any mediumistic discussion.

There were some intrinsic difficulties attending the subject which I learned of when I entered upon it more closely. Plato never committed his more mature metaphysical thinking to writing, and as a unified exposition. It is to be found partly in some discussions of his own, and partly in the writings of others, for instance his pupil Aristotle. From all these sources it may be pieced together. I found however that it has most conveniently been traced through critically by G. C. Field *(The Philosophy of Plato,* Oxford University Press, 1949). Field's treatment of the subject is from the standpoint of a classical scholar and – highly importantly – of a philosopher (holding the chair of philosophy at Bristol University).

The obstacles that have existed in arriving at the final thinking of Plato may explain why it is so little known to moderns. Marjorie wanted me to go into the metaphysic so that we could discuss it, with William Elton as medium, in the way we developed for dealing with special concepts in the situations of Chapter 16, *Physics* – where medium difficulty was strictly similar. In the result it became clear to me that Plato's thinking had much to say in a relevant way on the subject of mind; and moreover on that of energy as it is now understood in physics. It is of the more weight because in fundamentals at least it is analytic.

Plato had in the first place given much thought to what we are really concerned with in the flux of sense experience. This kind of experience is often highly fleeting and variable; yet in it we are certain we are relating to the enduring things which as centres of interest we call objects: things which – running through, and despite the transitory character of, the flux – can really matter. An object which we recognize in itself to be circular is seldom perceived in the sequence of actual events as a circular shape: it will – perhaps in all the many aspects we see of it – look elliptical, often maybe thinly elliptical. But we are positive we are concerned with a circular object. Then we may be certain that the object is really red in colour; yet in some lights it may appear very different, or scarcely coloured at all. Plato was deeply interested in the question of the enduring reality that pervades the vagaries of appearance. His thought ran on lines echoed today in psychological studies of cognition in sense perception; and in the search of science for the ultimate realities of the physical world. It was clear to him that we bring to bear concepts accessible to our minds in order to interpret the flux of physical events streaming in on us through our senses. The concepts he termed *the forms*.

Almost certainly his thinking on these lines derived from his being a mathematician. In mathematics the objects of thought are typically always the selfsame things – permanent; and for that reason they are relatively easy to contemplate. In real-life experience there is a sense running through what would otherwise be a chaos; and this sense lies in the discerned element of permanence. Something in the flux of immediate experience correlates with the essential permanence of specific form. Without such permanence in our experience life would be unlivable – we should be able to count on nothing. Plato's thought would beyond question have linked the general logical category of his forms to the geometrical forms he dwelt on as a geometer – which were indeed but particular instances of his forms.

This view of Plato, seeing the mind active intrinsically and constantly in interpretation, and finding as a result a highly significant thread of the unvarying throughout the immediate flux of experience, is fundamental to his metaphysical thought. Yet it is not the heartland of his general metaphysic. This heartland is the logic to which he was driven when he turned to the problem of *becoming* – to the fact of change which is encountered, in experience, in the discerned thread of significance. If the intrinsic activity of mind resulted only in the discerning of centres of interest that were *entirely* unvarying, there would be no such problem. Since the mind looks to the participation of the forms, that indeed might even be what one would expect of reality. But reality, as we meet with it, is not on such a pattern. How does it happen that the centres of interest which the mind perceives are subject to change in this way or that, to movement of one kind or another, even to creation or destruction and annihilation? The category of the forms, so helpful initially in Plato's thought, now had nothing to offer but difficulty. A concept which in its essential nature is incapable of entertaining change is not a concept to which to turn in the attempt to come upon an understanding of change. Empty coffers are no source of cash. The forms therefore held out no understanding of this problem.

The problem is illustrated in a particularly simple way by a paradox of Zeno of Elea. In the paradox Zeno pointed out that the flight of an arrow can be analysed as extensively as one pleases into a sequence of positions of the arrow. The procedure, which appears to allow of a complete analysis of the motion of the arrow, results in a set of elements of analysis not one of which contains the motion of the arrow. The positions of the arrow say nothing about the motion of the arrow in just the same fashion that Plato's forms, intrinsically permanent, are totally silent about change. The idea of the control of the arrow's flight escaped Zeno – he concluded that motion must be illusory.

In present-day physics the motion of an object is analyzed in relation to space and time in exactly the same way that Zeno analyzed the motion of the arrow. A point of great significance is that dynamics since Newton makes it fully clear – and most obviously so when the equations of motion are cast in Hamiltonian or Lagrangian manner – that considerations of space and time alone are inadequate to express a rational understanding of motion. In the Hamiltonian or Lagrangian formalism, the motion hangs explicitly on the associated energy. This energy is assignable to the motion and when it is assigned the motion can be worked out in detail: the motion is rationally understood in the sense that it can be predicted rather than left simply to tracing by observation.

It can be said that the energy is present to the space traversed and to the motion in this space. Notably the energy stands in the mathematics as a third parameter additional to the parameters of space and time. It *directly controls* the motion of the system. Since Einstein and his relativity theory in 1905, it is ranked equal in status with matter. Zeno was right that the motion of matter cannot be explained in terms only of space and time – but not in his conclusion that motion is therefore an illusion.

Plato found an answer to his problem of change that is greatly in sympathy with modern dynamics. He was clearly certain of the rightness of his form-analysis. But if, following Zeno, this analysis should be thought to offer a complete analysis of change then there was a real contradiction: the absolutely permanent must also be mutable. Therefore some major element – which was responsible for change – must have escaped the analysis. Such an element — on grounds of the rationality of reality – must clearly exist. Obviously also, and while entirely as real as the participating forms, it must fall outside the scope of the forms to describe – since they are incapable of explaining change. The intrinsic nature of the element must in consequence be form-less: a statement necessarily implying a transcendence of space. Such fundamental reality – like energy in physics – has always to be present to any situation of change. This in outline is the general metaphysic of Plato.

Plato's argument is an altogether general one; and it must, being so, include purely physical situations like that of the flying arrow. Modern dynamics is included, so it would seem, to a remarkably up-to-date degree.

Better to appreciate this last point consider first what the Plato analysis demands. It calls for three necessary participants to motion: space (because inevitably the forms must be entailed); time (because the situation is one of change); and beyond these and form-less – and so space- transcending – another fundamental and real element to which solely the motion is to be attributed. This raises the formal question: is the element identifiable with the energy that in modern dynamics attends the motion? The underlying role of the control of the motion is met with; and, very clearly, the element fits with the Einstein sense of energy in which the energy is as real as the matter with which it is associated. Can it be said as well that this energy in some way is such that it is to be seen as space-transcending? If it can then there is identity.

A well known experiment conducted by the Institut d'Optique Théorique et Appliquée at Orsay, near Paris, in 1982 (verifying with much care what seemed to have been shown by earlier experiments) bears significantly on the question of energy in its relation to space. The experiment was carried out by a team of physicists led by Alain Aspect. It was in regard to an argument first started by Einstein – indeed it was presented by him along with Podolsky and Rosen as early as 1935. In modern quantum theory, as Einstein observed, one particle of a pair in the so-called singlet state appears to be able to influence the other without any delay in the action whatsoever – and regardless of the space by which the particles may be separated. Einstein felt this instantaneous influence must be wrong. It must show a defect in quantum theory. He had proved impressively in his relativity theory that it is impossible for energy to cross space at a speed in excess of the velocity of propagation of light. It was impossible, he maintained, that the one particle of the pair should be able to influence the other except after an elapse of time at least as great as the propagation time of light between the particles. It is well agreed as a result of the experiment at Orsay that Einstein was wrong in his contentions; and that quantum mechanics is remarkably vindicated. But the experiment seems to leave matters in a state of paradox. If quantum theory actually is right, is relativity theory – so well established now – wrong?

The confusion of the Einstein-Podolsky-Rosen paradox undoubtedly rests with initial and tacit assumptions. Relativity, it is abundantly clear, is restricted to activity taking place by virtue of space-transport mechanisms – to energy carried by the propagation of photons for instance. It is in this sense that the theory is committed first and last to the activity of energy *within* space. Is quantum mechanics identically committed? If that is so then the paradox arising from the Orsay experiment stands as a real contradiction: the two prime theories in the physics of this century are in conflict. If, however, the influence extended between the two particles in the singlet state should be an activity of energy taking place in a fashion which *transcends* space then there is no contradiction. The activity would fall outside the scope of relativity mechanics. Nothing exists in quantum theory to prevent this view being taken – even if it seems strange in contrast to our customary thinking. It could be said that the Orsay experiment is a definite indicator of the actual nature of energy – that the experiment argues forcibly the idea of energy as ultimately a space-transcending entity; or *non-local* as it is often now put. Demanded by the Plato logic, modern scientific theory and experiment seem in a striking way to be expressing this. The concern of relativity mechanics is correspondingly that of energy confined to localization in matter.

Plato would undoubtedly have maintained the intrinsic non-locality of physical energy had he possessed the knowledge of dynamics now available to us. He would have seen such energy as one aspect of the broad category of motivation, transcending but controlling events, which was argued by his analysis. The Stoic philosophers following him were deeply interested in the content of the category. Plato himself was also interested – the content had to be worked out in any specific circumstance. First and foremost he saw the category occupied by mind.

Technically, mind is a proper candidate for the category; just as is physical energy. A distinctive thing about mind is the *purposive* aspect of its nature – in contrast with the random interactions of physical energy. When mind is active in a physical situation the course of events is characteristically different from that when the activity of mind is absent. The difference is an expression of intention.

Turning more closely to the nature of mind, it would have been profoundly interesting to put to Plato the bare facts of observation concerning the big-bang origin of our Universe. He would, looking to explanation, most probably have suggested that the originating eruption was a manifestation of intention. Going on to express to him the knowledge we have today in modern quantum mechanics he would no doubt have accepted as an alternative explanation that the eruption was purely a manifestation of physical energy. In either alternative, he could – understanding quantum mechanics – equally be counted on to see the *immediate* activity producing the eruption as that of physical energy; because it is physical energy alone that determines the states of matter. The eruption even if it derived from mind as the essential source must have come in the immediate sense in the guise of physical energy. Mind, more extensive in character than physical energy, cannot manifest itself in the world of material events except through the gateway of this energy: mind includes physical energy as an aspect of itself.

Plato's sense of the importance of mind as a self-existent reality active in the world of everyday events prompts me to say that, given his acceptance of a purely quantum-mechanical origin of the big-bang start of our Universe, he would nevertheless have insisted that the eventual emergence of life, and its continuance, were matters referring back to mind. The purely physical paroxysm of the birth of the Universe over and abated, events would have been able to fall very much into that broad picture of the developing pattern of life to which the logic of his analysis had carried him.

It was undoubtedly this mould to his thinking which dictated his terminology when it came to setting a name upon the generic transcendental reality thrown up by his logic. In the context of this mould the generic reality assumed for him above all else the particular significance of mind – the reality which is at the root of life. He named the generic reality *psyche*. *Psyche* is a Greek word with a common usage of the time conveying the idea of life. But meaning also *breath*, Plato's highly developed dramatic sense would have welcomed the name for reason of the vitality breathed into the intractable subject of mutability by his logic. Transparently a purely technical label it was however not perpetuated by Plato's successors. In Stoic philosophy Plato's *psyche* became *logos* – a term recognizing the essentially rational character of the thought processes that arrived at such conceptions of ultimate principle.

The use of the term *psyche* in this book does not have the generic meaning of the term in Plato's final metaphysic. It carries only the particular sense of mind.

Appendix VI

PHILOSOPHIC MATERIALISM

The subject is one of many complexions and is said to trace back to Greek atomism in the 5th and 6th centuries B.C. It is undoubtedly a conception of ancient thought. But as an influential force it is much more a mode of thinking of modern times in reaction to orthodoxy. Thomas Hobbes advanced it at the time that Descartes was advocating the total distinction between mind and matter. Hobbes's ideas are basic to modern conceptions of the subject; and comparison with the atomistic postulates of Democritus emphasizes the essential character of the materialistic principle in modern thought. Whereas in Greek atomism Democritus distinguished between mind and matter by his postulation of atoms of the soul besides the physical atoms of the whole corporeal system, Hobbes – in contrast – looked on the mind solely as the motions of the physical atoms that form the brain and body. The entire Universe (of mind and matter) was to be explained simply by physical atoms.

It was early in the present century that such thought began to capture the outlook of more than a small minority – perhaps because at that time there was increasing evidence to suggest that ultimate reality in science lay with particles: the newly discovered electron and then the atomic nucleus greatly supported the chemical conception of the atom. To present day ears it may come as odd to imply that the status of the atom was not fully accorded in the last century. The historic truth is that the great physicists of the 19th century had not looked to particles for final reality. They were very much field physicists. But the force of evidence it seemed had turned against them; and the mechanical materialism of Hobbes was underlined: now it appeared to stand as the spirit of science.

It has been well recognized that these purely mechanical notions face severe problems in the fact of consciousness. Hobbes had evaded them. His suggestion that the motion of the particles of the physical organism and of the brain must explain all mental facts was a suggestion *without saying how*. But it was a step taken in expression of the true essence of materialism: the aim to exclude by way of first principle all reference to mind in the sense of an ultimate entity.

The strength of the materialistic principle would be much greater had some elucidation been forthcoming, with time, to support the kind of promise made ever since Hobbes: that given the development of physical science it would most certainly become clear how this science can explain the various facets of consciousness. But despite extensive effort the principle remains purely promissory.

Possibly because of lack of success in this respect the principle has been much urged as a demand of logic. It is argued that the outlook is called for by the logical guide known as Ockham's razor. William of Ockham, a late medieval English Scholastic philosopher with a great interest in logic, had vigorously contended that *plurality should not be assumed without necessity.* It was a principle of much soundness. However it is hard to take seriously the notion that modern materialism is any expression of the famous dictum of William of Ockham. First it is abundantly not true to say that in materialism there is a discovery, in the natural sense of the word, of the purely physical origin of mental events. Consequently when materialism strikes out mind as an ultimate principle it needs – this principle in fact seeming to be necessary – to replace it by the assurance that mental events will eventually be found as simply physical. There is no real economy in starting concepts – nor indeed any true call of necessity from the Ockham principle. On the other hand many severe problems are created. And the implausibility of suggestions advanced to resolve the problems stands out acutely.

In instance of the problems, consider the conscious event of seeing a red object. The patch of redness present to one's consciousness is a mental fact. But it is not a fact which can be deduced from the existence, nature or activities of any of the elementary particles of physical science. A suggestion put forward to cope with this apparently insurmountable problem is the assertion that the redness is not a fact in itself; rather it is part of the reporting of a particular state of motion of the particles of the brain – a state which may be described as *the state of redness-seeing.* The contrivance of the wording is at least courageous in the face of overwhelming odds; but the truth is that it still leaves totally unabridged the hiatus between the mental fact of seeing redness and physical activity on the part of the brain. The words can be seen as an attempt to classify the experience – but doing no more than this they do not explain its origin. The hiatus is a yawning chasm which was fully recognized by Sir Isaac Newton when he was studying coloured light. Seeing a red patch you know the truth of the fact that you see the redness of the patch – there is nothing in physics from which any of this statement can be deduced.

Those supporting materialism who have felt sense perception to pose problems too great to be solved by talk like that of the state of redness-seeing have proposed alternatively that (in the absence of mind as a fundamental entity) it must be the case when matter is associated together in a sufficiently complex manner – like in the living brain – that in some way there then emerges a state of affairs in which the qualities naturally attributed to mind become present to the situation: the qualities like the ability to perceive redness and, moreover, in the circumstance to know that the sensation is being perceived. This conception of emergence bears perhaps the air, and with it the rational assurance, of an analytical derivation. But in reality it is – simply – a further hypothesis superadded to the Hobbes hypothesis to make good (if possible) the rational deficiency of the latter. Disappointingly, it is futile to ask in what precise way the deficiency is removed. *Emergence is* no more than a word used to bridge the unbridgeable rational chasm at the core of materialist ideas.

Among the sayings of Jesus addressed to the inner circle of the disciples and quoted in the "Gospel of Thomas" (long lost but recovered in a recent find near

230

Luxor) there is one saying which reads: "If the flesh has come into existence because of the spirit, it is a marvel; but if the spirit has come into existence because of the body, it is a marvel of marvels." The saying expresses what is undoubtedly the truth of the whole position.

However my main interest in this appendix is not so much to assess philosophic materialism as to look on its impact on psychical research. To the extent that such thinking was seen in the early phases of this century to be the spirit, or climate, of science it naturally acquired the idea of patterns of behaviour dictated by the laws of classical physics – or dictated so it was thought. In fact it tended to attach to these laws more weight than might be allowed by a professional physicist; and in principle it was felt the laws must be final and universal, and must operate in the sense of never being broken. That, vis-à-vis the paradox noted and considered in Appendix I, made it difficult to perceive psychical phenomena as part of what could be held a rational scheme of reality. Psychical phenomena – for those in the field of psychical research responding to the new climate – came to be termed in consequence *the paranormal*. The new terminology prevailed and the ultimate aim hitherto of seeking to explain such phenomena turned to one of explaining them away. This is the anti-realism I have considered in Chapter 14 and in Appendix IV.

Meantime, in the innermost circles of physics, dramatic things had been taking place. With 1924, and the few crucial years that followed, the pattern of physics changed like a change of pattern in a kaleidoscope. And it was with immense consequences, including the philosophical, that opened up a dazzling explosion in knowledge. Matter, for the first time ever became understood. Inevitably the particle lost its prime position. The wave-mechanical field and energy were looked to as the real ultimates. The formal structure of physical knowledge took a sharp change (Appendix I); and there was a very different – and necessary – new view of physical law. This vast revolution in physics occurred virtually unbeknown apart from the specialists of physics. The world at large is not aware that it is a commonplace in the new physics – and most importantly so – to see in the breaking of basic laws the source of new patterns of activity or existence. The new patterns may be of rare occurrence or otherwise; but, even if rare, they are still a part of the natural order – they exist, and no requirement to explain them away is seen in their manner of origin.

In the technical language of the new physics, any general pattern of behaviour (any for instance fundamental law of nature) is a *symmetry* of nature. *Broken symmetry* with this physics has in fact a vitally important role. The laws of conservation of energy and of conservation of momentum are examples of symmetries that are altogether central. Able now to understand the nature of particles it is realized by the new physics that no particle can exist except through the breaking of these basic symmetries. Without this broken symmetry the world would be totally undifferentiated and unknowable. Broken symmetry is the ground for more special kinds – more developed kinds – of activity and existence. It is essential to world building.

The new more penetrating understanding of physical reality is very different from the closed scheme of thinking that demands anti-realism in the psychical field. We are no longer concerned with the notion of particle activity which cannot break a set of prescribed fundamental symmetries of nature. Particles are the quantized stable-state expression of an underlying field and of physical energy. As such, they are derivatives from ultimates that conform to the open-endedness which, as shown in Appendix I, really describes the natural order.

Anti-realism might earlier this century have seemed to be called for by science. But it is apparent that such a call comes in truth not from science but from the materialist branch of speculative philosophy.